Soldiers in a Storm

Soldiers in a Storm

The Armed Forces in South Africa's Democratic Transition

Philip Frankel

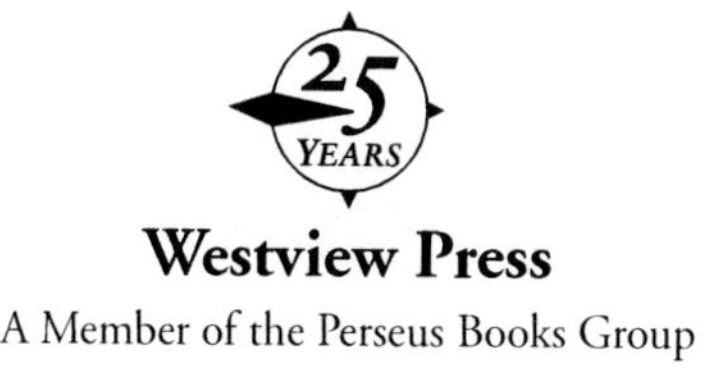

Westview Press
A Member of the Perseus Books Group

Published in 2000 in the United States of America by Westview Press, 5500 Central Avenue, Boulder, Colorado 80301-2877, and in the United Kingdom by Westview Press, 12 Hid's Copse Road, Cumnor Hill, Oxford OX2 9JJ

Find us on the World Wide Web at www.westviewpress.com

Library of Congress Cataloging-in-Publication Data
Frankel, Philip H.
Soldiers in a storm : the armed forces in South Africa's democratic transition / Philip Frankel.
p. cm.
Includes bibligraphical references and index.
ISBN 0-8133-3747-X
1. Presidents—South Africa—Transition periods. 2. South Africa—Politics and government—1989–1994. 3. South Africa—Politics and government—1994– . 4. South Africa—Armed Forces—Political activity. 5. Guerrillas—South Africa—Political activity. I. Title.

DT1970 .F72 2000
322'.5'096809049—DC21 00-032102

The paper used in this publication meets the requirements of the American National Standard for Permanence of Paper for Printed Library Materials Z39.48-1984.

10 9 8 7 6 5 4 3 2 1

Contents

Preface

Apartheid has been one of the great moral issues of our time. In fitting tribute, its passing has encouraged an explosion of literature seeking to explain why South Africa escaped the blood and civil war long deemed predictable and deserving for what arguably ranks as one of the most consciously vicious social systems of the twentieth century.

Some writings, cobbled together in explaining South Africa's unexpected negotiated revolution, have sought refuge in the extensive general literature on international trends toward democratization in the last decades of this era. A second category, linked to theories that emphasize the strategic role of elites in the movement from authoritarianism to democracy, have zeroed in on South Africa's leadership, particularly Nelson Mandela, to explain why apartheid avoided racial Götterdämmerung and, like its communist counterpart, imploded with a whimper. Still others have focused on such diverse variables as the peculiarities and increasing contradictions of apartheid as an instrument of repression in the face of heroic mass mobilization in the black townships, structural developments in both the domestic and global political economies, the changing balance of regional power that progressively tightened the noose on the apartheid state, or the role of strategic institutions and interest groups at the interface between government and civil society. Winston Churchill once made the point that the art and science of politics is to predict the future—and then explain why it did not happen. This certainly applies to contemporary analysts of South Africa.

In addressing this agenda, scholars and other writers may well derive valuable insight from the fact that democratizations seldom succeed when they are opposed by the military forces of authoritarian regimes and that their success rate is improved immeasurably should the military assist or otherwise display forms of social performance that do not discourage the emergence of democratic cultures and structures.

Militaries, a substantial body of universally recognized literature emphasize, are actually critical among public- and private-sector institutions in determining the initiation of democratic transitions—the shape, aspect, and ultimate sustainability of the democratization process. Given the enormous political influence wielded by the South African Defence

Force (SADF) under apartheid, particularly near the end, it is not unreasonable to assume that the armed forces were comparably important players in the local transition. Since postauthoritarian military behavior is increasingly regarded as vital to the short- to medium-term outcomes of democratization in other settings, it also seems reasonable to conclude that the South African trajectory into the twenty-first century will, in all likelihood, continue to be influenced by the psychologies and actions brought to the social arena by its soldiers.

Yet surprisingly, there has been no systematic, overall study of the sociopolitical role of the military since the mid-1980s, when the leitmotif—for myself and other military sociologists—was to "prove" that apartheid was a full-fledged, if creaky, garrison state driven by a tutelary military behind the masquerade of constrained civilian governance. Since then, despite extraordinary constitutional developments that have allowed South Africa to escape from the brink of the apocalypse—of which the armed forces have been an intrinsic if discrete part—very little has been produced to accurately demonstrate the link between military disengagement and the demise of apartheid; the internal reconstruction of the military as a facet of a new political dispensation with residual features of the old authoritarian order; and, perhaps most important, the persistent role of the "iron surgeons" in shaping public policy to protect corporate power and autonomy as South Africa moves past its second set of elections into the more advanced, consolidative stages of democratization.

Part of this has to do, no doubt, with the sheer pace of local developments, which makes it exceedingly difficult to pinpoint, least of all analyze, institutional aspects of the political landscape. Much like other writers who wrestle with interpreting the complex dynamics of a resurrected civil society, we must make sense of material that shifts and changes almost daily. Part of the analytical neglect of the armed forces has to do with the astounding achievements of civil society in pacting a political settlement that the military has seen to be in its corporate interests; but a consequence has been to move the generals into the shadows from the center stage they enjoyed during the last years of apartheid.

Certain hybrid peculiarities of the South African experience in democratization have also made it difficult to locate the local experience within the universal context of civil-military relations in somewhat less deeply divided yet democratizing societies. Finally, much like those elsewhere, the South African military has maintained an apparently conservative reserve and opaque appearance, resistant to external intrusion, which has discouraged most analysts—some associated with the antiapartheid struggle, others with the Truth and Reconciliation Commission (in its final stages at this writing)—from attempting to break through the bureaucratic barriers in probing the veiled norms and structures of military life.

The following work is constructed atop several intellectual pillars, some obvious, some less so. First, it seeks to feed (while feeding upon) the global experience of militaries that have entered civilian politics with a mixture of relish and reluctance, only to exit in the face of popular pressure from within their own ranks, political coalitions in civil society, and, in many instances, the international system. Although some of the concepts of this broader civil-military experience are not readily and directly transplantable across the social and historic boundaries that distinguish South Africa from democratizing counterparts elsewhere, there is, I believe, much that can be related to the military disengagement and civilianization already existing in the burgeoning literature derived from other examples.

Second, the work aims to add to the fairly extensive but uneven body of writing on the South African "miracle," which remains largely inexplicable (at least until analysts enjoy the twin luxuries of historic retrospect and newly unearthed material). That being said, the work is consciously iconoclastic in its focus on a specific network of institutions located within the state wherein recent experiences reflect the pregnancy, birth pangs, and nervous first steps of an emergent democracy. Insofar as it is possible to measure the progress of democratic transition, the South Africa experience is far more complete that that of many Eastern European countries, where nationalist xenophobia has undercut or neutralized the essential spirit of democratic pluralism, or Latin American countries, where ingrained state militarism lurks behind the ostensible democratization of governmental institutions. Yet the popular myths woven around the much-vaunted "rainbow nation" to which South Africans proudly and not unjustifiably lay claim belie a situation where the sociopolitical prerequisites for a stable and enduring democratic culture remain to be fully institutionalized behind the formal and procedural mechanisms set in place by national elections.

Nowhere are the traumas, difficulties, and cross-cutting agendas in building democracy more pointed than in the legacy inherited by the military. The armed forces are an index to both the past and future of the political system, and should the fledgling experiment fail, distort, or become unsustainable among the guardians of state security, it is extremely unlikely that it can succeed elsewhere in civil society.

The South African armed forces did not necessarily steer the timing and agenda of the transition to the extent of other societies where redemocratization followed on the heels of direct military governance. By the late 1980s, profound disquiet existed within the officer corps as to the long-term sustainability of "total strategy" as the programmatic foundation of apartheid.

Three distinct yet overlapping and loose factions emerged in the ensuing debate over the relationship between the corporate interests of the armed forces and the political environment: a small "liberal" group centered largely in the Air Force, a substantially larger managerial-technocratic concentration in the South African Army (SAA), and, spread across the spectrum but with roots in military intelligence, a "warrior" element (the classic *duros*) determined to perpetuate apartheid for a mixture of ideological reasons and bureaucratic self-interests. For reasons of space we do not have the opportunity to explore the complex dynamics of the power struggles that followed, many of which remained veiled in secrecy following the orgy of document-destruction that followed the end of apartheid and the creation of the Truth and Reconciliation Commission to examine, inter alia, the role of the security forces in human rights atrocities soon thereafter. In the event, the essentially conservative and numerically predominant "managers" were able to forge the coalition of internal interests within the military that were to define its political position once the critical decision was taken to enter into negotiations with the military wings of the liberation movements, Umkhonto We Sizwe (variously MK, or the Spear of the Nation), associated with the African National Congress (ANC), and, to a lesser (and later) extent, the Pan African Congress's Azanian Peoples Liberation Army (APLA). We therefore proceed directly in Chapter 1 to examine the mechanics and content of this complex dialogue that extended (at least in its most visible aspects) from the end of 1992 until the April 1994 democratic elections. The essential aim of this chapter is to link the outcome of these military-to-military discussions to the power relations that emerged at the historic moment of democracy and have continued to shape the internal and external behavior of the armed forces as a key element of the state bureaucracy during the early postauthoritarian period.

Chapter 2 covers the integration of the various statutory and nonstatutory armed formations present at the birth of the new democracy into a unitary South African National Defence Force (SANDF, or simply NDF), with all the institutional and political struggles attendant on forging erstwhile enemies into a new and cohesive postapartheid military. The apartheid state did not effectively collapse, and, reflective of the negotiated character of South Africa's transition, many of the normative and structural features of military existence were carried through into the new Mandela administration. The new political dispensation has nevertheless challenged the institutional prerogatives the armed forces enjoyed under apartheid, particularly in its last phase, and Chapters 1 and 2 deal with the transformative impulses and initiatives that have transpired in the armed forces as a key segment of the state bureaucracy.

Chapter 3 deals with the experimental experiences and challenges facing the new composite institution that is the SANDF in the absence of the formal foundational pacts that have characteristically delineated civil-military relations in other transitional contexts, with particular emphasis on attempts to build new cultures and structures appropriate to the civilianization of the South African military. Since the SANDF is no different from any other bureaucratic organization in seeking to protect its organizational interests and prerogatives at a time of political extrication, Chapter 3 also deals with various points of contention between the military and civil society as the former seeks to maintain its established corporate integrity within the overall framework of political disengagement.

Chapter 4 analyzes the current and controversial internal redeployment of the military in projects for national reconstruction and development sanctioned by the primary and secondary responsibilities assigned the armed forces by the new Constitution; the reworked concepts of national defense strategy dictated by democratizations; and the politics of rearmament, where the military has reemerged as a natural demand-maker following South Africa's readmission to the global arena.

This sets the tone for the Epilogue, which attempts to develop various scenarios for civil-military relations in the twenty-first century—in light of domestic developments (particularly social pressure to downgrade the armed forces as an integral part of the overall democratic project), as well as the broader literature on the role of militaries in early postauthoritarian societies.

It is a measure of the extraordinary pace of change in South Africa that it is virtually impossible to write an up-to-the-minute account of political developments, including civil-military relations. Although the postapartheid transformation project has encountered serious obstacles, the objective of building a discernibly "new" nation has forged ahead.

Unfortunately for the analyst of the armed forces, this means that what is true today may not be true tomorrow. This book is thus an exercise in hitting a moving target, with all the inconsistencies that this implies. Because of the retrospective advantage we already enjoy in viewing developments in the 1980s and early 1990s, the initial discussions regarding negotiations leading to the creation of the SANDF (Chapter 1), as well as the consequent attempts to forge seven military formations into a single working unit (Chapter 2), remain as valid today as they were several years ago. The task facing the analyst at this point is simply to unearth the congealed history. The history of the transformation in motion (see Chapters 3 and 4) is not, however, set in stone; there is always a temporal disconnect between the event and its documentary representation.

I have attempted to eradicate the obvious inconsistencies (including the names of people who have since left the scene), and I have reshaped the final chapter to reflect the perceptions of an observer posed at the leading edge of the new millennium. Yet some parts of the book remain cast in the truth and logic of their moment in history, and thus they should be judged on that basis. This includes, for example, the sections on secretarial and parliamentary control over the armed forces; defense legislation; SANDF peacekeeping; and much of the debate over defense versus development. I have left these sections much as they were originally written in the belief that they still convey the substance of the unfolding linkages between the South African state and its armed forces.

No one is responsible for the redundancy that inevitably creeps into any account of a contemporary social change—much as one finds in the South African military and its relations with a rapidly transforming civil society. Likewise, no one is ultimately responsible for the opinions expressed in this work other than the author. Yet there are countless people without whose input this work would have been impossible. Many of these persons were of exceptional assistance in providing me hitherto unavailable primary material in the form of previously reserved internal documents and reports, as well as countless interviews on the essentials and marginalia of military behavior. During the course of writing this book I was in particular honored by a request from the SANDF to write a history for the period 1990–1996 subsequently entitled, somewhat grandly, *Marching to the Millenium: The Birth, Development, and Transformation of the South African National Defence Force*. Chapter 2, Chapter 3, and, to a lesser extent, Chapter 4 herein represent minor revisions of that parallel "internal" work whose origin, spirit, and existence attest to a new ethos of transparency and public accountability in the armed forces. I am grateful to the SANDF for official permission to reproduce this important material from military archives for public consumption.

Militaries are nevertheless militaries, that is, functionally necessitated "closed" institutions; many senior personnel in intelligence and high command cannot be publicly identified—particularly if their views depart from official positions. I was impressed by the assistance I received from officers of different political persuasions; their contribution was invaluable. My inability to publicize their names should not detract from the debt that I owe them. Having said that, I would like to extend my thanks to two officers in particular: Major General Deon Mortimer, perhaps the primary architect of the integration that took place on the heels of democratic elections; and Brigadier General Marius "Mo" Oelschig. Major General Mortimer made important comments on the draft of *Marching to the Millenium* prior to its speedy clearance by military security, and Brigadier Oelschig provided me with extensive documentation from his personal collection on the military negotiations prior to South Africa's first democratic elections, held in April 1994. Thanks are also due to Brigadier General Marius van Graan and his administrative staff at Directorate: Corporate Communications, which facilitated many interviews with otherwise unreachable persons in the military establishment, as well as Colonel Craig Harrison, the arch-documentor of the Integration Committee, without whose proceedings neither *Millenium* nor the current work would have been possible.

Although we differed on many fundamental points of history and personal philosophy, I would like to thank the late General H.A. "Kat" Liebenberg, who, despite the ravages of a terminal illness, was an unparalleled source of otherwise inaccessible impressionistic information on the dynamics of the mission creep that infected the SADF in the last years of apartheid. I have dealt with this in a way that honors General Liebenberg's wish that I do not personalize the material, that is, provide detailed names of the key actors involved, some of whom now face applications for amnesty before the Truth and Reconciliation Commission. I would also like to express my gratitude to members of the British Military Advisory and Training Team (BMATT) who provided crucial documentation. The Military Academy at Saldanha Bay and various institutions in the Army, Navy, Air force, and Medical Service were always helpful when I visited. Similar warm feelings are extended to senior officers in the so-called nonstatutory forces, as well as former members of MK, APLA, and the Transkei Defence Force (TDF)—all of whom made themselves available for interviews in a candid and private capacity. Colonel Claire Bless of Medical Services provided me data without which I could not possibly hope to understand the collective psychologies and social relations at work.

I would also like to thank countless men and women at the military grassroots—the people in the ranks whose views will, I hope, instill a populist dimension into a product unavoidably designed for consumption by a discerning academic audience and the general public.

Many knowledgeable people and institutions in civil society have also been gracious in encouraging this work, offering suggestions and, where necessary, criticism over three years. Considerable use has been made of secondary resources, including military statements and articles and press reports. Dozens of interviews have been conducted into the labyrinthine world of military politics during the last years of apartheid and the transition period. I am indebted to fellow academics, retired military personnel, government officials, journalists, political activists across the party constellation, and various professional people with experience of military life. It is impossible to thank all of these individuals and institutions individually.

However, I would like mention several: Jakkie Cilliers and Bill Sass of the Institute for Security Studies—the Institute for Defence Policy at the initiation of my research—who reactivated my interest in South African civil-military relations a half-dozen years after the publication of my first book on the subject; Tom Lodge, my colleague at the University of the

Witwatersrand, who inspired my title; and various research assistants and erstwhile students, some now prominent members of the defense family, who have helped throughout the course of this complex project. Among the latter group, Tsepe Motume and Rocky Williams warrant particular mention.

On a personal note, I would like to thank my wife, Angela, and my daughter, Andrea, the doyen of my researchers. With her generation rests the responsibility of consolidating the struggle for democracy and justice at this turbulent tip of Africa.

Philip Frankel
Johannesburg

Acronyms

AA	Assembly Area
ANC	African National Congress
APLA	Azanian Peoples Liberation Army
AWB	Afrikaner Weerstandsbeweging
AZANLA	Azanian National Liberation Army
AZAPO	Azanian Peoples Organisation
BDF	Bophutatswana Defence Force
BMATT	British Military Advisory and Training Team
BNG	Bophutatswana National Guard
BT1/BT2	Bridging Training (Phases 1–2)
CDF	Ciskei Defence Force
CODESA	Congress for a Democratic South Africa
CPR	Certified Personnel Register
CSADF/ CSANDF	Chief of the South African (National) Defence Force
DCC	Defence Command Council
DIS	Department of Intelligence and Security (ANC)
DHQ	Defence Headquarters (Pretoria)
DOD	Department of Defence
DMI	Directorate Military Intelligence
DTL	Directorate for Transitional Liaison
GEAR	Growth, Employment, and Redistribution Program
GNP	Gross national product
IFP	Inkatha Freedom Party
IDASA	Institute for a Democratic South Africa
ISDSC	Interstate Defence and Security Committee
ISS	Institute for Security Studies
IWG	Integration Working Group
JMCC	Joint Military Coordinating Council
JPSCD	Joint Parliamentary Standing Committee on Defence
MCC	Military Command Council
MDC	Military Disciplinary Code
MK	Umkhonto We Sizwe (Spear of the Nation)
MRG	Military Research Group

NCCAC	National Committee for Conventional Arms Control
NCO	Noncommissioned officer
NCPS	National Crime Prevention Strategy
NDF	National Defence Force
NIA	National Intelligence Agency
NIS	National Intelligence Service
NPKF	National Peace-Keeping Force
NSF	Nonstatutory force
NSMS	National Security Management System
OAU	Organization of African Unity
OPDS	Organ for Politics, Defence, and Security
PAC	Pan African Congress
PDSC	Plenary Defence Staff Council
PIOC	Parliamentary Integration Oversight Committee
PIP	Psychological Integration Program (Medical Services)
PMORD	Personnel Maintenance Office/Reception Depot
PRWG	Personnel Rationalisation Working Group
RDP	Reconstruction and Development Program
SAA	South African Army
SAAF	South African Air Force
SADC	Southern African Development Community
SADF	South African Defence Force
SAMS	South African Medical Services
SAN	South African Navy
SANDF	South African National Defence Force
SAP/S	South African Police/Services
SCD	Sub-Council on Defence
SCSJ	Select Committee on Security and Justice
SDA	Special Defense Account
SDU	Self-Defense Unit (ANC)
SF	Statutory force
SPP	Strategic Planning Process
SPU	Self-Protection Unit (Inkatha)
STSC	Short-Term Service Contract
TBVC	Transkei, Bophutatswana, Venda, and Ciskei Defence Forces
TDF	Transkei Defence Force
TEC	Transitional Executive Council
VDF	Venda Defence Force

It could so easily have been different because they [the security forces] had the physical means to turn the country into a bloodbath of frightening proportions.

—Adriaan Vlok, former National Party minister of law and order, in testimony for amnesty before the Truth and Reconciliation Commission, quoted in *The Star* (Johannesburg), July 22, 1998.

History causes the military problem to become the essence of the political problem.

—Lenin, in a 1921 speech.

1

Negotiation: Forging the Military Pact

If military-political affairs were only left to a few efficient and reliable officers, the officers would soon agree to everybody's satisfaction.

—*Helmuth von Moltke, "The Elder" (1800–1891).*

The enemies front is not the objective. The essential thing is to crush the enemies flanks . . . and complete the extermination by an attack on his rear.

—*Alfred von Schlieffen,* Cannae *(1913).*

Contemporary democratic transitions take on forms that reflect power relations between elite incumbents and opponents seeking to dismantle authoritarian political systems. Some transitions are speedy to the extent that history has eroded the foundations of authoritarian power in a manner that precludes elites negotiating from strength. Others are substantially slower because of equity in power between the protagonists, one consequence of which is that the political arrangements governing the emergent democratic system become heavily dependent upon trade-offs of interest, complex political deals, and give-and-take in aligning agendas. All transitions, however, require negotiations of some sort or another, including political gamesmanship not only between stakeholders in civil society but also between military actors. This is especially the case where each player, as in South Africa, possesses their own armed forces.

Prelude: Talks about Talks, 1991–1993

It is semiofficially acknowledged that the first tentative and vague contacts—the proverbial talks about talks—between the SADF and MK (the armed wing of the ANC) took place in 1991, although there is some evidence to suggest informal discussions occurred between individuals from the South African military and MK as early as ten to fifteen years before. Certainly the Directorate Military Intelligence (DMI) and the Department of Intelligence and Security (DIS), the intelligence arms of the SADF and the ANC respectively, were in touch, if only to "penetrate" the other long before F.W. de Klerk's groundbreaking speech of February 1990, which opened the way to political reform. The content of this speech, which politically legalized the ANC and its allies in the liberation movement, nevertheless stimulated communication, with both parties—SADF and MK—meeting secretly on several occasions from May onward to address technical military issues arising out from the Groote Schuur Agreement, the product of the first formal talks between the ANC and the South African government.

Commonality of political interest was soon evident despite the distance between the opposing parties. As at the Congress for a Democratic South Africa (CODESA) meetings, where the two, major political parties were determined to dominate outcomes behind the appearance of democratic multilateralism, the MK and the SADF agreed to exclude the "homeland" and other nonstatutory forces from participation in future discussions in order to avoid "complications." Neither the small Azanian National Liberation Army (AZANLA) nor APLA (the military wing of the Azanian Peoples Organisation [AZAPO] and the Pan African Congress [PAC]) were, in any case, inclined to enter negotiations prior to the transfer of power; neither was MK (the largest of the liberation armies) especially keen to form a united front with these smaller and ideologically divergent organizations in deciding on the future of a new national defense force. The SADF, with its equally monopolistic inclinations, was not about to consult with its clones in the homelands and thus conceded that their presence would imply recognition of the so-called *bantustans*.

In any event, both parties were suspicious of the largest of these armies, the Transkei Defence Force, whose wily leader, General Bantu Holomisa, had been playing a complex political game to build a support base among the SADF, the ANC, and the PAC simultaneously. MK was also "painfully aware that in many respects the technical expertise and formal training of the Transkei, Bophutatswana, Venda, and Ciskei (TBVC) forces was a threat to its own role as the SADF's major negotiating adversary."[1] Holomisa and these forces were eventually to throw in their lot with the ANC when they were finally admitted to negotiations in November 1993. By then, however, the major decisions had been taken. This, plus the absence of other nonstatutory forces, did not "reduce the validity of negotiations"[2] but, as we shall see, posed several problems that would become evident once the armed forces amalgamated after the elections.

By early 1993, however, political negotiations in civil society at CODESA were beginning to deadlock as the ANC and the National Party—the two biggest players in the game—ran into disputes over essential questions, principles, and procedures with regard to power sharing. The SADF and Umkhonto now decided to take the initiative and enter into bilateral negotiations, for continued political uncertainty had obvious implications for the military balance of power between the state military and its opponents. Neither of the key negotiators at the Congress for a Democratic South Africa (CODESA, convened at the World Trade Centre in Kempton Park east of Johannesburg, ultimately brokered the agreement that led to the 1994 democratic elections), Roelf Meyer (lead negotiator for the government/National Party) and Cyril Ramaphosa (chief negotiator for the ANC) was seen to be especially well equipped to address the specific issues inherent in a military pact; perhaps more important, neither enjoyed the full confidence of the respective military leaderships. From the SADF perspective, Meyer, who had enjoyed a short and not particularly distinguished career as de Klerk's previous minister of defense, seemed insufficiently forceful to be entrusted with the important business of securing the corporate interests of the armed forces under some new, as yet unclear political dispensation. His association with de Klerk, the archetype Machiavellian and cynically self-serving politician (in the view of some generals), had further damaged Meyer's image as the person to negotiate the appropriate "fit" for the military within a postapartheid framework. The comparably sleek Ramaphosa, who had been involved in the struggle only on the internal front, was equally uncongenial to the hard men of MK, who, like their SADF counterparts, began to feel that direct military-to-military talks were needed.

As civil leaders appeared increasingly incapable of managing the violence outside the negotiating chambers, both sets of military leaders were reinforced in their mutual concurrence that it was essential to secure a degree of internal order so that political negotiations could continue. Both MK and the SADF were deeply concerned that "unstable elements"—APLA, the Afrikaner Weerstandsbeweging (AWB), and, to a lesser degree, the Afrikaner Vryheidsfront—could derail political negotiations, but neither felt it could act unilaterally against military formations that were either ideologically akin or sentimentally inclined toward the opponent. In the case of the SADF, action against APLA or rogue elements in MK would have unacceptable political spin-offs; neither could its own leadership be seen to take decisive action against the militant white right wing, with its strategic pockets of support in the Commandos (largely white rural units), in the part-time forces, and in the military mainstream—unless MK could be recruited into an initiative under the umbrella of a "national" peace force.

"The purpose of negotiations," noted an SADF official at the time, "is to find the best possible way to *jointly* manage conflict before, during and after elections."[3] Unstated was the view that MK appeared to be "on the bare bones of its arse," with limited logistical control and infrastructure for its widely dispersed cadres in the Republic and camps to the north of the border. Confident that it could maneuver proceedings from a position of strength, the SADF welcomed intensified bilateral talks that, it believed, would catch MK off-balance.

These views were shared by the senior leadership of the South African Police (SAP, the old apartheid police), which, like its military counterparts, was deeply disturbed by the escalating political violence in the run-up to the April 1994 elections. The SAP, however, was reluctant (or institutionally incapable) of participating in the full-blown strategic management plan for elections—nor was the SAP especially welcomed by the military. Hence, the military bureaucrats were at the center of various efforts (by now launched on mandate from the Defence Command Council [DCC]) to devise a system to protect national and corporate interests in the unstable, unpredictable conditions of transition. Since the legalization of the ANC, the SADF had in fact begun provisionally examining the various costs, benefits, and options attached to transacting with MK, and during 1992 efforts were stepped up to work the variables into a systematic, if unfortunately termed, "total strategy" for negotiations. As the SADF recognized, this involved, inter alia, setting "minimum baselines" for the principles and process of eventual integration of all forces into the new national defense force that would inevitably follow elections. During 1992, for example, SADF strategists at Operations Division, because of several difficulties inherent in bringing the various armed formations together, toyed with the idea of "joint arrangements" with MK rather than full integration prior to elections. These included time constraints with elections looming, the possible diminution of SADF command and control once MK became part of a single defense force, and subsequent internal conflict within the SADF, including resistance from the "platteland," that is, rightist elements in its part-time component.[4] Ultimately, full preelectoral integration was elevated to the top of the agenda (for the SADF, if not MK), since this would simultaneously secure the armed forces the legitimacy they required; facilitate SADF participation in a National Peace-keeping Force (NPKF); and, perhaps most important, lock MK into a system of institutionalized control before the transfer of power to an unpredictable Government of National Unity.

The internal debate then turned its attention to the comparative costs and advantages of integrating MK members as a group or individually. Initially, there was a strong case for the latter: This would assist quality control over new MK recruits, maintain SADF hegemony, break MK cohesion, cream off its leadership (who could be anticipated to be among the first to apply for admission), and assist the inculcation of SADF organizational culture. Collective integration, in contrast, would compel MK to release information on its depots, organization, and personnel, notwithstanding the downside to this option—the economics of the exercise, the risk of "SAW troepe" (i.e., the national armed forces) being placed under MK commanders with their political commitments, and, once again, resistance from the right, both inside and, to a lesser extent, outside the military establishment.

Eventually the decision settled on the collective approach, so long as it would not impede SADF constitutional responsibilities and operational effectiveness. MK would settle for nothing less, and integration en masse held out several crucial symbolic and strategic advantages. At the metaphorical level, it would build local and international credibility for the SADF as a participant in a truly "popular" force. MK would be challenged to match this bona fides, and if it did not (or so it was calculated), it could be labeled as destructive to the transition process. Less prosaically, the collective approach would halt the dangerous tendency of MK cadres to disperse or exfiltrate throughout the country; it also spread the burden and responsibility for managing the mounting political violence.[5]

Debates of this type formed the backdrop to the first officially acknowledged bilateral contacts between the SADF and MK. As we have implied, they are still veiled in mystery, although it is commonly accepted that the intelligence services in both camps—the National Intelligence Service (NIS), Military Intelligence, and the ANC's DIS—were important brokers in bringing together the military men as well as the ANC political leaders. Various clandestine meetings took place from the beginning of the 1990s, most at the Dome (the Military Intelligence College in the eastern suburbs of Pretoria), and they enabled each side to come to a direct appreciation of the other. NIS and Military Intelligence were in close contact with Mandela through intermediaries who visited the future president after he was transferred from Robben Island to Pollsmoor Prison on the South African mainland prior to his eventual release; Thabo Mbeki, whom the intelligence agencies contacted in both Europe and Africa; "Terror" Lekota (subsequently premier of the Free State region); and, above all, Joe Modise, who was correctly appraised as heir-apparent to the Ministry of Defence (MOD) under the proposed new government. From the purely military perspective, these first minor contacts were important not only in clearing up mutual misperceptions but also as a means of bonding the soldiers despite their political differences and historic enmity. While it would be an exaggeration to say, as some former SADF leaders do in retrospect, that reconciliation began in the military years before civil society, the personal relations quietly forged between individuals among the two major armed formations while the politicians were posturing were significant in circumventing the institutional obstacles that arose once deliberations became more serious, public, and formal. Certainly both armies realized that, in the absence of a military pact and irrespective of any political deals, South Africa would be reduced to a wasteland that neither wished to inherit.

Once power-sharing negotiations got under way, mechanisms were put in place to coordinate negotiation strategy on a more regular and formal basis. In late 1992, General "Kat" Liebenberg, Chief of the South African Defence Force (CSADF), volunteered the SADF to energize negotiations with Neil Barnard, chief of NIS; shortly thereafter it appears that delegations met at a secret venue east of Pretoria. Principles were placed on the table, although both parties emphasized that these were not "negotiations," as the ANC had only "suspended" the armed struggle. Nevertheless, agreement was reached on several basic principles that eventually shaped the military component of transition, such as the apolitical and nondiscriminatory nature of a postapartheid military. SADF's insistence on maintaining a large part-time component in the future defense force as a matter of economy soured the somewhat brittle atmosphere, largely because MK equated this arrangement with conscription, the maintenance of the white Commandos, and minority power in general. This reinforced the SADF perception, which it would later turn to its advantage, that MK had little information on the specialist aspects, structures, and chain of command of the South African armed forces, despite a good general knowledge of military matters. To the relief of the SADF, MK accepted the need to maintain high professional standards but then asserted that they could not be barriers to speedy affirmative action to make the military more representative. Since the SADF favored what it termed a "natural" rather than "forced" color configuration, the gathering, according to all accounts, stiffly teetered to conclusion.

Round One: Admiralty House, Blenny, and the First Bilaterals

In March 1993, SADF and MK members appeared together in public for the first time at a conference on the future of the Navy organized by the Institute for Defence Policy (now the Institute for Security Studies, or ISS). A similar meeting to set the tone for real military negotiations took place in the same month between MK and representatives of the South African Air Force (SAAF), ostensibly to discuss acquisitions policy regarding new training aircraft for the SAAF. Though officially sanctioned by Mandela, the meeting began badly, according to SAAF participants, with Modise and Mojo Motau of the ANC launching into rhetoric about past injustices. Thereafter, as the participants warmed to each other, discussions focused on a variety of issues, including the international arms embargo on South Africa, the need for the SAAF to adopt a defensive posture, and the role of local defense industries in assisting other African airforces. The SAAF representatives left pleasantly surprised by the level of general knowledge about military aviation on the part of their MK counterparts.[6]

This informal encounter ushered in the main event on the negotiations calendar: bilateral talks between the armed forces of the South African state and the military wing of the ANC at Admiralty House in the Simonstown naval base in Cape Town on April 23 and 24. At this auspicious and groundbreaking event, the SADF delegation consisted of CSADF General Liebenberg, Lieutenant General Georg Meiring (chief of the Army), Lieutenant General J. Kriel (chief of the SAAF), Major General J.P.B. Erasmus (chief of Military Intelligence), Brigadier J.W. Sonnekus of the Army, and Dr. Neil Barnard (head of the National Intelligence Service). Its ANC counterparts on this occasion were Joe Modise (commander of MK), Siphiwe Nyanda (chief of staff, MK), Joe Nhlanhla (chief of DIS), its adjutant chief, Mo Shaik, Matthews Phosa (head of the ANC's legal department), and a prominent civil rights lawyer, professor Fink Haysom. The South African Navy, the small but historically "liberal" arm of the SADF, was conspicuous in its absence; there was no formal agenda, but the meeting was cautiously publicized as an event to negotiate mechanisms for the management of ongoing political violence while clearing up "possible misunderstandings and misperceptions" on both sides of the military equation.[7]

The initial part of the two-day meeting was dominated by presentations by senior SADF officers on the mission, strength, and organization of the SADF, ostensibly to acquaint MK with its structure and workings. Since MK was already acquainted with the skeletal and basic information provided in the charts and organigrams placed on display, this extended exercise was not only tedious (according to participants) but also perceived for what it was intended to be, namely, a conscious policy to intimidate and confuse MK with a mass of technical information designed to project the enormous complexity of the SADF and its preponderant strength over any of the liberation forces. Given its self-presumed superiority, the SADF then proceeded to raise concerns about MK weaponry and to advocate that both its firepower and personnel, upon the brink of repatriation to South Africa, be placed under the command and control of what its representatives termed the "statutory" military. This was further broadened with the introduction of the notion that any joint force established to maintain internal order also be placed under the authority of the *wettige veiligsheidsmag*, that is, the "lawful" military.

MK understandably rejected these principles for discussion, what with their underlying allusions to Umkhonto inferiority and their less-than-veiled suggestion that the armed wing of the ANC bow before SADF hegemony. While MK had no objection in principle to subjecting its armaments and personnel to the oversight and control of external structures, these must, it argued, not be the SADF (whom it presumed to be an equal negotiating partner) but a higher political authority, such as the proposed Transitional Executive Council (TEC) vaunted by the civilian negotiators at CODESA. In the interests of mutuality and balance, the SADF should place itself under the authority of the TEC as well. The principle of joint control by a multiparty political authority for preelectoral purposes should, MK added, also be extended to any new peacekeeping force. This could conceivably be either the TEC or an independent electoral commission, both of whom would be mandated to "prevent an impact on the political playing field by the security forces" before elections and during the process of postelection amalgamation. The SADF, equally understandably, did not concur at this point.

Although the first Simonstown meeting ended in a tentative impasse (an expected outcome), the event is important in setting the tone and logic that dominated discussions over the military "pact" as a component of overall transitional negotiations for much of the run-up to the April 1994 elections. It is understandable, as neither party at the table, at Admiralty House and long thereafter, approached negotiations with deep-seated feelings of reconciliation. Since one side had not defeated the other, the self-satisfaction of the SADF, rooted in its superior numbers and technology, was more than matched by the arrogance of MK in the atmosphere of political victory.

From Admiralty House to the Joint Military Coordinating Council (JMCC) that was to come on line nine months later to guide the new National Defence Force (NDF) into democracy, neither party could entirely come to terms, perhaps even less so than their civilian counterparts, who working toward an interim constitution at the World Trade Centre, given the complex political and military contradictions inherent in a situation of "negotiated revolution." As in the civilian realm, however, the antagonists at Simonstown were, for better or worse, interdependent, and this sense of symbiotic futures eventually drove the sides together regardless of mutual antipathies, surface conflicts, strategic maneuvers, and wranglings over detail. The tendency of the SADF and MK to drift toward a common negotiating language despite the state strategy to disorient their opponents also appeared at this early stage once MK made it evident that it would not be bludgeoned into agreements that were incomprehensible. Armed with political astuteness, MK, as we shall see, was able to drive the debate from the complex technicist heights to relatively simple terms of communication on the blunt issues of transferring power. This "popularization" factor enabled MK to shape the agenda to a far greater degree than professional soldiers, and at Simonstown and succeeding venues the plan of the military to "fight political battles through projecting its specialist knowledge on technical matters" counted very little in what emerged as a straight political battle in which MK promised to deliver on the legitimacy that the SADF required in return for incorporating erstwhile opponents into the national armed forces.[8]

As at the political pact negotiated at CODESA, time constraints imposed by the April 27 deadline held the military parties together and, ultimately, forced conclusions that worked, in many respects, to the advantage of MK. Despite the tense atmosphere and disagreements at Admiralty House, the two-day meeting ended with a decision to establish three working groups to address the leading-edge issues in periodic follow-up discussions during 1993 and, to a large extent, in the deliberations of the JMCC that followed at year's end.

In the first instance, the Simonstown meeting was called to establish some joint military mechanism to facilitate governance in a climate of political violence—both at present and in the anticipated future, when the TEC would come to fruition to guide South Africa into elections. Already prior to the Simonstown meeting, the concept of the Sub-Council for Defence (SCD) within the TEC had been mooted, and, at Admiralty House, considerable if fleeting attention was given to its terms of reference in exercising control over the various security forces. The exact mechanics of the relationship between the proposed SCD and TEC remained unfinished business by the end of this meeting. Yet there was agreement that the role of the SCD would be to oversee all armed formations "insofar as their activities would impact" on the process leading up to and during elections—even as SADF and MK remained independent bodies. This subtle arrangement was acceptable to both parties, as neither was especially enthused with the prospect of being constrained in freedom action prior to the establishment of a new unified military on elections night; yet each wanted a loose joint administration to monitor the actions of the other.

With an eye to exercising some degree of control over MK, the SADF also raised its concern about the continued training of MK members outside the country, then generously proposed the establishment of assembly points within the Republic where both local and repatriated MK troops could be concentrated for training on a joint basis with SADF logistic support and, if required, international supervision. These assembly areas (AAs), the SADF intimated, would constitute the first practical step toward integration and the development of a new national defense force. But MK would not be drawn to the urgency of beginning integration along this route, largely because concentrating its forces in camps surrounded by the SADF would render them vulnerable. Although the SADF continued to argue that since the ANC would probably win the elections it made no sense to delay integration, MK remained firm that the process should start only after the creation of a government of national unity. This did not, however, preclude initial preparation.

Third and finally, both parties turned their attention to the immediate creation of the transitional NPKF comprising all parties and dedicated to maintaining the peace process. Since the SADF and MK reflected the will of their political masters—that negotiations be sustained in support of a political settlement—the leaders accepted the principle of such a force as well as the need to immediately investigate such technical issues as composition, training, budget, and possible deployment. At this point supposition was that the proposed NPKF (the peacekeeping force) would eventually blend into the NDF after elections. Foreshadowing later developments, the parties failed to reach consensus on questions of command and control over the NPKF.

In early May, the SADF sat down to articulate a follow-up negotiation strategy in a series of meetings at Blenny, on the edge of Pretoria, attended by the most prominent members of the High Command. These included General H.A. "Kat" Liebenberg, General Georg Meiring (as well as four other senior Army officers), head of military intelligence General J.P.B. Erasmus, and the most senior officers of the Air Force,Lieutenant General J. Kriel and its subsequent chief, Lieutenant General W.H. Hechter.[9] Doubts were expressed whether it was possible to complete integration before elections, but it was decided to make a maximum effort to "bind" MK and other military formations into long-range arrangements while political power remained with the National Party.[10] Skepticism was also expressed over the efficacy of a *gesaamentlike vredesmag*(community peace force of civilian and military personnel), but the Joint Peace Force (as it was then termed), it was decided, should proceed, if only as a device to neutralize the nonstatutory military formations through a system of joint training and common activity. The Army was to play a dominant role, and at least 50 percent of the peace force would be SADF as a prophylactic against ulterior purposes.[11] Other formations would be "understudies," and it was important, according to participants, that unstable elements—including the AWB—be "kept busy."[12] A minimum seven-month training program was anticipated, and it was strongly emphasized that anything shorter would undermine the whole initiative.

AAs were, the meeting agreed, an important device in this process of concentration, provided the SADF maintained maximum control over their management. "Sincere" international observers from the Eastern bloc would be welcomed to oversee the process, but Australians, Canadians, Americans, and Cubans would be excluded from participation "at all costs." Insofar as monetary costs were concerned, the financing of the AA process would come from sources outside SADF. When the Air Force indicated its concern that its role required more highly specialized personnel than mere infantrymen, SAAF was assured independence in selecting its own integrees from the AAs. None of these decisions—indeed no concessions at all—were to be revealed to MK until it agreed to release accurate statistics on MK manpower.[13]

During late May 1993, a small group of SADF members was also appointed to work with MK on specific problems arising from the first talks. This included Generals Erasmus and Kriel as well as Brigadier "Mo" Oelschig and Colonel "Callie" Steijn of the SADF. On the MK side were Rashid Patel, Mojo Motau, and Refiloe Mudimu. From May 26 to June 10, this group worked closely and hammered out several key issues.

Command-and-control matters, which were to dog the bilateral and multilateral meetings for the remainder of the year, however, remained stumbling blocks. On the proposed JMCC (the Joint Coordinating Council at the time), for example, disputes remained over its functions, activities, and relationship with the future SCD. As was to be the case long after this initial working group had been terminated, discussions were frequently interrupted as negotiators moved out to consult with principals on alternatives, including the possible creation of two committees, one under the existing MOD (which would remain an SADF bastion until elections), the other (responsible for the NPKF) under the direct authority of the TEC. Talks also focused on the possible creation of a Joint Coordinating Committee for Integration, also to be established under the SCD, "in consultation with the Minister of Defence."[14] Ultimately, agreement was reached on what was to become the JMCC under the authority of the SCD.

The NPKF also had a mixed experience on a range of issues, from the most technically mundane to matters of command and control. Even at this early juncture the SADF began to doubt whether such a formation could be effectively trained and deployed before upcoming elections. Still, an NPKF held the possibility of concentrating MK's dispersed and potentially dangerous members and represented an alternative to the AAs where MK would in fact not assemble. Since it was also a common political interest that such a force be established to maintain the social environment for ongoing political negotiations, consensus in principle was quickly reached and a series of work groups established to identify details of NPKF operations, logistics, communications, finance, and other functional matters translate the concept into reality.

The NPKF, it was generally agreed, would be a paramilitary force tasked to prevent physical violence, to intervene where necessary, to apprehend agitators through coordinated action with law-enforcement agencies, and, more broadly, to level the political playing field by providing protection for free political activity, crowd control, and the protection of polling stations to be determined by the Independent Elections Commission.[15] Agreement was also reached fairly easily on the NPKF financing, which would come from the state and not SADF coffers, with possible supplementary assistance from the international community.[16] Issues such as logistical support, equipment, daily maintenance, uniforms, and vehicle colors (light blue) were quickly dispensed.[17]

Yet as both players constantly looked over their shoulders to assess the political consequences of their decisions, the less technical and more political an issue the more difficult it was to reach a meeting of minds.

The composition of the NPKF, for example, quickly became a bone of contention. Both parties conceded that the mission of the NPKF required the force to be legitimate, representative, balanced, and fully integrated down to the section level. Both also agreed that all armed formations consisting of South African citizens be included, but this necessarily spilled over into the sensitive issue of the status of the homeland armies—statutory armies from the viewpoint of the SADF, *bantustan* creations from the perspective of MK. Since both sides were reluctant to overcommit resources to an experimental military venture outside their own control, however, pragmatism took precedence over principle. When the homeland armies agreed to the use of their facilities should the NPKF be deployed to their areas, both MK and the SADF swung into agreement.[18] The NPKF was therefore to consist of approximately 1,000 MK troops, one battalion each of SADF and TDF forces, as well as smaller contributions from the defense forces of the Ciskei and Venda (part of the homeland armies/*bantustans*).[19] Whether the NPKF should also include police personnel from the homelands and the SAP was also a minor issue, resulting in the eventual decision to include only military personnel working in close coordination with police authorities.

Even then, disputes arose as to what constituted an "armed formation." Since the peace process up until elections was punctuated by sporadic acts of violence from militant groups on both extremes of the political spectrum, the issue arose as to whether such elements as APLA and the AWB should (or could) be neutralized through an invitation to subscribe to involvement in the NPKF. MK, for its part, was favorably disposed to include APLA—the military wing of the rival PAC—as part of upgrading the numbers of the "liberation armies" but could not conceive the possibility of working alongside the racists in the AWB. Similar antipathy toward the paramilitary AWB, whose existence and unpredictability challenged SADF hegemony over the statutory forces (SFs), was felt among more moderate SADF leaders, who were not prepared to cooperate with APLA until the PAC officially terminated the armed struggle. This point was strongly underlined to Joe Modise by Dr. Neil Barnard of NIS when the various parties met at the World Trade Centre in September.[20]

Consequently, it was decided that no organization could obtain membership in the NPKF should it participate in violence or use or continue to use violence as a policy to achieve political ends.[21] Still, differences arose over recruitment criteria and the size of the NPKF. Given the wide range of its support base in townships and the historically important role of black youth in the mass mobilization that was to erode apartheid in the 1980s, MK was inclined to support including anyone over sixteen as part of a peace force of some 10,000 men. With a view to excluding the common *klipgooiers* (stone-throwers) and minimizing logistical investment, the SADF preferred a minimum admission age of eighteen and a force component of about 3,000.[22] Ultimately, in December, it was agreed that the minimum age would be sixteen (with preference for more mature candidates) and that logistical planning would take place on the basis of an initial intake of 3,000, rising to a possible 10,000 should circumstances warrant.[23]

Although both parties concurred that the NPKF be schooled in doctrines of minimum force, training issues were also controversial. There was a common view that international assistance be recruited to facilitate the training process, with less certainty on whom should be approached to render help. MK, given its background, favored the United Nations, some of the former Soviet bloc countries, or a "cocktail" of forces in the face of SADF preference for European or British help, given the roots of the nation's armed forces in the commonwealth tradition. Since both sides were suspicious of encouraging intervention by a third party, it was decided to approach the British as the least potentially dangerous of all possibilities. It is partially a measure of the technical and political wranglings that took place during 1993 that a special subcommittee to address training issues on a multilateral basis did not convene at the Army College until December.[24] Here again, at root were the tedious matters of command and control. The SADF preference—that political control of the NPKF be vested in the existing minister of defense in order to kick-start training as soon as possible—was unacceptable to the MK, which remained unwilling to grant authority for the military side of the peace process to an "apartheid structure" at the expense of the TEC. The SADF, in turn, rejected this view, as the TEC was geared to come on line only months before elections, and this would make it impossible to effectively train the NPKF in peace-enforcement functions.

A series of alternative formulas was then placed on the table in June to break the deadlock. These included a system of joint control between the TEC and the MOD, the administrative "attachment" of the NPKF to the MOD, and even the creation of some new third body with power over NPKF leadership.[25] MK, however, continued to adhere to the view that the logic of the NPKF as a joint instrument in the peace process demanded its establishment under a joint political authority such as the JMCC under the TEC. In effect, a great proportion of NPKF business, including training, was deferred until the emergence of the JMCC in January 1994. By that time, the SADF had concluded that the entire elaborate plan was fatefully delayed by MK "obstruction" and that it was practically impossible to fully emplace the NPKF to fulfill its mission. SADF enthusiasm for the initiative declined even lower, which, as we shall see, sealed the NPKF's abysmal failure in the end.

Scoring Points: Mid-1993

As the NPKF slid to the margins of the SADF agenda, long-range questions about the nature of the NDF that would follow upon elections moved to center stage. The issue of eventual integration, as we have noted, figured in the first Simonstown talks, and as various bilateral and multilateral meetings succeeded through 1993, it became increasingly urgent that agreement be reached on the character of the postelectoral armed forces.

Here again some issues eased into consensus while others became caught up in interminable wrangles, both on and behind the scenes, as the various players jockeyed for advantage. Article 16 of the TEC Act, for example, eventually made provision for a committee (or committees) of specialists to lay down guidelines for concentrating both locally and externally based MK personnel, but the AAs quickly emerged as a primary point of conflict. The siting of AAs at Wallmansthal, De Brug, and Hoedspruit was not especially problematic for MK, once the SADF offered its own facilities as reporting points by September.[26] Yet some SADF senior leaders were less than enthusiastic at having to assume the responsibility for feeding thousands of "former terrorists" at Wallmansthal who would be concentrated "on the doorstep of the PWV" (the Pretoria-Witwatersrand-Vaal Triangle), especially near Pretoria.[27] The existence of three reception depots nevertheless conformed with SADF policy to limit the number of AAs to a minimum as a means to reduce logistic investment.[28] The decentralized arrangement also alleviated ANC anxiety that its members would be "cordoned" and rendered strategically vulnerable.

The logistics of the AAs to which the specialist committees were referred were also relatively smoothly decided despite MK insistence as early as May that the responsibility for payment and maintenance of those assembled rested with the South African state once cadres returned from across the borders.[29] Questions of remuneration for integrees, which would dog the whole process at a later stage, now surfaced, but MK dropped its pitch that support also be extended to the dependents of integrees once it became evident that this was beyond SADF philanthropy.[30]As always, however, "security" issues, that is, matters of command and control, resurfaced, with the two parties in virtually diametrical opposition with regard to AA management. Unlike the NPKF, whose existence was largely a sideshow in the grand scheme of integration, AAs were a keystone in the development of the new NDF—and, as a consequence, both teams of negotiators dug in their heels. As the minority party, MK could not conceivably bargain away its powers in these areas without placing itself at the mercy of its opponents. To most MK leaders, the concept of concentrating their members at specific sites was tantamount to military emasculation. Throughout the organization there was the well-founded belief that MK troops, once concentrated, could become proverbial sitting ducks. While both parties recognized that assembly must necessarily precede integration, MK was determined to secure maximum autonomy over the process, the more so as SADF negotiators at various meetings rubbed feelings raw by referring to the AAs as vital mechanisms of "control" necessary to assist integration.

To say, in the words of one SADF commentator, that MK had "problems with the SADF's understanding of command, control and security" at the assembly points is, in historic retrospect, an understatement.[31] While the SADF held out several options for the AAs, including international oversight worked through the JMCC, or joint control under the SCD, MK clung doggedly throughout 1993 to the principle that the sites should be under its own sole authority, including complete MK autonomy with respect to daily routine, training activity, security, and even weapons.[32] At the third bilateral meeting in September, for example, MK indicated that it saw no function for the SADF in any manner or at any level in the AAs apart from facilitation between the AAs and the SCD. When questioned on whether this was appropriate given that the SADF was making available its own resources and facilities for assembly, MK replied that this was irrelevant. Command and control at all levels and in all areas, MK insisted, was vested in the forces who occupied those facilities; as an added security measure, MK also required control over the immediate perimeter of any such area.[33]

At the next bilateral meeting the following month, the SADF responded that since one of the primary purposes of the AAs was to foster integration the existence of an independent controlling force was totally unacceptable in principle. MK demands for its own bases "in order to prepare its own forces for integration" were, its spokesmen added, entirely incompatible with the principles of joint planning and preparation for integration, and an armed force with its own weapons, training programs, and responsibility for security was intolerable. At the meeting, understandably, they agreed to "terminate" its unproductive discussions and request a meeting of principals.[34]

At the November bilateral, however, the same conflicts arose, with General Erasmus taking MK to task for articulating demands outside the spirit of joint understandings developed by the principals, that is, Modise and General Liebenberg. MK replied, justifiably, that SADF demands that it surrender its personnel and weapons was also outside the spirit of bilateral cooperation: What applied to one party should apply to another. For good measure, MK added that in its judgment the SADF was discriminatory, devious, prescriptive, and arrogant in its refusal to treat MK from the outset as an equivalent army. This augured badly for the future of integration, which MK saw as a genuine merger of forces and not the absorption of MK into the SADF. When SADF negotiators responded sharply by accusing MK of ongoing negative criticism, the meeting once more broke up in an atmosphere of unbridgeable dissensus.[35]

Issues pertaining to the governance of the AAs were further aggravated by SADF's somewhat heavy-handed tactics to bludgeon MK into decisions by linking the command-and-control issue in the AAs to a "package" involving assembly, the future of the NPKF, the selection of cadres for eventual incorporation into the new NDF, and their training—indeed, the whole integration project.[36] This package, which the SADF saw as a means to resolve a host of outstanding issues through a quick and single intervention, quickly went awry. Faced with the overwhelming power of the SADF, MK felt threatened and determined to address issues on a sequential basis, with control of the AAs in the forefront.

Because it was technically impossible to design the proposed assembly until criteria had been developed on what constituted a "member of an armed force," MK's persistent refusal to be pinned down on this point, or even to release accurate figures on the number and musterings of MK personnel available for selection and assembly, made matters even worse. SADF intelligence sources had indicated that MK probably had a "proper" membership of about 12,000 on the basis of Modise's guesstimate that about 5,500 cadres were still outside the country in camps to the north in June 1993. It was also suspected that Modise and a small circle of senior MK personnel had data on the "approximate" ranks of its members in top-secret files at ANC headquarters.[37] In the climate of mutual distrust and political bargaining, however, it was unrealistic to expect MK to reveal its vital manpower statistics even were it actually in a position to do so in the disorganized climate of early transition, with some members in distant camps and others dispersed in the streets outside the negotiating forums.

MK's inclination to consider anyone who claimed to be a member as a means of inflating its size was a source of ongoing consternation to SADF military planners and strategists, who had a natural interest in confirming the strength of their opponents; it was impossible to plan assembly in the absence of exact arithmetic on the quantity and quality of MK membership. MK could not (or would not) provide this essential information—this was to go on years after 1994—and the SADF came to the conclusion that there was mala fides. MK insinuations at one point—that it might consist of as many as 80,000 members, 16,000 of whom were available for immediate integration—were greeted with a mixture of anger and derision by the SADF, confirmed in its worst suspicions. As SADF pressed harder for accurate answers, MK became (or appeared to become) more evasive in a spiral of rapidly accumulating and mutual recriminations.

At the outset of discussions, MK was characterized by one senior SADF leader as being full of "hatred, suspicion, mistrust and feelings of revenge that . . . break through the thin crust of courtesy at almost regular intervals in reaction to what is considered to be the slightest provocation."[38] Some of these feelings were reciprocal, despite the ostensible willingness of SADF negotiators to forgive and forget. In contrast, MK members tended to constantly "hark back to the evils of apartheid, the ravages of minority oppression, the iniquities of the Bantustans, the sufferings of the innocent etc."[39] All of this was irrelevant anathema to the apolitical, technicist professional soldiers in the SADF, who resented being privately labeled (according to military intelligence) as "creatures of the National Party" in Umkhonto strategy sessions; thus they held to the position (as they would continue to do), that under apartheid they had simply followed the commands of a legally constituted political authority. MK was not especially persuaded; neither were its representatives especially happy with the condescension that they constantly detected behind what were (at least to the SADF) sincere attempts to "educate" MK in the logistical implications of the demands they were making. This sometimes encouraged the SADF to embark upon a policy, described by one of its generals as "shaking MK into reality," which, given the sensitive atmosphere, further complicated relations.

As in the civil negotiations, however, familiarity bred through working together eventually produced a degree of mutual respect that broke through the hostility on both sides. Unlike CODESA negotiations, however, the military discussions were bilateral until the end of 1993, when the TDF, Venda Defence Force (VDF), and Ciskei Defence Force (CDF) were finally admitted, which tended to reinforce the polarity. There were no highly skilled facilitators such as a Roelf Meyer or a Cyril Ramaphosa (whose personal ties influenced proceedings at the World Trade Centre), and, to make matters worse, there were several highly combustible personalities on each side of the military table. On one occasion, two of the more volatile military leaders had to be separated by the intervention of General Meiring when the discussion over command and control of the AAs degenerated into verbal abuse and an imminent threat of physical violence. Inevitably, the passage to a meeting of minds was slow, erratic, and punctuated by regression. The recurrence of conflict over the more sensitive aspects of command and control pointed to a deeper malaise that was, understandably enough, at its most intense at the start of discussions and throughout 1993, as it was between erstwhile enemies, neither of whom had militarily defeated the other, but both of whom acted as if they did.

To the irritation of the SADF, MK leaders aspiring to senior positions in the new NDF hypocritically criticized the historically top-heavy SADF.[40] MK was also utterly dismissive of the TDF, the most developed of the statutory forces after the SADF itself but which MK derided as a Disney-type *bantustan* formation. If the standards of the TDF were comparable to the vaunted standards of the SADF, so MK pointedly joked, its own officers should have no difficulty in obtaining prime positions after elections.[41] With their similar "distinct attitude of superiority and arrogance towards the SADF," one SADF negotiator complained, "it is clear that they [MK] consider themselves to be the victors." They are, he continued, "critical, suspicious and/or negative about any suggestions emanating from SADF members and, despite their evident lack of understanding of purely military matters, believe that their opinions and solutions are superior to those of the system [i.e., the SADF]."[42]

Not that the SADF was always a model of moderate good sense and camaraderie in its search for consensus. While insisting that negotiations between professional military men were of a different caliber and ilk compared to political talks, SADF negotiators, like civil negotiators (and those in MK), maintained a keen if not always discernable eye to strategically exploiting the weakness of their opponents. From the outset, for example, SADF negotiators were alert to MK concerns with status, career paths in the new NDF, and rationalization. As early as the March 1993 meetings between MK and the SAAF, designed to "test ideas," Air Force Intelligence had detected deep anxiety in MK over rationalization,[43] and this became a chord on which the SADF could (and would) play as a means to extract concessions. While the documented proceedings make little or no mention of informal quid pro quos, the SADF appears to have given some assurances about long-lead rationalization and MK promotions in the new military hierarchy—"to reflect the national composition of the South African population"—in return for MK concessions along a range of issues from the NPKF to the AAs.

SADF negotiators were, as we have already noted, also convinced that they could speak from a position of relative strength despite having lost the political struggle. MK, in their perception, were disorganized, financially strapped, and, it was widely believed, a growing liability for the ANC in its search for an overall political settlement.[44] There was widespread belief among SADF leaders that once the ANC became a full-fledged political party it would lose its financial and logistical wherewithal as a liberation movement to support MK in its camps.[45] This ultimately implied a multipronged game plan to steamroll the MK into agreements where possible, protracted and wounding negotiations—"one should not be overhasty"—and recruitment of the other military formations—the TBVC armies, the Inkatha Freedom Party (IFP), and even the Afrikaner Volksfront—to roll up MK with deathblows in a final multilateral arena.[46]

MK, however, proved a far more wily and tenuous opponent than anticipated. Its "stubbornness" and "single-mindedness," of which the SADF frequently complained, enabled it to grind down discussions to the basics in a way that, as we have intimated, effectively neutralized the SADF on its technicist high ground. Within the parameters of their limited conventional military experience, MK negotiators were, as even the SADF was forced to admit, well prepared,[47] particularly in the business of strategic evasion and extracting political advantage from the most mundane of issues.

Joe Modise, the ostensible minister of defense for the ANC over many years, was highly regarded by SADF generals who had been alerted to his capabilities by Military Intelligence; lesser MK leaders, who eventually went on to prominent positions in the NDF, such as political commissar Andrew (later Major General) Masondo, were "experienced negotiators" notwithstanding what the SADF saw as a "lack of depth" in intricate issues of military strategy and force design. This combination of military and (above all) political skills was particularly evident on integration matters where MK was adept at avoidance behavior designed to prevent it from being locked into hastily devised "administrative arrangements" sold by the SADF under the seemingly innocent label of "taking the process forward." MK was also master at what the SADF characterized as "politically expedient revelations" that violated the confidentiality of the negotiations process, and there were frequent complaints from the state side of "leaks" that compromised SADF positions. A case in point was the contentious press statement by Siphiwe Nyanda in September 1993 suggesting the SADF be "confined to barracks" during forthcoming elections.[48]

Protests by the SADF at the following bilateral largely eliminated the use of this MK tactic thereafter, but in general the SADF lacked the skills in political maneuver honed by MK through years of Byzantine survival activity on the international front. Members of the SADF's DCC had actually undergone short workshops in political negotiations and change management once the prospect of talks became imminent, but this was an incremental, belated counter to the accumulated political maturity of some (but by no means all) MK members, who led discussions from a broader, universal perspective. While conceding the managerial supremacy of SADF negotiators, MK appreciated, correctly, that their opponents were hampered, as they put it, by years of "political solitude." Hence their frustration, or, as former MK leaders prefer to deem it, "stagnancy" at this level.

Yet SADF intelligence that MK members were "dying of malaria in their African camps" and sought speedy repatriation and the end of the armed struggle at any cost was not so wide of the mark and helped soften MK defenses. Most MK facilities and logistics were pitched north of the border, and sudden repatriation meant a dispersal of forces, institutional disorganization, and personal confusion that the SADF could turn to its advantage. Still, the condescending proposition that the ANC would shop its military arm as the price of political peace was grossly inaccurate despite early warnings, articulated by one senior SADF officer, that the "arrogance" of MK extended to its own political masters.[49] Although not itself immune from the temptations of political intervention, SADF and its observers were surprised if not shocked by the apparent tendency of MK "to brook no interference, delay or criticism from politicians when it came to the creation of a new defence force."[50] In practice, the military wing enjoyed considerable if not unrestrained influence in the higher realms of the ANC at this critical point, when it was necessary to secure the military foundations of the transition. Consequently, it was the cart that frequently drove the horse along the track of negotiations—at least at this historic moment.

Forging Consensus: The Run-up to Elections

For the duration of negotiations in 1993, the core of the SADF agenda revolved around five cardinal objectives: political stabilization to make elections possible in the first instance; a "nonpolitical" military thereafter to assist reprofessionalization and inhibit a reverse replication of the "total strategy" years under an ANC government; adherence to "international standards" of some sort as part of the tested recipe for protecting national security; a two-tier structure to maintain the established distinction between full- and part-time forces; and general amnesty. "Despite certain positive achievements in our talks with MK" three months after Admiralty House, "there remains a lot to be done before we can really expect to see eye to eye on the more important issues."[51] So wrote a senior SADF negotiator shortly after Admiralty House. In the months that followed, however, as the politicians forged ahead and the soldiers sought to keep pace, much was in fact done to achieve agreement on the key principles (if not exact mechanics) despite different agendas, personality clashes, and the stealth and posturing of mutual suspicion.

The bottom line was that neither military stood to gain from civil war, and as violence mounted with elections on the horizon, the two sides were drawn to each other even while remaining apart on the exact dynamics of their relationship. On the SADF side, MK's initial threats (or, as some would later allege, promises) to "replace" the military establishment were dismissed as laughable and utterly unrealistic given the actual bargaining power of MK. From the earliest contacts, senior leaders in both the ANC and MK had in fact privately conceded that anarchy would result if the SADF were dismantled in the midst of the transition—even if such was possible, which it was not. Ironically, the power of the SADF became the guarantor the political system that the ANC sought to inherit, and once MK leaders absorbed this point (as they quickly did), any further talk of radically transforming the military in the foreseeable future was reduced to empty if politically correct public verbiage. Unfortunately (and this was to have major implications later), little was done by MK leaders to effectively communicate this reassessment of negotiation strategy to foot soldiers, who continued to be fed on a far more heady and appetizing diet.

Despite its inherent suspicion of the SADF, MK also hoped to secure an advantageous military settlement to match the triumphs in the political arena by the ANC's civilian leaders. This meant, inter alia, a merger of armed formations to whose command structures MK leaders would have access according to the general principles of power sharing articulated in the civil arena, career mobility for its cadres emplaced in the lower ranks, and the institutionalization of nonracial, democratic values in the new national organization. Differences in these values existed inasmuch as SADF and MK came from two vastly different military cultures, but integration was seen, at least on the MK side, as a genuine joint venture. Initial bombastic rhetoric about fundamental "restructuring" of the armed forces once again soon gave way to more practical considerations once the SADF succeeded in marketing the complex necessities and requirements of a conventional military to protect national security under an ANC—or any other—government. MK, former SADF leaders insisted, appeared to believe that simple displacement of the general staff was all that was required before a genuine "people's army" came into play. There was very little understanding of the complex logistics involved in organizational transformation at the middle-management level, so breaking down MK magnetism to a people's army became one of the planks in the SADF's negotiating platform beginning at Simonstown.

In the end, despite the tussles over "standards," MK leaders (if not their followers) could find very little with which to disagree when the opposition talked of the need for a modern defense force, particularly in such highly technological arms of service as the Air Force (where MK had insisted that standards, hopefully British, be maintained since the first MK-SAAF contacts).[52] At a later meeting at Shell House at the beginning of 1994, MK had even gone so far as to admit that it was concerned that its "African standards" (at least in the field of military aviation) would not receive international accreditation, and this created space for SAAF negotiators to press (as they constantly did) for extensive bridging training as part of the price of incorporating MK into the SADF.[53] Subsequently, MK was to fully grasp the nettle.

During the 1993 bilaterals (as well as in internal SADF discussions), such values as civilian supremacy over the military, the constitutional accountability of the armed forces, and their representivity, apolitical character, and respect for democracy and human rights had also been affirmed by both parties.[54] These, after all, were norms for which the ANC had struggled and that the SADF saw as building blocks for institutional reprofessionalization. The principle of an apolitical military was quite congenial to ANC politicians and the more professional soldiers of MK, most of whom had been "internationalized" in countries, be it India, Cuba, or the Soviet Union, where professional militaries have traditionally been maintained on a tight civilian leash, be it of the constitutional or party variety. In the last analysis, there was surprisingly little distance between a great many of the broad principles of civil-military relations on the part of a "unconventional" MK, on the one hand and, on the other, an SADF leadership conscious of the need to reconstitute itself after the damaging experiences of late apartheid.

Both parties had little difficulty with the question of a part-time component of the armed forces and the potentially more explosive issue of general amnesty. While MK was inherently suspicious of the part-time and Commando components of the SADF, which it saw (not entirely without justification) as a repository of right-wing racism, its vision of a people's army could not exclude the notion of a professional core linked to wider society by a system of part-time service. Although the Citizen Force system had been a vital tool for militarization under apartheid, a future democracy held out the medium- to long-term possibility of including a mass of black volunteers that would eventually give the armed forces real roots within the community. Since the professional core, with its part-time network advocated by the SADF as a possible force design for a future military, was also the most cost-effective means to structure a postapartheid military in a future where less money was most likely to be spent on defense as opposed to reconstruction and development, the core/part-time option was also attractive to the more economy-minded among MK's leaders.

Despite its enormous political and humanitarian connotations, general amnesty for both sides in the apartheid struggle was also relatively unproblematic, and agreement was reached at an early stage in the negotiation process. Arguing in terms of hard political realities tinged with institutional self-interests, neither the SADF nor MK were particularly enthusiastic to rake over the coals of human rights violations in a way that would create a dangerous and mutually reinforcing spiral of recriminations upon the very birth of democracy.

The common concern of both parties with stabilization also implied politically neutralizing the small but dangerous groups of extremists spread across the political spectrum, from APLA on the left to the AWB and (in the course of time) General Constand Viljoen's Afrikaner Volksfront on the right. The political costs of acting against the AWB or Viljoen, with his powerful profile in the military establishment, were as unacceptably high to the SADF as was the risk of MK, acting against its fellow "liberation movement," persisting in its armed struggle—sometimes with covert assistance from its own renegade members. Neither the militant right nor left could, however, be expected to participate or stand aside at democratic elections that transferred power according to the polite prescriptions developed at CODESA unless some highly persuasive incentive, such as immunity from prosecution for acts committed during transition or under apartheid, could be offered. Both the SADF and MK cohered in marketing this view, albeit not very successfully, to the radicals (and associates), who by this time had come to fundamentally distrust the principals. Nevertheless, the two sides had a common political interest to reign in their rogue elements in the interests of elections, and this tended to set the atmosphere for wider cooperation on some of the more thorny human rights issues.

Both the SADF and MK had engaged in acts against (or for) the apartheid regime, commissioned (or commissioned with the connivance) of some of the very leaders of the now "respectable" armed forces sitting around the negotiation table. General and mutual amnesty was consequently a blanket to cover several all-around difficult problems. Subsequently, during a series of very private discussions with the most senior SADF leaders early on in negotiations, consensus was quickly reached in cavalier fashion that papered over the moral content of the pressing human rights issues. Throughout the negotiations MK was constantly reminded, gently, firmly, and (on social occasions) jokingly that the SADF had the capability to exercise its power to derail the whole transition at any time it chose through activating "Plan B" (this innocuous-sounding backup was allegedly a disinformation exercise to force a negotiated solution with the threat of a nonexistent coup or, worse, an outright plan by right-wing elements in the Army and intelligence to sieze power and head off elections) in whole or part. Rather than call this lethal bluff of potential coup (which would set the country on a course to civil war), some MK leaders began to hint obliquely, at the earliest stages of negotiations, about the possibility of an overall historic amnesia. Modise, it is rumored, when pressed lightly by the SADF generals at a lavish barbecue in early 1993, generously "guaranteed" that Nuremberg-style trials and investigations of *military* personnel of any persuasion did not (and would not for the indefinite future) form part of the ANC perceptions of a new South Africa.

Quite apart from the fact that this neat arrangement effectively coldshouldered the SAP, which now became the sacrificial lamb for apartheid atrocities, it remains unclear whether this commitment to wipe clean the historic slate in the interests of both military formations represented Modise's personal convictions—a slip of the tongue—more than an actually policy suggestion from MK and the ANC. Certainly, SADF leaders, in follow-up consultations to verify the position with other senior ANC personnel, came to the conclusion that the future minister of defense had accurately represented the official position of the ANC government-in-waiting. This, as we shall see later, was the root of major political conflict in civil-military relations that would come after democratic elections.

In the shorter term, however, all this implied that once the reciprocal barriers of suspicion and double agendas had begun to erode the way was relatively clear for the two parties to move forward even while struggling for strategic advantage. Somewhere during the course of 1993—observers differ in their retrospective observations according to political agenda—the communication barriers began to break down in the bilateral discussions, easing the way to the multilateral forums that came on line toward the end of the year, and, ultimately, the first meeting of the JMCC in January 1994. Observers also disagree on the meaning and consequences of this development, with some fixed in their opinion that it was during this process that a mildly disconcerted MK effectively caved in on integrative transformation in the face of intense and aggressive pressure. Be that as it may, a more charitable view is that mutual compromises began to take place toward the middle of 1993 once the SADF "surrendered" its demand for preelectoral integration and the parties agreed to the "absolute necessity of a general amnesty" after elections in the interests of reconciliation.[55] Thereafter, the building blocks of the military pact began to fall, albeit erratically, into place.

As early as May 1993, MK began to make subtle indications, peppered with public asides characterizing the SADF as a limb of apartheid, that it was not uncomfortable with the idea of a civilian-controlled army based on the retention of high organizational standards. While the exact nature of these standards remained unclarified in a way that would thwart integration for years after elections, MK conveyed the message that its own experience of African militaries—including those of the homelands—had led it to a new appreciation of the importance of military efficiency and professionalism. There was no reason, communications implied, not to accept the professional norms advocated by the SADF as long as they were not manipulated to exclude MK personnel from positions of real influence within the new command structures.

The SADF would not make unequivocal commitments to affirmative action for disadvantaged race groups, which it saw as a recipe for internal conflict and the dilution of professionalism. Lack of capacity and skill in the management of a large-scale conventional military organization, the point was frequently made, would inevitably reverberate back on MK once its leaders had assumed positions of power and prominence under new conditions of public accountability. Like other established military organizations, SADF and its negotiators were extremely reluctant to violate the existing chain of command with horizontal political appointments that could foment discontent among and demoralize the lower reaches. Nevertheless, once the SADF held out the olive branch of senior appointments of MK personnel into the upper reaches, accompanied with promises of bridging training to ensure all MK members the opportunity to compete with SADF personnel on merit irrespective of background—that is, once it provided the proverbial sweetener—the deal was virtually struck.

Earlier in the negotiations, MK had also raised the issue of the so-called lost-generation youth and its own members who might not be suitable or may not wish to make the military an ongoing career. This reflected the fact that MK, since the first repatriation of its leaders to South Africa, had been recruiting aggressively so as to bring larger numbers to the negotiating table. Since the campaign had been pitched at all and sundry, accompanied with promises that the military offered limitless and long-term possibilities of employment, MK now found itself painted into a corner with an "overflow" problem. Future rationalization, which the SADF played upon to soften its opposition, struck fear into MK, faced with the possibility of acute public embarrassment if not a breakdown of discipline in its own ranks. ANC leaders (the SADF knew) had already expressed concern to their military wing about widespread social disorder on the heels of repatriation as disillusioned cadres turned to criminal activity in cahoots with the mass of questionable local personnel whom MK had recruited indiscriminately. Urgent assembly was therefore a matter of national security, and it was left to MK to find some sort of creative smokescreen to facilitate its negotiation without losing face.

From early on in negotiations, the issue of some sort of mechanism for easing national unemployment had been raised by MK as a means to address this problem of its own making. Aware that MK had hoist itself on its own petard, the SADF primly remonstrated that it could not be expected to accept everyone into its ranks and that the ANC should take responsibility for its own actions. When, however, it generously conceded that a Service or Youth Corps could accompany possibly integration—which required assembly to get off the ground in "sound administrative terms"—this was welcomed by all as the means to manage a potentially explosive situation for MK in particular.

The Service Corps was, of course, a sideline issue in overall negotiations. Nevertheless, it is interesting and emblematic of the subtle gaming and trade-offs on more serious issues taking place, often in private, behind formal discussions and, in some cases, within the internal frameworks of both the SADF and MK. Generally speaking, the DCC remained relatively coherent throughout negotiations once initial decisions to talk around the strategic creation of a new NDF under postapartheid conditions had been taken. This did not preclude idiosyncratic differences and disagreements over interpretation as game plans were put into implementation in highly charged circumstances, but for the most part the DCC presented a united front that reflected a genuine sense of internal unity.

While there were differences in style between Army and Air Force leaders (the latter sometimes seen as a touch too "soft"), there were hardly any substantive conflicts over content and strategy at the negotiation table. This reflected the fact that the military hard-liners, by the beginning of 1993, had either been marginalized or converted to managerial values by the weight of peer opinion (as in the case of CSADF General Liebenberg). The personal influence of Liebenberg' successor, General Meiring, was also decisive not only in facilitating relations with MK but also in a wider social realm that ultimately embraced a diversity of strategic political leaders such as Constand Viljoen, Ferdi Hartzenberg of the Conservative Party, APLA, and the IFP's Chief Gatsha Buthelezi—all of whom were engaging in dangerous brinkmanship until the last days of the transitional government. Meiring's relations with Viljoen were ultimately critical in allowing elections to go forward, as was the mutual accord almost immediately struck up with the future president, Nelson Mandela.

On the MK side of the equation, a comparable cohesion existed, partially bred by sudden, direct contact with a gargantuan common enemy and the exhilarating possibility of power after years of external exile. It was this dual coherence in the maze of transactions and subtransactions forming the stuff of negotiations on a soldier-to-soldier basis that eventuated, toward the end of 1993, in both parties agreeing to "accept the facilitated strategic planning process currently in use by the SADF" and to establish a formal pattern of joint work groups for corporate decisionmaking on the operations, personnel, logistics, and finance of the proposed NDF.[56] The tone was thereby set for an extended discourse over the military pact through the work of the JMCC in early 1994, the various postelectoral White Papers that followed, and, eventually, the Defence Review brought to culmination four years later.

The Interim Constitution, in the process of formulation in civil society, was (and remains in final form) the origin point for the mandate of the NDF. Since neither party viewed a politically neutral defense force as problematic (albeit for different reasons), both were able to quickly agree that the future armed forces be apolitical in both character and orientation, subject to parliamentary accountability as described in Articles 226–228 of the proposed Constitution. This aligned perfectly with ANC desires to politically neuter the armed forces based on their observations elsewhere in Africa, the conceptions of civil-military relations among the small professional leadership of MK, and SADF leaders seeking reduced political interference in the restoration of their own professionalism. The rider that the NDF be "inclusive" satisfied the SADF's quest for a newly legitimate and representative military while addressing MK's desire for incorporation.[57]

Both parties cohered fairly quickly in the view that the NDF comprise a permanent professional core force with part-time reserve components based on advanced technology compatible with international standards. While the nature of these standards would (and will) continue to remain uncertain for years, MK conceded considerable ground in eventually accepting a balanced rather than the restructured force that it had initially demanded at the negotiations table. This, the SADF reassured MK somewhat condescendingly, was the price for combat efficiency in a modern military arena.[58] Since all NDF members appeared to be infanteers who would now be trained up to the conventional military competency according to the criteria for advancement defined by the SADF (albeit under third-party supervision), this was, in retrospect, the recipe for MK absorption. The transformation of the armed forces, as MK saw it in terms of the democratic project, was now on the back burner.

Both the SADF and MK nonetheless came to a common understanding of organizational posture in their determination that the NDF be primarily a defensive force in the protection of national sovereignty and territorial integrity in line with constitutional prescriptions but maintain a strategic deterrent capability to discourage aggressive states. Rationalization, the SADF accepted, would begin only after the completion of integration, during which a Service Brigade would be established to assist redundant MK members. Preparations for integration could begin preelectorally, but as MK had lobbied, the actual process would take place only once the Government of National Unity had been established.

While conceding that the Military Disciplinary Code (MDC) would require review or amendment in light of the new social circumstances, the SADF once more managed to assert its institutional hegemony through the provision that all laws relating to itself be transferred to the proposed NDF at the outset, not excluding the existing Defence Act of 1957. Neither party could take issue with questions of collateral utility, and both agreed that the NDF assist other state departments, where necessary, to preserve life, health, property, and the maintenance of essential services. As a gesture to the reconstructionist agenda of the incoming ANC government, the SADF agreed to help with socioeconomic uplift and, subject to various constitutional provisions, to cooperate with the SAP in upholding law and order. (Both these commitments would resurface to haunt the NDF shortly after its formal establishment).

On the international front, a similar specter was raised by the decision to deploy the NDF in the resolution of regional problems through preventative diplomacy, in the first instance, and collective security actions at a later stage. After some initial resistance, the SADF also agreed, somewhat gratuitously, to the inclusion of the word "national" in its new name—but only after midnight on the day of elections. With a view toward the long-term future under an interim Government of National Unity, the SADF pressed that the executive be given power over the military only with the agreement of both deputy presidents (one of whom one would inevitably a Nationalist) and the Cabinet (in which the National Party would figure). When this was resisted, the proposal was adjusted to decisions governing the appointment of the Chief of the South African National Defence Force (CSANDF) and the deployment of armed forces in defense of the Republic or in compliance with international obligations. Ultimately, when SADF leaders felt more comfortable with Mandela, the Interim Constitution would provide for wider presidential control (subject to parliamentary approval) over both the appointment of the

CSANDF and use of armed forces.[59] It has been suggested that the various delays until this consolidated series of agreements in late 1993 are attributable to the presence of "inexperienced negotiators on both sides."[60]This, as we have suggested, is to overlook the technical-managerial skills brought to negotiations by the SADF, on the one hand, and the political astuteness of MK delegates arguing from positions of organizational weakness on the other.

The sparse collection of writings that document the SADF's "desperate" quest for popular support as the driving force in negotiations also tends to overstate and simplify what might be termed the "legitimacy factor." First, legitimacy was not on the market at any price, and it was only after negotiations conducive to corporate interests that skeptical officers in the SADF began to buy more fully into transitional negotiations. It boggles the imagination to believe that the SADF was actually "received back with joy . . . [as] the most popular force ever to have been deployed" in the volatile East Rand townships after the pathetic withdrawal and then disbanding of the NPKF, to which we will turn later.[61] Nevertheless, surveys conducted in early 1994 just prior to elections do indicate distinctions in the minds of some township dwellers between the military and police as enforcers of peace.[62] The SADF had previously conducted a campaign to win residents' support, which heightened the belief in military circles that the SADF could indeed win some hearts and minds in the black areas—subject to the important proviso that it could establish and then *sustain* concrete stability in the short term rather than more amorphous national acceptance farther down the road. Doing so, however, required community and, ultimately, ANC-MK cooperation in a guarantor capacity. The SADF, in other words, wanted more legitimacy on a nationwide basis rather than legitimacy per se.

There is also some debate over whether MK could have manipulated the legitimacy factor more effectively to extract additional concessions from the SADF once the latter had recognized MK as a fellow, if inferior, fighting formation with deep, symbolic roots in the community. The ANC, it can be argued, was far less reliant in its negotiations strategy on its armed wing than were the Nationalists, and MK was merely a means to greater political ends envisioned by ANC leaders at CODESA. Once assurances of loyalty to the new interim constitution were obtained from the SADF in a series of meetings that apparently took place between SADF leaders and Mandela during late 1992, ANC incentives to back its own small military to the hilt rapidly diminished. In the military negotiations, some MK representatives were distinctively weak-wristed once they had obtained what they saw as the first prize: an amorphous "civilian control" over the military. After the elections, when MK cadres were faced with the practical consequences of earlier decisions taken by their leaders, this lack of attention to detail during negotiations quickly translated into widespread suspicions that the rank-and-file had been sacrificed on the altar of political expediency.

Many issues were indeed kept off the agenda of the 1993 talks or were given limited exposure. Some of these, such as the future of the Citizen Force and the Commandos, would be detailed only after elections, as would more problematic matters such as the downsizing of the armed forces and the mechanics of civilianization. Complex questions linking budget to force design could not conceivably be effectively explored given the time constraints governing negotiations and uncertainty over public policy on defense matters in future South Africa. There was a widespread view, later operationalized in the Defence Review after elections, that "defense in democracy" required extensive public consultation; this would, by nature, be a postelectoral exercise.

Some of the more delicate personnel and human resources issues that were to dog integration for years after the elections were purposefully downplayed so as to avoid derailing negotiations once the hard questions of force design and posture had been decided. Throughout the negotiations, the SADF had, for example, been extremely sensitive to questions of affirmative action, even while conceding the vague need for equal opportunities as part of the package for a new representative military. By the end of 1993, the standards of the proposed NDF were rapidly displacing questions of command and control at the apex of the conflict agenda, but MK did not press its case for inclusion of affirmative action commitments, partly because of inadequate time to talk through the matter, and partly because of the possibly unwise belief that "enough guarantees existed in the [proposed] Bill of Rights to ensure this."[63] As we have intimated, many other questions—all of which were to bedevil the armed forces at a later stage in their history—were simply papered over and consigned to the future.

Transitional Arrangements: The SCD and JMCC

With the creation of the Transitional Executive Council in November 1993, the Sub-Council for Defence was created within the network of subcouncils to implement the work of the transitional government. The SCD, with eight members, had been previously deliberated at CODESA, whose third working group proposed that the body "acquaint itself with developments concerning defense and military formations at all levels of government" and that it "take steps to identify and promote all developments in this field . . . that impact favourably upon the levelling of the playing fields and free political participation." The SCD, it was proposed, will also take "all steps to identify and prevent within its powers all developments . . . which in its opinion will impact adversely upon, peace, stability, free political participation or the transition to democracy."[64] A TEC-SCD workgroup was established toward the middle of the year by MK and the SADF. Since both were deeply concerned that forces to its respective left and right would act to violently prevent or disrupt elections, it concurred that the SCD be vested with multiparty control, oversight, and monitoring power over "all armed forces so far as the activities of these would impact on the political process leading up to and during elections."[65]

An earlier gathering of the SADF at Blenny had advocated that the SCD be given the power take any measures to resolve conflicts by nonviolent means, develop relations with other subcontinental states, maintain professional norms and standards, and promote representivity in the armed forces "subject to the principle that females are not employed in a combative capacity."[66] This last provision, as we shall see, was to later become a bone of contention between the patriarchal SADF and MK leaders, with the latter's insistence on gender equality at all levels. The SCD was nevertheless also given a mandate "to pronounce on circumstances under which a military force may be deployed in an operational capacity within the borders of the country,"[67] and most of the long-debated provisions of earlier meetings were incorporated into the military sections of the TEC bill.

To bolster the powers of the SCD, the bill also directed the TEC to formulate a code of conduct to which all military forces would adhere;[68] to audit and supervise their arms and armaments;[69] to investigate the conduct of any military force and its members;[70] and to "recommend appropriate disciplinary measures" where necessary.[71] Significantly, these provisions virtually echoed, word for word, those contained in official communiqués of the SADF's Operations Division some months prior.[72] The TEC was also given the power to commission "research into any relevant matter,"[73] the nature of which had also been explored previously in SADF circles and in the internal workshops it convened at midyear. This research covered almost two dozen items central to the restructuring of the armed forces after elections, including such issues as parliamentary control over the military, the relationship between the executive and the armed forces , amendments to the existing Defence Act, and the manpower policy, control, composition, and organization of a postapartheid defense force.[74]

The influence of the earlier workgroup in which SADF Operations was decisive was also reflected in Articles 10–14 of the TEC bill (on the SCD), which gave the TEC responsibility for the establishment and control of the proposed NPKF. Article 10 defined its composition (all military forces and every policing agency under their control), Article 11 its command structure (a NPKF Command Council representing all participants), and Article 12 its establishment process, "having due regard also to the interests of women." Subsequent articles dealt with technicalities such as uniform, insignia, and, in Article 14, the resolution of conflict should it arise between the NPKF Command Council and the SCD.

Bilateral negotiations during 1993 had echoed the view prevalent in SADF Operations that the SCD also oversee the planning and preparation of the integration process leading to the future armed forces. This was included in Article 2(g), whereby the SCD was given the responsibility for the planning, preparation, and training for the future South African defense force. This included the eventual creation of a "committee of experts" to manage designated assembly points and to make finale decisions on their budget.[75] In terms of the bill, each military force agreed to acknowledge the authority of the TEC[76] and to keep the SCD informed on a continuous basis of its conduct and deployment.[77] Nevertheless, the command structure of each military formation was to remain independent on matters of internal administration, while the existing minister of defense would retain the power "to make, amend or repeal regulations concerning defense force conduct, functioning, structures and deployment" under the mandate vested him by the Defence Act of 1957.[78]

As in civil society, apartheid and its foes entered the transitional government with mixed feelings and half-satisfied agendas. While all parties recognized that a transitional government was a essential component in the process of eventually sharing power, the main players in civil society—the ANC and the Nationalist Party—were both concerned with exploiting the new institutions to best position themselves prior to the decisive electoral moment. This was particular true of the Nationalists, since it was reasonable to expect that the ANC would emerge as the overwhelming victor—if, that is, free and fair elections took place on April 26.

Similarly, in the military arena, by the end of 1993 some SADF leaders were still anxious over MK's "destructive and revolutionary" attitude to the defense force[79] despite their having already notched up several impressive negotiated successes behind the public image of a "new destiny" of peace, reconciliation, and democracy embracing all military formations.[80] Much in the tone and design of the new SCD reflected talks throughout the year in which the SADF had played a decisive role. By May 1993, a month after the Admiralty House meetings, a proposed SCD was already on the agenda, and for the rest of the year the issue figured among the welter of talks on the NPKF, the AAs, and the character of a new national military after elections. Eventually, the SCD emerged within the wider framework of the TEC, with its emphasis on multiparty control in both the civil and military sectors. Both the SADF and MK had certain difficulties with this arrangement. MK, for example, was less than enthusiastic over the powers derogated by the TEC bill to the sitting minister of defense, who was a member of the Nationalist Party. Given the limited life span of the SCD, it could not conceivably fulfill its charge to draw up a new code of conduct, and this meant that MK would be exposed to the existing Defence Act until it was redrafted sometime in the indefinite future.

Nonetheless, both parties supported the SCD in broad principle because, we have noted, it allowed each military formation to monitor the other while maintaining its internal autonomy. This was important for the SADF, which was opposed to a system of preelectoral joint management yet feared a breakdown in the MK chain of command that could spill over into social disorder and political violence. The SCD was, however, especially important for MK since it had no other institutional alternatives for exercising statutory control over the SADF. As far as the SADF was concerned, the SCD had double value in that it allowed for institutionalization of the registered gains from negotiations over the preceding months while providing means to manufacture additional capital. Since the SCD was also part of a wider framework, eventually including the JMCC at the level of policy implementation, the advent of the TEC was also regarded by the SADF as an additional means to impress upon MK the level of organizational complexity and depth of professionalism in the statutory forces. Hence, the TEC was welcomed on both sides of the military equation, particularly by the SADF, whose leadership believed the SCD must be "seized with enthusiasm"[81] and then moved quickly to exploit the political opportunities inherent in the new system.

Both militaries were determined to utilize the various loopholes in SCD arrangements to maintain freedom of behavior insofar as possible within the framework of overall SCD authority. This meant cementing relations with the SCD but with a degree of distance designed to keep the SCD as unobtrusive as corporate interests demanded.

From the outset, SADF leaders determined to keep contacts with the new transcending body as formal as possible while cultivating it (and the MOD) to project influence over MK. In October 1993, two months before the SCD, SADF Operations determined that "contact between Defence Headquarters and the SCD is . . . expected to be official and structured" but that "every attempt is to be made to foster and to establish a spirit of trust, understanding, support and cooperation."[82] "The SADF," it was also noted, "must position itself before the activation of the TEC in terms of the establishment of procedures, channels and systems of communication and [liaison] with the SCD."[83] Since May 1993, the SADF was concerned with developing what it termed "interaction mechanisms" between the SCD and the various military formations with a view toward communicating information on SCD activities, findings, and pronouncements.[84] This was a polite formula for monopolizing the flow of information around the SCD.[85] In October, a special Directorate of Transitional Liaison (DTL), under the command of the Chief of Staff: Operations, was established: It's "primary objective was to promote the preparation for and transition to a democratic order."[86] That meant facilitating relations between the SADF and the SCD, including the strategic transmission of communications into and out of the SCD, aligning communications with SADF doctrine and policy, and feedback between the SCD, the CSADF, and the DCC of all "selected and relevant material."[87]

The SADF had also keenly recognized the public-relations value of the SCD, which, in its opinion, provided a unique opportunity "to promote the image of the SADF as a professional, apolitical force dedicated to the defence of the [Republic of South Africa]," no less to the members of the SCD and MK.[88] The SADF could afford to be generous on this point, hence the insistence of the DTL's chief, Brigadier Oelschig, that "everything be done to strengthen the existing bona fides of the SADF."[89] Thus the DTL would once again provide all stakeholders with public relations–type "orientation" on the mission, organization, command, control, and, above all, professionalism of the existing conventional forces. This would include briefings and visits to the DCC and the various functional sections of the SADF (i.e., personnel, operations, logistics, etc.) by key players with interests in defense-related matters. This was in line with SADF-DTL policy to "encourage, possibly provoke [MK] to make known their own ideas, views and perceptions on a quid pro quo basis."[90] Since this facilitation was largely the prerogative of the SADF, however, the SADF enjoyed a virtual monopoly of what would (or would not) be exposed to scrutiny. Hence, ANC visits to such organizations as the Coordinating and Joint Intelligence Committees, the Joint Security Committee, and the State Security Council "may be considered," but no official documents were to be handed over in any circumstances.[91]

Arrangements were also made to monitor illegal activities by the ANC-MK, both before and after the TEC bill, as a means to counter similar allegations that might be made against the SADF. Based on recommendations from Military Intelligence that the ANC was actively seeking information to compromise the SADF, a comprehensive list of ANC violations was to be compiled with urgency from information provided by all arms of service to a nodal point in Intelligence Division, and then "held in readiness [by the DTL] to be submitted to the SCD on request by the Minister of Defence at an appropriate time."[92] Since the DIS of MK and the ANC was in fact manufacturing similar political material on the SADF, both sides would be remarkably quiet about illegal actions by their various operatives (and their friends in extremist circles), both before and during the transitional government. This was fully in accord with the spirit of the agreed principle that general amnesty was essential for the maintenance of the military pact.

The 1993 negotiations, the Strategic Planning Process (SPP), and the TEC bill together provided for a council within the SCD framework to implement its wide-ranging mandate. Article 2(j) of the bill referred to a "coordinating council" to facilitate between the commanders of all military forces represented on the SCD, and, when required, "to report and make recommendations to the [SCD] concerning any matter relations to [its] functions."[93] Seeing itself as the last bastion of white rule and determined to negotiate as many details on the design of the postelectoral military as possible before handing over power to the Government of National Unity, the SADF had already to a large extent prejudged the issue. In July it had conceived a joint committee, the eventual Joint Military Coordinating Council, to become involved in tactical and operational planning for integration, including such matters as whether there should be AAs (and, if so, how they should be structured), the "disposal" of those deemed unsuitable for integration, and the general process of eventual demobilization.[94] Hence, it welcomed the JMCC as the implementing device in the SCD package—the more so if it could continue to shape the content and spirit of military transactions.

The policy of MK, in contrast, was to delay making commitments on the military pact for as long as its limited capacity allowed and, insofar as possible, to leave unfinished business until after elections, when ANC dominance of the political system would vastly increase its leverage over the military. Still, the momentum of political negotiations at CODESA gathered pace as elections loomed over the horizon, and the SCD offered the option to relocate negotiations from loose bilateral and multilateral meetings into a statutory forum; the JMCC was a natural accompaniment to this process. The JMCC now became the primary site for power struggles over the future of the armed forces.

Both military formations were ambiguous as the JMCC moved into its first meeting in January 1994, because the SCD-JMCC framework limited their independence of action. Yet the JMCC, as a joint institution, provided each with a mechanism to exercise a degree of supervision and control over the other in the experimental and inherently unstable conditions of transition. As we have noted, this tension was expressed in the provision that the JMCC exercise joint control subject to the provision that all participants remain in command of their internal administration, meaning, in the case of the statutory forces (i.e., the SADF and the TBVC homeland armies) that they would continue to be governed by existing defense legislation as reflected through the Interim Constitution.[95] The new organizational mechanism, as we have also noted, was nevertheless of particular importance to the weaker party—that is, MK—because it now theoretically extracted the SADF from the sole authority of the state or the ruling National Party in the preelectoral period. Since the governing SCD was a predominantly military body, the JMCC was also not especially prohibitive to both MK and the SADF in allowing both militaries to maintain a degree of power in shaping their mutual relations without excessive intervention by politicians.

The JMCC was defined as a joint military organization to cross-cut the April 1994 elections, so it continued to function until late that year, even after Mandela assumed the presidency following the ANC's overwhelming victory at the polls. In the short term, however, its mandate was to facilitate joint planning and regulation of the military component of transition into and through the electoral period on a virtual daily basis. Given the wide range of agreement in principle and procedure already reached by the time of its birth, the JMCC was therefore largely a mechanical entity, its purpose to refine and articulate the enormously complex body of practical details and concrete arrangements often overlooked by analysts but inherent in military disengagement. The fact that disengagement in this instance involved the coming together of two historic antagonists—each of whom saw itself as the armed wing of the "victors" in the apartheid struggle—rendered the tasks facing the new TEC even more problematic.

Apart from its difficult short-term charge, the JMCC was also vested with the long-term and intrinsically more controversial mission to "formulate a strategy based on the analysis of [South Africa's] defence situation and perceived threats for the period 1994 to 2004" in accord with the SPP of the SADF, into which MK had been incorporated.[96] From that would flow a commonly designated force design and structure for the new NDF that would integrate the various military formations in the medium term and rationalize thereafter. The JMCC, it was anticipated, would function until the emplacement of a new DCC at some point following elections, although in the preelectoral period it would work alongside the existing DCC under SADF in accord with the principles of autonomy pertaining to the various military formations within the SCD-JMCC framework. CSADF General Meiring and Siphiwe Nyanda (chief of staff, MK) were appointed cochairs of the JMCC at its first meeting on January 12, most of which was given over to defining the organizational characteristics of the new body.

The JMCC was, in its way, an extraordinary vehicle for military disengagement in an extraordinarily complex political and military situation.[97] It was also, in the words of one commentator, "a unique joint planning exercise involving previously implacable enemies,"[98] which, according to the official communiqués, "reached consensus on most of the critical issues facing the process of forming the SANDF."[99] Given the uncertainty and confusion of the transitional situation, the mass of working groups subordinate to the plenary worked reasonably well on the whole to fulfill their mandate, that is, to produce the framework for new NDF to support elections and protect national security thereafter. Personal relationships forged during initials contact in 1993 were consolidated, mutual respect grew in some instances, and MK was reinvigorated by news from the World Trade Centre that the ANC could obtain a better political settlement than expected. Neither the SADF nor its opponents were inclined to disrupt the symbiosis and interdependency of interests that had emerged during first-round negotiations.

Still, there was hard bargaining to be done as the various parties sought to secure and institutionalize these interests within a very tight time frame. As in the negotiations that preceded it, the JMCC was heavily pressed by the pace of political negotiations deadlined for culmination in elections on April 26. If anything, the JMCC, sandwiched between the establishment of the TEC the preceding November and the elections, was under even more pressure to make preelectoral decisions and then to self-destruct as quickly as possible so that "normal" military institutions could be emplaced to steer the difficult and immediate tasks of integration. In these circumstances, much as in initial military negotiations and those over the Constitution itself, many issues of consequence to the future NDF were left partially explored or papered over in order to reach quick decisions.

The JMCC, with its hard managerial logic, also seriously underestimated the social and political dynamics at work in the very human business of converting many military formations into a unity, and some of its plans for integration were clearly preposterous even before the end of its life span. At its penultimate session (the twenty-first overall), for example, it approved another "final" integration plan that 15,000 NSF members would be assembled during 1994, that bridging training be completed forty-two weeks later, that 27,000 NSF members be trained by the end of 1995, and that the "last" intake be of 4,000 further personnel in August of that year.[100] While some doubts were expressed as to whether this was feasible given the size of the Army's training institutions, this took no account of some fairly obvious medium- to long-term problems (e.g., the Certified Personnel Register [CPR]) that would come home to roost once integration was up and stumbling.

In the short-term, however, the situation worked to the advantage of the SADF, which, with its strategic planning capacity, complex organizational structures, and breadth of technocratic personnel, was able to shape the process of sorting through highly complicated data by the very nature of its participation.

The political abilities of MK displayed during the 1993 negotiations were now of considerably less value when it came down to hammering out exact organizational details and military minutiae. While MK was able to bring many skilled negotiators to the table at the plenary and the multitude of work groups and sub–work groups that eventually grew under the JMCC umbrella, its human resources were stretched very thin quantitatively and qualitatively to varying degrees. The Military Research Group (MRG), which had been invaluable to MK as a specialist support group during the 1993 talks, was excluded from direct participation in the JMCC along with all other unrecognized nonmilitary formations. Although this did not rule out informal consultation, some MK leaders, to the delight of the SADF, were now less than welcoming to white civilian inputs, however "progressive."

In the so-called nonstrategic committees, where subgroups were formed around such issues as human resources (including gender) and where talks had a distinct political component, MK functioned fairly adeptly. On specifically strategic issues in the military mainstream—on obtuse matters of logistics, operations, and other questions related to conventional defense management that the SADF heaped upon it—MK frequently floundered, as would be the case for much of the early period of integration. Except among its strongest personalities, MK disorientation was rife at this level. Many of its representatives have recollections of being buttonholed minutes before crucial meetings so that MK would have a presence of some sort or another; of unbriefed and unprepared participation on complex military matters where they were clearly disadvantaged; and of being recirculated from one workgroup to another in quick succession.

The SADF, still driven by Beaufre-type prescriptions (i.e., the "total strategy" concept of General Andre Beaufre, that militaries remain uncompromising in achieving compromises in political negotiations), did little to alleviate the plight of their breathless counterparts, most of whom could not keep pace with the rigorous schedules (determined by the SADF's own Directorate of Strategic Management) to keep talks on track. Some MK representatives, in historic retrospect, even suggest that the organizational differentiation that took place—the whole panoply of special and sub–work groups insinuated into the process—was part of a conscious strategy by the military establishment to wear down MK delegations.

In the higher reaches of the system—that is, in the SCD—where the principals met the atmosphere was considerably calmer despite its location at the communications nexus between the TEC and the JMCC. Here, however, personality considerations were important in easing the way for the SADF to cast its long shadow. Generally speaking, the SADF leadership was not at all displeased with having to address a ostensibly compliant Modise or Ronnie Kasrils, their archenemy. Both, it was anticipated, would come into the Government of National Unity—Modise as minister of defense, Kasrils as his deputy—and considerable pains were taken to cultivate the pair, despite the personal contempt felt in some quarters (both have since been replaced). Had other individuals come into the MOD after elections, the SADF would have been less than happy. As it was, the armed forces of the old regime had a fairly full measure of the two key civilian officials who would be concerned with military affairs in the postelection government.

In the early months of 1994, the long-awaited National Peace-Keeping Force came on line amid widespread premonitions, in both civil and military circles, that it could well turn out to be a monumental disaster. Tasked to perform a multitude of complex yet ill-defined functions very late in the transitional process, the NPKF actually accomplished virtually nothing of its mandate to ensure free political activity, least of all to promote the wider objectives of nation-building. While virtually all significant stakeholders in the civil and military sectors recognized the political and symbolic necessity of creating some sort of peacekeeping initiative to build a climate conducive to fair and open elections, none could, despite months of deliberations, decide on its exact military mechanics. This ongoing haggling, particularly over who should control the NPKF, persistently delayed its implementation. In retrospect, most commentators feel that it would have made no difference—indeed, that it would have saved many wasted human, financial, and organizational resources—had the NPKF not existed at all.

Part of the abject failure of the NPKF has to do with the fact that it was established in an administrative vacuum within which very little preparatory work had been done to ensure its functioning. Other problems that dogged the NPKF included the tendency of all parties to define their participation according to political self-interest, poor logistic support, hostility on the part of both Military Intelligence and the SAP, and, in the last analysis, rejection by community structures in the volatile townships east of Johannesburg to which the NPKF was briefly deployed.[101]In any event, at midnight on April 26, 1994, the SADF ceased to exist, and in a culmination of the process of political trade-offs and mutual bargains that had driven both civil and military negotiations into a pacted democracy, the SANDF came into existence. Despite widespread expectations that General Pierre Steyn would head the SANDF, his participation in the 1992 Commission of Inquiry had seriously discredited him among leading elements in the armed forces, most of whom remained at ease but also as they were: conservative, Army, and Afrikaner. Unsurprisingly, General Meiring was designated chief of the SANDF, whose "tradition of discipline, courage, innovation, loyalty and success" would now become the probable yardsticks for a postapartheid defense force.[102] Neither the SADF nor MK had entirely realized the objective once described by Beaufre of remodeling or restructuring the adversary.[103] Yet transition also involves setting rules and procedures that determine the balance of power in future institutional configurations, and at this level, where SADF "standards" were to remain the organizational bottom line, the military establishment had cause for celebration. For all intents and purposes, the SADF had weathered the first storms of democratization with a new name, banner, and, most surprising of all, the majority of its rigging still largely intact.

Conclusion

Who were the ultimate victors in the great game of transitional negotiations? Was it the SADF, whose monopoly on the organizational base from which to build a new national defense force enabled it to dominate the discourse over postapartheid military power? Or was it the much-maligned nonstatutory forces, essentially MK, whose political astuteness compensated for their lack of conventional military power? Was the result of negotiations ultimately a win-win rather than zero-sum situation, whereby all parties failed to achieve their objectives but eventually sacrificed and walked fulfilled into democracy with at least most of their objectives intact? Or, almost five years into democracy, were there only losers, Pyrrhic victors in the course of time, whose achievements will fade as South Africa moves farther into its new political dispensation?

On the face of it, the SADF appears to have achieved more than it surrendered in the complex maze of familiarization talks, formal bilaterals, multilaterals, and, perhaps most important, the undocumented one-on-ones, which together make up the stuff of negotiations. Much of the evidence for the less public occasions when MK and the SADF came together remains hidden behind barriers designed to protect those still in positions of influence six years after the culmination of negotiations resulting in the April 1994 elections. Yet on the surface the SADF appears to have been the winner because it reached one of its primary goals: setting the basic terms for the process of integration following elections. From the outset, the SADF was determined to maintain its standards—the entrenched institutional values at the center of its organizational culture; those in MK and the APLA would have to adapt to them. At the end of talks, it appeared that at least the MK was willing to do so in order to reach a military settlement for a truly national defense force.

The SADF thus had every cause for satisfaction depite appearances, and history will look kindly upon the liberation armies. Already, six years after later, many of the original arrangements so carefully negotiated in 1993–1994 are in tatters, partly due to rapid democratization, partly because SADF negotiators failed to see past the horizon. History inevitably resides in the long term, and, in appreciation of MK leaders, negotiations were never the narrow, material, and largely once-off debates over military issues that fit so neatly (and continue to fit) into the strategic managerial paradigm of MK's SADF opponents. On the contrary, most MK leaders regarded negotiations as a stage in a much more sweeping and longer political process within which the peaceful transition to democracy was one facet of a broader project that would ultimately be appropriated in the name of the South African people.

Under the circumstances, it was discursive and largely irrelevant whether agreement was reached on such apparently burning technical issues (at least for the SADF) as, for example, whether the new NDF would maintain so-called standards. Such standards were vacuous in the real world, as was just about anything else leading up to an election in which the political compatriots of MK would—as both MK and SADF negotiators recognized—inevitably come to power. Most of the debates were, in the end, surrealistic, because they were based on the presumption (which everyone recognized as false) that the old military establishment could somehow (and in some inexplicable way) defy the noose of history and emerge in some form reminiscent of a political order on the brink of redundancy.

Negotiations between the military formations were, in a sense, so easy and successful not because the SADF was so overwhelmingly potent, as some analysts believe, but rather because MK was simply not prepared to dig in its heels on arrangements that might compromise peaceful democratization and were themselves transitional in terms of developments in the political arena. Most SADF personnel never quite cottoned to the fact (or cottoned only too well) that whatever was decided could never quite stand the test of time and that history, fueled by its own logic, was loaded to the advantage of MK. MK leadership, although technically uncompetitive from the obtuse technoperspective of the SADF, was also deeply schooled, through a mixture of choice and necessity, at the critical interface between military and political affairs in a fashion that was, with individual exceptions, way beyond the exact comprehension of their SADF opponents, locked as they were by years of total strategy within the strict boundaries of traditional military ideology. In practice, the SADF was in a sense desperately apolitical, whereas MK, during the 1993 talks, both in public and especially in private, were masters of strategic dissimulation and political avoidance. These skills went way beyond the straight military dialogues to which the greater majority of SADF leaders were accustomed, with which they felt comfortable, and to which they linked their corporate identity in the process of reestablishing their legitimacy atop the ashes of apartheid. If the SADF insisted on the maintenance of standards, then let it be, so the ANC argued, since this would be swept aside by postdemocratic history. If the SADF, with its circumscribed perspectives, demanded bridging training, then also so be it; that would have little meaning in the long term.

In the end, then, the mental barriers bred by apartheid on its enforcers, their desire to cement the uncementable, the origins and fluid historic perspectives of MK—all this conspired to give MK a superior edge in appreciating the historic moment. Power, everyone knew, would eventually reside with the political masters of the MK the day after the elections. All knew deep down that after a diplomatic period of time when the ANC had consolidated its power base—be it three years or five—MK would inevitably begin to make the necessary changes to the military pact as circumstances required, no matter how fine-tuned within a wealth of sealed and signed agreements. In Chapter 2, we turn to the changing nature of the so-called military pact under the shifting power relations of fledgling democratic South Africa.

Notes

1. See Mark Shaw, "Negotiating Defence for a New South Africa," in *About Turn: The Transformation of the South African Military and Intelligence*, ed. Jakkie Cilliers and MarkusReichardt (Midrand: Institute for Defence Policy, 1995), p. 19.

2. Ibid., p. 20.

3. South African Defence Force (SADF), Working Paper in Preparation for SADF/ANC Discussions on Unrest/Conflict Before, During, and After General Elections. No Date/Reference (Oelschig collection).

4. Ibid.

5. Ibid.

6. Memorandum, Chief of the South African Air Force to Chief of the South African Defence Force, March 23, 1993, LMH/G/IGLM/203/2/18

7. Bilateral Meetings SADF/ANC(MK), April 23–24, 1993, Admiralty House, Cape Town. Unpublished Notes and Proceedings, N.d., Oelschig collection.

8. Shaw, "Negotiating Defence," p. 19.

9. Notes: Meeting of the Workgroup of the SADF Negotiating with Other Internal Forces at H.S. Ops 061030B, May 1993, Oelschig collection.

10. Confirmatory Notes: Meeting of the Workgroup of the SADF Negotiating With Other Internal Forces at Blenny, 101200B (May 1993).

11. Notes for Communication to Chief of the Army and Air Force: Chief of the Army Conference Room, 111500B (May 1993).

12. Confirmatory Notes: Meeting of the Workgroup at Blenny.

13. Confirmatory Notes: Communication at Chief of the SADF on Standpoints for Further Negotiations with the ANC(MK) (Monday May 17, 1993).

14. Notes on Discussions, June 3–4, 1993 (amended June 10, 1993, Oelschig collection).

15. Ibid.

16. Ibid.

17. Conference Notes on Multilateral Talks Held at Fontana, November 26, 1993. N.d., Oelschig collection.

18. Conference Notes: Discussions of the Multi-Party Planning Group on the Establishment of the National Peace-Keeping Force, December 9, 1993, South African Military Intelligence College No. 9, December 1993.

19. Conference Notes: Fontana.

20. Notes on a Meeting Between SADF and MK at the World Trade Centre, Kempton Park, September 7–8, 1993, Oelschig collection.

21. Notes on Discussions, June 3–4, 1993.

22. Notes on Negotiations, 27/Y/93, July 27, 1993, Oelschig Collection.

23. Conference Notes: Discussions re: NPKF.

24. Ibid.

25. Notes on Discussions, June 3–4, 1993.

26. Notes on Bilateral Working Group WRT Specialist Committee, WTC, September 8, 1993 (Oelschig Collection).

27. Submission to the Defence Command Council General Kritzinger, Chief of Staff Operations, September 15, 1993, Hs/OPS/311/2/27 (UOR).

28. Ibid.

29. Observations on MK-SADF Working Sessions May/June 1993. Correspondence from Brigadier M. Oelschig to Major General J. Erasmus, June 21, 1993, MO/DTL/ONDER H3/Doc.

30. Notes on Bilateral Working Group.

31. Bilateral Discussions SADF/ANC, September 16, 1993, Leerverwysing AFD/INL/ 205/1.

32. Confirmatory Notes: Second Meeting of the Bilateral SADF/MK Working Group, September 16, 1993. Fax from Colonel Steijn to Major General Botha. DTG 22163OB, September 1993.

33. Confirmatory Notes: Third Meeting of the Bilateral SADF/MK Working Group, September 30, 1993 (Oelschig Collection).

34. Confirmatory Notes: Fourth Meeting of the Bilateral SADF/MK Working Group, October 6, 1993 (Oelschig Collection).

35. Notes on the Meeting of the Bilateral Between the SADF and MK on November 2, 1993 (Oelschig Collection).

36. Confirmatory Notes: Second Bilateral Meeting; Bilateral Discussions SADF/ANC, September 16, 1993.

37. Observations on MK/SADF Working Sessions, May/June 1993.

38. Ibid.

39. Ibid.

40. Ibid.

41. Ibid.

42. Ibid.

43. Memorandum: CSAAF to CSADF, March 23, 1993.

44. Ibid.

45. Ibid.

46. Bilateral Discussions, SADF/ANC, September 16, 1993.

47. Observations on MK/SADF Working Sessions, May/June 1993.

48. Confirmatory Notes: Second Meeting of the Bilateral.

49. Observations on MK/SADF Working Sessions, May/June 1993.
50. Ibid.
51. Ibid.
52. Memorandum: CSAAF to CSADF, March 23, 1993.
53. Memorandum: Chief of the South African Air Force to Chief of the South African Defence Force, January 27, 1994, LMH/HvLMS/311/2/TEC.
54. Report: Transitional Executive Council/Sub-Council on Defence (TEC/SCD) Working Group, June 2, 1993/Proposed Terms of Reference for the TEC/SCD: Notes of Workgroup on South African Defence Force Negotiations with Other Internal Forces, Blenny, 10120B, May 1993.
55. Confirmatory Notes: Multilateral Talks, November 26, 1993.
56. Confirmatory Notes: Second Multilateral Meeting of Commanders of Armed Forces. Fax Colonel C.S. Steijn to Brigadier M. Oelschig, No 141500B, December 1993.
57. Bevestigende Notas: Werkgroep vir Riglyne No. 21. Fax Colonel C.S. Steijn to Brigadier M. Oelschig, No 221400B, December 1993.
58. Achievements of the SADF in the Negotiating Process (CSADF Internal Communication Bulletin No. 2, 1994), January 2, 1994.
59. See Section 62(4), Interim Constitution
60. Shaw, "Negotiating Defence," p. 25.
61. Ibid., p.24.
62. Chris de Kock and Charles Schutte, "The Public's Perception of the National Peace-Keeping Force at Deployment at Katorus (Midrand: Institute for Defence Policy, NPKF Research Project, May 1994).
63. Shaw, "Negotiating Defence," p. 26.
64. Ibid., p. 22.
65. Proposed Terms of Reference: TEC/SCD, Appendix A to CS/OPS/OG/503/1, June 21, 1993; Report of the TEC/SCD Workgroup, June 2, 1993 (Oelschig Collection).
66. Proposed Terms of Reference for the TEC/SCD, Blenny, May 1993.
67. Proposed Terms of Reference for the TEC/SCD, Notes of the Workgroup, SADF Negotiations with Other Internal Forces, Blenny, 10120B, May 1993.
68. Transitional Executive Council (TEC) Bill (SCD Section), Article 2e.
69. TEC Bill (SCD Section), Article 9a.
70. Ibid., Article 2c.
71. Ibid., Article 2d.
72. Proposed Terms of Reference for the TEC/SCD, June 21, 1993.
73. TEC Bill, Article 2f.
74. Proposed Terms of Reference for the TEC/SCD, May 1993.
75. TEC Bill, Article 2k.
76. TEC Bill, Article 16.1.ii.
77. TEC Bill, Articles 2a/b.
78. TEC Bill, Article 7.
79. Proposals for Exchange of Strategic Ideas, Views, and Perceptions: Directorate for Transitional Liason to Chief of the South African Defence Force, HS/OPS/S/302/S
80. "Facing the Future," *Salut*, May 1994.

81. Communication and Liason Between the SADF and the Sub-Council on Defence of the Transitional Executive Council, Appendix A, October 4, 1993, CSADF Directive 3/6 DD.

82. Ibid.

83. Communication and Liason Between the SADF and the Sub-Council on Defence of the Transitional Executive Council, CS/OPS/501/5B, October 1, 1993, Appendix A.

84. Proposed Terms of Reference for the TEC/SCD, May 1993.

85. Ibid.

86. "Facing the Future," *Salut*.

87. Communication and Liason Between the SADF and the SCD of the TEC, October 4, 1993.

88. Ibid.

89. Proposals, Directorate for Transitional Liason to CSADF.

90. Ibid.

91. Ibid.; Communication and Liaison Between the SADF and the SCD of the TEC, October 4, 1993.

92. Ibid.; Communication and Liaison between the SADF and the SCD of the TEC, October 1, 1993.

93. TEC Bill (SCD Section), Article 2(j).

94. Proposed Terms of Reference TEC/SCD, June 21, 1993; Communication and Liason Between the SADF and the SCD of the TEC: Ref AThe TEC Bill. Operations Division, October 4, 1993, Appendix A, CSADF Directive 3/6 DD.

95. See 236(1) of the Interim Constitution.

96. "Facing the Future," *Salut*.

97. For a detailed discussion of the mechanics and deliberations of the JMCC, see Philip Frankel, *Marching to the Millennium: The Birth, Development, and Transformation of the South African National Defence Force* (South African National Defence Force: Directorate of Corporate Communications, 1998).

98. Shaw, "Negotiating Defence," p. 21.

99. "Facing the Future," *Salut*.

100. Joint Military Coordinating CouncilSession, 21/Dec261/7:19

101. See, for example, J. Anglin,"The Life and Death of South Africa's National Peace-Keeping Force," *Journal of Modern African Studies* 33(1) (1995): 21–52.

102. Bill Sass, "The Union and the South African Defence Force, 1912–1994," in *About Turn: The Transformation of the South African African Military and Intelligence*, eds. Jakkies Cilliers and Markus Reichardt (Midrand: Institute for Defence Policy, 1996), p. 138.

103. See J-P. Charnay, *Essai general de la strategie* (Paris: Editions Libre, 1973), p. 9.

2

Caesarian Section: The Birth of the South African National Defence Force

The designs of generals should always be impenetrable

—*Flavius Vegetius Renatus,* De Re Militari *(438 A.D.)*

Successful generals make plans to fit circumstances: but do not try to create circumstances to fit plans.

—*General George S. Patton,* War as I Knew It *(1947).*

Democratization involves diversity, specifically the accommodation within the political mainstream of various forces, institutions, movements, and political relations previously excluded. The "resurrection of civil society" referred to by legions of contemporary transitologists is reducible to a single core issue: How does a new democratizing system, beset by past legacies and current cleavages, accommodate the multiplicity of interests generated by the opening up of a political regime to new actors? This is the crux of the transition in South Africa today, the agenda behind the agenda of the new Constitution, the interaction between the formerly privileged and the newly empowered and between an old order, comfortable in its understanding of a racial system sanctified by time, and liberators carrying an agenda to reshape history.

These issues resonate across the civil-military divide in which the military has been the preserve of the ruling class, its membership now challenged by new claims to institutional association that transcend the established criteria of race, class, identity, and political reliability that previously defined who was appropriate for military service, who succeeded within it, and, at bottom line, who was vested with supreme responsibility for national security. New political dispensations inevitably place pressure on those of military rank to reevaluate the nature of the state they serve. The new dispensations also imply redefinitions of military service among those traditionally excluded from the military and the sources of state power. Ultimately, democratization (and disengagement) means flux within military personnel and, hence, the entire system they represent. The challenge to the armed forces in "managing" democracy and retreating to the barracks lies ultimately in their capacity to adapt to the dynamics of new and frequently unfamiliar social conditions without irreparably damaging their institutional capability.

The South African National Defence Force that emerged at midnight on April 26, 1994, was no more than a nominal entity. Despite the hard bargaining and preliminary infrastructures set in place by the Joint Military Coordinating Council during early 1994, a legitimate and "national" defense force did not exist for all practical purposes at that dramatic moment when all South Africans went to the polls for the first time in history. At this point the new NDF still remained to be built, and the task of translating the military pact into reality, of forging a coherent and representative armed force from the seven armed formations that stood by at elections, was to preoccupy the military and civil society. It continues to do so today. This chapter is about this enormously difficult process of integration (which remains, in many respects, inconclusive even as South Africa runs up to its third democratic elections), its achievements despite the odds of bringing together historic enemies, and what remains to be done in this critical facet of democracy-building and consolidation.

The primus inter pares of the seven formations requiring consolidation into one cohesive military in April 1994—the central player in the integration drama that was about to unfold—was (and remains) the old South African Defence Force, whose gargantuan size and organizational differentiation virtually preordained that it provide the framework for integration from the outset. Equipped with all the complex and highly sophisticated attributes of a modern conventional military, the former SADF has been the giant among the competing militaries: MK of the African National Congress, APLA of the Pan African Congress, and the TBVC, or homeland, armies. In the nexus of the new NDF, the old SADF has inevitably and despite resistance set the pace of integration, if not its exact character. Alone among the formations in integration, it has had the administrative systems for large-scale organizational management. This implied that regardless of the decisions in the political arena (and despite the ANC's electoral victory) SADF leadership would inevitably be at the cutting edge of any changes to the armed forces before, during, and after transition.

This was already evident in the 1993 negotiations and the subsequent staff work of the JMCC, both of which accepted the predominance of SADF standards and procedures as the starting point (but not necessarily the endpoint) for regenerating a system of armed forces in line with the new political dispensation emerging after April 1994. Like the other players in transition, both civilian and military, the SADF carried its own agenda into the new South Africa—a sense, as it were, of what this institutional reordering in the military should and should not involve. In line with transitional circumstances, this represented a mixture of innovation and tradition, a reconciliation of old and new. In short, the SADF desired to align the new military with the emerging political order as a means to secure legitimacy and assist reprofessionalization in the wake of the damage to corporate interests inflicted by apartheid. Yet this was tempered by a keen eye to maintaining the institutional supremacy of SADF norms and standards among the various armed formations in the newly constituted NDF, as the SADF had believed that they were best suited to protect national security.

Needless to say, this has not gone over well with MK and the smaller but strategically important APLA. Both recognized the need to maintain a combat-effective military to oversee democratic consolidation. Yet their origins in the populist military environment of the liberation struggle made it difficult, if not impossible, to casually accept their opponent's cautiously transformative agenda, which, they rightfully suspected, presumed that the old military would remain first among equals.

How should power be allocated in the armed forces to reflect changing power relations in civil society? What should the military look like at the end of amalgamation? Different visions were brought to these questions during the very first contacts between the SADF and MK. Thereafter, they were the heart of the epic struggles waged in succeeding years over the spirit and logic of military integration.

Soft Options: The TBVCs

The old homeland armies tended to be on the margins of these dramatic developments. Indeed, if integration has been as a stage dominated by two or three main actors, then the bit players have been these four armed formations despite their constitutional designation alongside the SADF as statutory forces. Uncomfortably positioned between the mammoth SADF and the so-called nonstatutory forces (MK and APLA), the TBVCs (the TDF partially excepted) have never quite enjoyed the political leverage of the others. Subsequently, their integration was far less disruptive, less problematic, and infinitely more regulated.

Prior to April 1994, the JMCC Strategic Planning Process had already laid down a specific procedure for bringing the TBVC grouping into the NDF. This was later reinforced by the Public Service Act, promulgated by presidential proclamation during 1994. As statutory forces, the TBVC armies were not to be "integrated"—this singular honor was reserved for nonstatutory elements—but simply "translated" into the NDF. What this meant was an audit or verification of the qualifications, status, and merits of each TBVC member according to South African public service standards, followed by official emplacement in the ranks of the new armed forces. Three months after democratic elections, however, with integration in the offing, it was by no means certain that this technical exercise could be easily accomplished. In all the TBVCs, there was considerable anxiety as to how the four smaller armies, essentially cloned from apartheid, would fare under the new political dispensation.

In the Eastern Cape, for example, British military observers from the British Military Advisory and Technical Training Team (imported to facilitate the implementation of the military pact) noted poor base facilities, low morale, and considerable potential for unrest in the Transkei and Ciskei armies.[1] TDF soldiers in particular were reluctant to submit to any audit that appeared (in the eyes of their officers) to demean their professional status and standards relative to the SADF. Nor were many TBVC personnel especially happy with the provisions for medical examinations laid down in JMCC procedures for translation.[2] Speedy translation was consequently advocated by the BMATT in order to allow the NDF to maintain command and control,[3] but during 1995 and 1996 verification of TBVC soldiers was often made difficult by absent or inconsistent personnel information on homeland records. Fortunately, much of the required information on fellow statutory forces was also available on NDF computer systems, so all that was eventually required was a relatively straightforward search and update that ultimately did not pose structural challenges to administrative systems.[4]

Insofar as verifications revealed TBVC soldiers to be "substandard," arrangements were made for retraining according to individual requirements. As we shall see below, relatively few TBVC personnel actually fell into this category because of similarities in military background with the SADF. Exceptions were in the more unusual musterings, such as special forces, to which members of the TDF and Bophutatswana Defence Force (BDF) were beginning to be translated toward the end of 1994. During November of that year, complaints were raised to parliamentarians of the Joint Parliamentary Standing Committee on Defence (JPSCD) that specialist training of this type did not take place jointly with SADF personnel, that TBVC instructors were not in situ, and that the majority of instruction was in English or Afrikaans rather than in the vernacular.[5] Yet various measures were introduced by the NDF in the following year to counter these and other similar feelings of marginalization, including the joint training exercises on tactics and survival that the TBVCs had demanded.[6] During 1997, in Eastern Cape Command, for example, "vision" exercises to psychologically reequip TDF and CDF officers for the new NDF environment had been introduced and were proving noticeably successful.[7]

Although translation was theoretically conceived as an essentially administrative process driven by "fixed parameters" that did not require value judgments about the statutory forces,[8] certain tensions indeed emerged in the process; they were precursors to far greater problems encountered when the armed forces came to the much more complex and substantial business of merging nonstatutory forces with the NDF.

Struggles over benefits (a familiar issue) surfaced in TBVC-NDF relations as well, since the smaller statutory armies generally enjoyed better service conditions and fringe benefits. By the early 1990s, for example, CDF soldiers were the best paid soldiers in southern Africa, and all of the TBVC armies were uneasy at the prospect of losing privileges under the public service provisions imposed on members of the new NDF. The TBVCs had all followed generous promotion policies during the apartheid years so as to promote their officers as quickly as possible in a bid to engender personal loyalty. This was not entirely discouraged by their South African mentors, who had stakes in maintaining their compliance; in some instances, such as the Transkei, they could not be discouraged, as the military leaders of the homelands took their independence quite literally. The result was that the TBVCs came to the multilateral negotiations of late 1993 with top-heavy military structures staffed by officers with considerable expectations.

The nationalization of the TBVC additionally posed problems of social dislocation, for they were regional armies not favorably disposed to dispersion throughout the country. As early as September 1994, Transkei and Ciskei personnel were complaining to BMATT that the new dispensation would cause considerable hardship to themselves and their families.[9] To a degree, this remains a problem. One solution, raised early in integration, was to simply absorb the TBVCs into the various regional commands of the new NDF, but this ran into MK objections that the principle of a national army precluded the old homeland armies continuing in their traditional areas of operation.

Relations between the TBVCs and the NSFs were, in any case, fairly fragile given the origins and repressive role of the TBVC formations in the apartheid system. Behind the fiction that they had been established to protect the territorial integrity of what MK and APLA defined as *bantustans*, their raison d'être was mainly to repress internal dissidence at the behest of the apartheid government. All the TBVCs came to the negotiation table in one fashion or another carrying the burden of apartheid history. Their capability had been projected mostly against people who now represented MK or the PAC, with whose military forces they were now expected to amalgamate politely. Quite apart from the pervasive view among MK leaders that the TBVCs were bush soldiers under South African surrogacy, there were strong feelings about what these supposedly inferior militaries had wreaked upon followers of the liberation movements. The Bisho massacre of September 1992, in which many ANC supporters were killed by the CDF, complicated the military negotiations the following year, as did the experience of the defunct National Peace-Keeping Force (where, it was rumored, TBVC personnel, particularly the CDF, were paid higher salaries than their MK counterparts). Now that the various military formations were engaged in a competitive struggle for status and resources in the newly formed NDF, MK and later APLA were not about to stand back and allow these apparently underqualified and largely despised miniformations to dominate the arena.

Much the same negative feelings applied to the BDF, which in MK eyes had been a tool of the "illegitimate" Mangope administration. The refusal of the BDF to ultimately prevent the demise of their patron stood them in better stead when it came to the redistribution of power in the nascent NDF after the 1994 elections. Still, the BDF was a late-comer to the JMCC, and along with the other TBVCs it had played a very limited role in shaping the agenda of integration determined in the 1993 bilaterals. Those key negotiations had also excluded the TDF, the largest (if not necessarily the best-trained) in the TBVC group; its leaders, General George Matanzima and then General Bantu Holomisa, had acted astutely to position the TDF politically between MK, APLA, and the SADF as integration became imminent. During 1993, for example, the TDF inexplicably increased in size by almost 40 percent, and its senior officers had begun to move rapidly upward. Yet this less than subtle strategy only partially secured its relationship with any party, since its motives and agendas were ultimately obvious and distrusted by all.

Mutual suspicion—which would characterize the whole process of integration, whether of SFs or NSFs—soon surfaced as claims were staked to the rewards of translation. MK leaders had cautiously courted the TDF during the multilaterals of late 1993 and were aware of its political value in the ongoing jockeying for institutional power in the new NDF. Still, MK leaders were not about to compromise their own supporters and, at least in the early stages of integration, were quick to label benefits sent the way of the TBVCs as "discrimination." For their part, TBVC leaders were aware that they were small game in the overall contest and were also quick to see discrimination in favor of the NSFs when benefits flowed in that direction. For example, at early South African Medical Services (SAMS) placement procedures, the VDF protested what it saw as preferential treatment for MK, similar to that in the failed NPKF.[10] Here again we see the allegations and counterallegations that characterized debates at placement sites as NSFs were being integrated. Fortunately, the Sub-Council for Defence had foreseen this possibility and, in this instance, expanded the verification committee to include additional representatives from the TBVCs and the NSFs. In another foreshadowing, BMATT, which had been originally conceived as a facilitator only between the SADF and the former NSFs, was also somewhat reluctantly invited to expand its role in verification and adjudication to include the TBVC formations.[11]

Given the natural difficulties of forging a military where smaller participants are determined to protect their corporate interests, the process of translating the TBVC forces has, in historic retrospect, gone reasonably well. Despite the various maneuvers of the TBVCs in the JMCC and after the April 1994 elections, most of the problems of translation have tended to take on an administrative rather than political character susceptible to management within the statutory framework. Section 236 of the Constitution, for example, was an important instrument for diffusing potential conflict, protecting as it did the contracts of TBVC members. As we have already noted, the administrative compatibility between the various SFs assisted the creation of a single computerized personnel system. While this was sometimes uneven because the TBVCs could not or would not provide data as and when required, the dimensions of the problem were never of the magnitude that the Personnel Maintenance Office/Reception Depot (PMORD) was to encounter when it came to the task of attempting to make sense of the human resource aspects of integrating the former NSFs. Relative to this wider exercise in military amalgamation, the incorporation of the TBVCs was also small in scale and, above all, simplified by the structural similarities between the various statutory armies. The TBVC armies collectively made up less than a third of the numbers who had to be brought alongside the SADF into the new NDF after the 1994 elections; they used much the same equipment and to varying degrees had been exposed to the same training systems and standards.

Although the historic relations between the TBVCs and the SADF have varied considerably, this has not seriously inhibited the new system of arrangements in which many militaries have, in a sense, become one. The BDF, for example, was an extension of the Bophutatswana National Guard (BNG), whose 125 men were originally trained and equipped by the SADF in preparation for Bophutatswana's "independence." Two years later, in November 1979, the BNG was itself translated into the BDF, which eventually came to integration with a force of some 4,000 men, two colonels, seven lieutenant colonels, and twenty majors, most trained to SADF standards. With the exception of basic, section, platoon commander, and basic officer training, all VDF training was also undertaken by the SADF. The latter had also played a directing role in the development of the CDF; thirty-eight of its 318 members were SADF instructors when the CDF was formed in 1983. Two years later, Ciskei President Lennox Sebe was requesting the withdrawal of South African military personnel. With Brigadier Oupa Gqozo heavily dependent on South African military support during the early 1990s, however, the Ciskei had become a virtual SADF fiefdom for seconded officers. By mid-1990, SADF officers occupied all the primary functional positions in the CDF and, following another coup attempt the following year, still more SADF officers were filtered in to ensure the political loyalty of the local military.

Dependency on South Africa was somewhat more convoluted in the case of the TDF when Generals Matamzima and Holomisa moved to establish closer ties with both the ANC and the PAC. Following the creation of the Transkei in 1975, however, the TDF received substantial SADF equipment for a fifteen-year period. During the 1980s, most TDF personnel were trained in counterinsurgency along with other TBVC soldiers in South African military institutions, at least until the end of the decade, when it became clear that a new political dispensation was on the cards. Already in the late 1980s, SADF officers were suspect of political meddling, and relations began to erode following the 1987 coup that brought General Holomisa to power. By the early 1990s, the atmosphere for South African advisers was distinctly hostile as Holomisa moved to diversify the Transkei's military contacts. Many TDF officers were now being sent on staff courses to other parts of Africa, and that, as we shall see, was to create several problems after democratization in the issues of placement and accreditation.

The standards of the TBVC armies also varied significantly at the point of political transition, with some personnel having been rigorously trained by the SADF, others less so. At the initiation of postelectoral translation, for example, the VDF had only five majors who had completed the junior staff course of the SADF and no warrant officers first-class. In any event, few homeland personnel ultimately required much in the way of the bridging training eventually advocated for MK and APLA because most were already schooled in the conventional framework favored by the South African armed forces.

Three of the four formations in the TBVC grouping were also largely neutralized as political actors when it came to translation and integration. The VDF, with 1,300 men, was too small to be consequential, whereas both the BDF and the CDF were disempowered by popular mobilization in early 1994. Although the BDF still remained a relatively significant military force in 1994, its political influence was undermined with the collapse of the Mangope government, after which it was forced to modulate its aloofness to the integration process and meekly seek admission to the JMCC as one among several minor actors. The CDF also withered as a political actor during early 1994 with the withdrawal of its South African "consultants" and "advisers," who made up the core of its leadership.

For its part, the SADF moved quickly to rein in the TBVCs, whom it saw as natural, albeit minor, potential allies for the anticipated integration struggles with APLA and, above all, MK. Due to their largely luxuriant promotion policies during apartheid, all of these formations were relatively top-heavy institutions and could provide black officers, trained to SADF standards, to meet the constitutional and political demands on the NDF as a representative military. Senior officers in the TBVCs were clearly vulnerable to overtures from the new NDF, whose decision that all TBVC ranks and salaries could not be decreased during translation has been extremely important in greasing the translation process and addressing the anxieties in the TBVCs over career prospects in the new armed forces. The sudden (and, one suspects, political) elevation of many TDF officers just prior to integration was, for example, casually overlooked; the great majority, along with the TBVC counterparts, were simply translated into equivalent rank in the NDF despite concern in some circles (read: MK and SADF) that many lacked the necessary competence. The eight TDF colonels who became brigadiers during 1992 are illustrative: Seven remained brigadiers five years later, despite the fact that few actually passed the NDF's Senior Staff Course, and one (Brigadier Ntsinga) had been elevated to the rank of major general alongside Major General Matanzima. Rank equivalency as a principle of translation has been applied lower down in the rankings, although many TBVC noncommissioned officers (NCOs) have also risen rapidly along with their superiors. Rank equivalency has also been applied to the white officers of the TBVCs who have consequently been incorporated into the post-1994 military.

Distribution of the NDF's institutional largesse has not been perfect. Almost six years into integration, some of the lowest ranking former TBVC personnel were still not entirely satisfied with the natural predisposition of the NDF to prioritize the integration of the former NSFs. This view has to some extent infected their superiors, who, it is sometimes surmised, bring a dangerous legacy of coups, political agendas, and unwarranted expectations to the transitional armed forces. Be that as it may, most of the administrative milestones of translating the TBVCs into the new armed forces identified in JMCC deliberations prior to 1994 were reached relatively quickly, efficiently, and effectively. Already by June 1994, the small air wing of the TBVC group, its infantry, and its medical corps had been clearly placed under the control of the Chief of the South African Air Force, the Army, and the NDF Surgeon-General respectively. Already by September 1994, the operational command of the NDF had been consolidated with the TBVC armies designated for incorporation into the existing system of territorial commands with new uniforms and equipment.[12] The former TDF and BDF now fell, for example, under Eastern Province and Northern Commands respectively.[13] Already by April 1996—a mere two years after initiation of the process to develop a new national defense force—its leadership could confidently report that some 10,600 of 11,500 former TBVC members "who integrated are still in service and are already being operationally deployed and utilised."[14]

Hards Cases: The Liberation Armies

The logic governing SADF relations with its erstwhile opponents in MK and APLA has been considerably more problematic. Not only has the arithmetic been different (MK put forward some 33,000 men and women for amalgamation, APLA 6,000), but both organizations also reflect the populist conditions of the antiapartheid struggle. As was already evident in the 1993 negotiations, both MK and APLA bring substantially different values and cultures compared to those internalized in the vast conventional structures of the SADF. Both MK and APLA subsequently proved to be far more intractable to change and incorporation compared to their TBVC counterparts.

Much of the history of MK and APLA remains to be written. Nevertheless, only a small proportion of their personnel were on active service at any one time in the antiapartheid struggle: when this did occur, it was generally in the form of in irregular warfare involving small units with considerable tactical autonomy.[15] While some MK soldiers gained experience in conventional warfare as South Africa moved to support various insurgent groups ranged against the de facto Angolan government following the Portuguese withdrawal after 1974, many of the military skills acquired in the underground war against apartheid were (and are) not readily transferable to the large-scale, high-tech, professional environment of the SADF. Some 400 MK members are estimated to have received staff and specialist training in administration, ordnance, logistics, and intelligence. Yet the standards of this training in such diverse places as Zambia, Libya, Tanzania, and Uganda—"hardly well-springs of military professionalism," according to one condescending commentator[16]—are not necessarily commensurate with those in the SADF, nor with the internationally recognized principles for conventional military organization endorsed by the JMCC as part of the overall democratic settlement.[17]

The culture gap between the SADF and the NSFs, along with the size discrepancies, consistently fueled MK-APLA fears of absorption and more fundamental distinctions of attitude regarding discipline, command, and control in relation to understandings of military life—all of which complicated the task. Ultimately, amalgamation has not only required technical training programs to upgrade MK and APLA members seeking to continue life in the ranks; it has also demanded more complex, controversial, and difficult initiatives to align values and attitudes in a way that transcends the origins and sociologies of the SADF and NSFs.

During the course of integration, the former SADF element in the NDF has not always been especially sensitive to these subtle distinctions. In accord with its ethos, the SADF has approached integration in a consciously technocratic manner, blending various principles for organizational restructuring imported from the corporate world with concepts, decisions, and procedures inherent in the political transition. Early in the transformative process, for example, SADF leadership approached specialist managerial consultants in the private sector with expertise in such esoteric disciplines as change management, institutional development, and policy control in multicultural environments. Deloitte and Touche, the multinational management consultancy, was consequently contracted to design and implement Project Optimum for the transformation of the armed forces using the hard managerial principles with which SADF leaders felt (and still feel) most comfortable.

In approaching the integration project, moreover, the SADF was also guided by policy and administrative guidelines derived from negotiations concerning democratization of the armed forces as well as its own institutional experiences. These included decisions of the SCD that provided for the use of SADF systems and facilities in germinating the new NDF, including "special procedures . . . for the placement of all the constituent forces of the NDF."[18] Provisions of the Interim Constitution also formed part of the conceptual framework for integration, particularly Section 224(2), which formally recognizes legal distinctions between the SADF, the defense forces of the TBVC states, and the NSFs.[19] Ultimately, the normal personnel procedures of the statutory forces would also be included in the JMCC's SPP in forging a multidimensional recipe for an exercise in military amalgamation that is, in many respects, quite unique in contemporary history.

Within this political-managerial framework developed in the run-up to the April 1994 elections, amalgamation was seen to involve a carefully articulated and sequential process that would result not only in the unification of the various military forces into a single unit—the new NDF—but, more fundamentally, in the conversion of NSF members from guerrilla-style to conventional military cultures and structures. Hence, the process developed in the JMCC was specifically planned to begin with certification when NSF personnel would present their credentials in petitioning for inclusion. This was manifest in the Certified Personnel Register to which the ANC had formally submitted the names of some 28,000 MK members prior to its closure on the night of elections. Since the PAC was not initially party to this arrangement because of its continued resistance to the electoral process, APLA names were added shortly thereafter. The eventual CPR, once APLA had been included, tallied 32,888 names.

Assembly followed the CPR, at least in the SADF's retrospectively overdelineated game plan for integration. In June 1994, two months after elections, cadres from the liberation armies began arriving en masse in South Africa from camps north of the border in a repatriation exercise that was to continue over many months. Seventy official intakes then took place between April 1994 and April 1996. Initially, MK members were assembled at the Wallmansthal camp near Pretoria, where most intakes were conducted, their APLA counterparts at the De Brug camp near Bloemfontein. This was initially considered politically desirable. One "mixed" intake nevertheless took place at Hoedspruit in the Eastern Transvaal in June 1994, and with the eventual closure of De Brug in early 1996 NSF members were brought into the armed forces together largely irrespective of political membership.[20] Separation in terms of origin at Wallmansthal AA was nevertheless largely maintained. While some intakes have been reserved for female cadres in order to assist administration and avoid social conflict, such segregation has also not always been effective. Gender and party mixture, in spite of neat planning, characterized Intake 6 in August 1995 (675 men and 287 women, 209 of whom were from MK and 78 from APLA).[21]

Most intakes at Wallmansthal consisted of some 1,500 persons (in line with the estimated administrative capacity of the camp), while those of APLA at De Brug involved some 1,000 persons at a time.[22] Further small and initially unplanned intakes of about 150 cadres continued throughout 1996 and into 1997, largely because of the dribbling pace of reporting to the AA. Most integrees have been designated for Army service at the outset, and intakes for the other services have been conducted somewhat separately. The SAMS, for example, began its own assembly in October 1994, and thereafter small numbers of MK and APLA personnel seeking musterings in the SAMS were assembled separately at Voortrekkerhoogte as a matter of convenience.[23] Integration into the Navy (SAN) and SAAF involved assembly at Army points, after which the relatively small number of cadres seeking to join those branches would be selected, recruited, or otherwise filtered out. The conclusion of the assembly phase of integration was planned for the end of 1997 at the latest.

Placement to determine rank, salary, and bridging requirements has constituted the third element in the strategic trajectory. This has been implemented through placement boards that have consisted, in the case of MK, of members of the six constituent forces (excluding APLA), the NDF functional directors, and representatives of BMATT, which arrived in South Africa soon after the elections. In the case of APLA, placement boards have consisted of representatives from APLA, the NDF, and BMATT. The historical absence of rankings in MK has complicated the placement process, despite a hasty attempt by MK to rank its members at the outset of integration. These did not, however, conform to SADF criteria and, in order to diffuse conflict, provision was made, on BMATT's suggestion, to establish a preselection system whereby integrees were subject to functional tests, after which a recommendation regarding proposed rank could be made to the main placement board.[24]

Final decisions on placements remained, however, with the placement board, which in making a determination would consider such criteria as educational qualifications, previous experience, the results of preselection tests, age, NSF seniority, and military qualifications. In assessing academic qualifications, emphasis has been placed on the "appropriateness of such qualifications to the task which the person is expected to do."[25] This has resulted in the somewhat anomalous situation whereby persons of the same rank receive different salary packages. In the event of unproven academic qualification, provision has been made for specially designed potential tests agreed to by all relevant parties. Ultimately, all new members have been the right to appeal decisions of the placement board to an appeal board, whose members correspond to those of the placement board itself.[26]

Decisions of placement boards have taken the form of a letter of appointment that cadres can either except, reject, or appeal. On acceptance, officers have been provided with temporary commissions while other ranks are attested and their details included on the personnel system. Given the manpower requirements of the SAA and the overall infantry character of the NSFs, approximately 90 percent of integrees have been filtered into the SAA. As of 1997, 7 percent have been placed in the SAMS, 2 percent in the Navy, and a mere 1 percent in the highly specialized ranks of the Air Force.[27] A handful of cadres has gravitated toward chaplain and intelligence service, although portions of each arm have also moved into intelligence. In the SAA, for example, 569 cadres were attached to SAA intelligence as of March 1996.[28] The NDF has a flexible service system, and in the integration process most NSF soldiers with less than seven years' experience have normally been offered short-term service contracts (STSCs) of two years, which are technically renewable. This has, however, also been coupled to rank, with most privates and corporals on short-term service and staff sergeants and warrant officers on the medium- or long-term system. Special provisions have also been made for NSF personnel regarded as "deserving cases" or those with special abilities. Hence, placement has involved a fairly complex and not readily discernable procedure whereby two privates could, for example, end up on very different service systems, each with different benefits.

NSF soldiers, according to one official source, "have been disadvantaged in the past and should therefore receive such military training to fully qualify them for the rank which they now hold."[29] Bridging training is also inherent in the important principle articulated during negotiations that all personnel in the NDF conform to international standards, and letters of appointment issued to NSF personnel contain commitments to this type of personal upgrading. The Army, with an estimated bridging capacity of 10,000 persons at a time, has subsequently established twenty-four bridging training units to which personnel are assigned following placement. Other arms, which have inducted far smaller numbers of integrees, have established a further twelve facilities:[30] five units in the Air Force, three in the SAMS, three in the Navy, and one in Military Intelligence. Because of the particular requirements of these services, course content varies quite substantially from that in the Army. Bridging training has nevertheless generally been conceived as a two-stage process beginning with basic orientation (BT1), consisting of a twenty- to twenty-five-week course dependent on service in accord with a syllabus originally negotiated by the JMCC. Phase BT2 (formation training), following instruction in the basic skills of conventional soldiering, has been dedicated corps/service training and is designed "to bring ex-NSF personnel up to the required standard for his/her specialization/arm of service."[31]

NSF personnel appointed as officers had to undergo similar training, albeit in shortened form, followed by courses scheduled according to mustering or rank. After completion of this more advanced course, all integrees were assigned to their parent units or headquarters for operational deployment. This does not, however, exclude further career development training where, for the only time in the process, courses are conducted jointly by all members of the forces. The result is a continuous (and administratively difficult) circulation of personnel between units and courses taking place over the years. Integration bridging training was initiated in January 1995 and was fully operational by the middle of that year. Conceived in the wider sense of career development, however, bridging training could conceivably continue into the indefinite future, particularly in the case of the former NSFs seeking upward mobility in the new NDF as career officers.

Such is the theory of integration. The practice, however, has been far different. Looking back to the first tentative steps to create the new NDF in the immediate aftermath of the April 1994 elections, it would be fair to say that very little has corresponded with the neat strategic prescriptions originally laid down. On the contrary, the whole process, from first-stage certification to full incorporation, has been constantly bedeviled by pressures and problems that could not be conceived at the outset or entirely anticipated by the political decisionmakers in civil society and, perhaps more important, the military planners. Few of either, it appears in retrospect, took full account of such factors as the natural desire of the SADF to impose its own institutional agendas on the implementation of the actual process; the NSFs equally natural resistance to the possibility of being absorbed into the mammoth SADF; different military cultures; clashing political interests; poor communications between the constituent forces; and, in the last analysis, reciprocal distrust.

Many of the governing decisions, negotiated in principle with difficulty in the JMCC, its various working committees, and the SCD prior to April 1994, have actually had little practical meaning when translated into operational criteria at the grass roots—be it in the assembly areas, training programs geared to reconfigure MK cadres, or social relations within mixed units. In some cases, policy mismatch has been due to poor communication, but in others, as BMATT regrettably indicated early on in the process, there have been "deliberate attempts to overturn agreed or JMCC procedures" on both sides.[32] At Wallmansthal from the outset, BMATT noted, former MK and SADF representatives on the ground had clearly different interpretations of the rules of integration despite concurrence by their leaders in the JMCC or negotiations. Downward communication through the respective military hierarchies, the observers added, was then so poor that the "learning curve is steep for all concerned."[33]

The political logic of transition has also demanded that amalgamation take place with excessive speed. In the days following April 27, 1994, MK was under extraordinary pressure to accommodate its repatriated cadres who were flocking into the country, and the SADF viewed with anxiety the presence of large numbers of previously hostile soldiers, many still under arms, in a society whose electoral foundations had yet to set up. Both parties subsequently favored quick concentration and placement, with the result that amalgamation was initiated without the necessary support structures firmly in place. Neither side at the grass roots, British military observers noted, fully understood the detailed mechanics of what had been decided in the JMCC. Neither had time to transmit what little was understood down through the military hierarchy to on-site staff at AAs like Wallmansthal. Hence, for much of its early history integration was almost entirely haphazard, largely experimental, and a learning process for all participants.

MK, in the opinion of some observers, had little understanding of the options attached to amalgamation, while the SADF feared its consequences. With little common knowledge or consensus on selection criteria and procedures on both sides, the placement boards inevitably became potential sites of struggle where the inherent tensions between (and within) former enemies broke regularly to the surface. At Wallmansthal, for example, former MK members who accepted positions on prescreening or placement boards were threatened with violence as sellouts by their own comrades on several occasions.[34] Former SADF leaders were naturally concerned with the impact of placement decisions on the morale of their own forces and were determined to monitor changes to the organizational hierarchy as closely as possible. MK, to make matters worse, naturally approached the placement boards as vehicles to advance its members into positions of rank and seniority and, in so doing, consolidate its presence in new NDF structures as soon as possible. Conflict was inevitable.

The first placement/manning board in the Air Force, for example, immediately ran into problems over the number and quality of MK representatives, none of whom could produce official credentials as to rank or experience to the satisfaction of their former SADF counterparts. In seeking to break the impasse, it was decided to integrate one MK member as the brigadier that he claimed to be; thereafter matters went off well, with no BMATT adjudication required.[35] Even then, the representative concluded, MK "clearly has misunderstandings or misconceptions about the SAAF's view on integration."[36] At later placement board proceedings, MK personnel were frequently intractable in their demands on ranking, partially because of their belief that it was conscious SAAF policy to downgrade former NSF ranks as far as possible. This was reinforced by false comparisons with Army placements where cadres were perceived to be receiving higher ranks on the grounds of age and experience.[37] Similarly, six hours were required to make four placements in the first senior placement board in the Navy—and then only with constant BMATT intervention to ensure a continuation of proceedings. Deep suspicion was evident on all sides, setting the tone for many future deliberations, and "all were unhappy with the way placement had been conducted."[38]

As integration proceeded the situation did improve, and BMATT, in the end, was ultimately required to adjudicate in only a small proportion of cases (less than 10 percent in the Army).[39] BMATT and the prescreening boards nevertheless differed quite substantially with regard to sensitive appointments, particularly in areas such as Military Intelligence, where BMATT saw its observation as especially unwelcome. At Chief of Staff Intelligence (CSI), the loss of files on the personal particulars of the small batch of MK integrees seeking intelligence positions was widely interpreted in the beginnings of integration as part of a covert action. This was, however, a source of some amusement to BMATT, since prescreening was clearly haphazard over all the armed forces and did not, at this point, appear to make use of the minimal information placed before it by PMORD in any case.[40] In the less controversial atmosphere of SAMS, in contrast, integration was assisted by a very positive attitude on the part of all concerned from the beginning, and most placements proceeded with ease and mutually agreed concessions.[41]

As could be expected following years of mutual antagonism, neither side approached integration with fraternity or collaborative spirit. This was particularly true as one moved downward in the ranks and away from the policy nodes at the senior leadership level, where, all things considered, relations were remarkable good. At De Brug, where the remnants of the discredited NPKF had been concentrated following its one and only disastrous outing into the field, demoralization and mutual suspicion were at a premium. Disinterest and cynicism abounded, with integrees hostile in equal measure to NDF camp organizers and their own commanders.[42]

From the MK perspective, the presence of BMATT after elections was important, not only in enhancing its claims in the vast military network of the SADF but also in providing intervention to sort out its internal problems. Hence, the first visit of BMATT personnel to ANC national headquarters at Shell House in Johannesburg was greeted with "delight." The British noted a "deep-seated anti-apartheid feeling" that was to continue inevitably right into the integration but did not detect "a general anti-white fervour."[43] "Strong [racial] prejudices under the surface of many individuals" nevertheless surfaced as integration proceeded,[44] especially (but not exclusively) on the SADF side, where the arrival of BMATT was viewed as intrusive behind the hand of hospitality extended to its members. The new, if hardly existent, MOD had urged BMATT to be proactive, and this enhanced the view in former SADF circles, notably in Military Intelligence, that the British were tools of ANC politicians who should be "frozen out" whenever possible. BMATT quickly reciprocated by concluding that there existed various "hidden agendas," within the Army in particular.[45] Consequently, when BMATT proffered advice on organizational matters to NDF leaders, it was frequently ignored, circumvented, or simply labeled as interference. The first meetings between BMATT and the Army were formally correct yet distant: This, in the opinion of the British representative, was "probably the result of their self-generated organizational failures" to which the British drew attention.[46] In August 1994, moreover, the BMATT commander was directly informed by the SADF that its tendency to make observations and proffer advice exceeded its charge to validate and adjudicate and "was irritating to some." Its opinions, it was bluntly suggested, should be voiced only when called for.[47]

In the first few months of integration (late 1994), relations between stakeholders were fragile all around and fairly poor in some instances. Initial relations between BMATT and the Navy, for example, were particularly problematic when, to the surprise of all concerned, several hundred MK cadres indicated that they wished to serve not in the relatively low-tech environment of the Army but in the Air Force and Navy. The appearance of cadres with some naval expertise produced confusion in the SAN and then a hard emphasis on standards. When confronted with ten Soviet-trained personnel (and a further 440 MK applicants on the CPR) at the beginning of integration, SAN agreed that personnel without naval experience were "recruits" outside the boundaries of JMCC agreements, were inadmissible for placement as integrees, and should be returned to the Army. This was not appreciated either by MK or BMATT, with its commitment to the "spirit of integration" defined by the provisions of the JMCC, nor by the Army, with its natural reluctance to become a dumping ground for rejects from other services.[48] This "large and unresolved problem" at the time was compounded by the refusal of SAN representatives on the first senior placement board to accept the rankings put forward by the handful of MK naval officers—whereupon MK walked out of the proceedings. BMATT, as facilitator, subsequently suggested that MK accept lower ranks with higher seniority, but this was initially rejected by the Chief of Staff–NDF Personnel as a violation of civil service rules governing terms of employment.[49] Conflict over contracts then emerged with the Navy, insistent upon offering only temporary admission should it benevolently agree to accept a proportion of MK recruits without experience.[50]

Ultimately the ten senior MK naval personnel agreed to accept one rank lower than that requested and were transferred to the Naval College at Gordons Bay for further training. Two hundred twenty-four of the lesser MK cadres were then accepted from the total batch for bridging training at the naval base at Saldanha, leaving the remainder at Wallmansthal "feeling disappointed and, in many cases, very bitter."[51] Adding insult to injury, SAN then insisted that the senior MK personnel at Gordons Bay, some commanders in their mid-thirties, wear midshipmens' uniforms until such a time as orientation training was completed.[52] Unsurprisingly, roughly three months after arrival, BMATT was forced to dramatically conclude that "it is now becoming clear that there are elements within SAN [at both junior and very senior levels] who not only do not support the integration process but are actively trying to torpedo it." "The integration process," it was added cuttingly, "is beginning to resemble a damage-limitation exercise."[53]

This was perhaps a somewhat premature judgment that fortunately did not pertain to all services at all times, least of all as integration moved into higher gear during 1995 when it developed a better track record. Still, insensitivity and pettiness frequently fueled conflicts over human resources that continued to punctuate the entire process. For much of the integration, the NDF resisted moves to compromise basic standards and procedures, particularly in the high-tech services. The NDF, its critics alleged, was often insensitive to MK demands, impatient with the lack of MK rankings, and positively alienated by MK's tendency to inflate its members' status before the placement boards. There was, in the opinion of many former SADF leaders, a general lack of understanding of the nature and consequence of various musterings.[54] The Navy, it was said, was "generally reluctant to give any credit to any MK military experience because they do not regard it as relevant."[55] And this reflected the more general NDF view that was dismissive of "previous external training which is either not relevant or not up to the required standard."[56] This has necessarily fueled differences over placements between the NDF, the BMATT facilitators, and MK, which was itself divided on some of these matters. While senior officers such as General Sephiwe Nyanda (the new CSANDF) have always strongly affirmed "professional standards at an international level,"[57] such sentiments have not always been entirely shared among the more politicized cadres of MK and APLA lower down the rankings. Here, the self-same standards have been seen as mechanisms for institutional marginalization and the maintenance of former SADF hegemony over the command apparatus of the new armed forces.

Throughout integration, conflicts over standards and status have inevitably turned into mutual allegations of discrimination. Promotions have also become an especially contentious issue, as JMCC agreements did not address promotions policy on the misplaced assumption that integration would be a short-term process extending over twelve to eighteen months at maximum. Since NSF members were not yet bridged in the early part of integration, vacancies tended to be filled almost exclusively by former SADF personnel already wait-listed for promotion, and this understandably angered MK and TBVC members.[58] During early 1996, for example, former NSF spokespersons alleged that most to all promotions were benefiting former SADF members to the exclusion of other constituent forces and called for an overall review of promotions policy.[59] With the initiation of bridging training at the beginning of 1995, moreover, the debate had already sharpened as former NSF people came up against the hard realities of formal instruction. Many certainly came to the conclusion that they were being acculturated into former SADF systems of norms and values as part of an overall absorption project, particularly when people failed to meet training criteria. In the specialist services outside the Army, many former NSF personnel aspiring to be pilots, seagoing naval commanders, or medical practitioners were also beginning to encounter difficulties by mid-1995. Some were subsequently remustered—much to their anger, according to their actual skills level.[60]

Generally speaking, the NDF has tended to enjoy more leverage than the former NSFs on the standards issue—on legal, political, and professional grounds. Section 236(8)(d) of the Interim Constitution specifically subordinates NSF membership in the NDF "in accordance with normal employment policies and terms of conditions and service" in the absence of any alternative provisions.[61] The political deal brokered between MK and the SADF during negotiations (particularly the former's recognition of the maintenance of international standards in the proposed NDF) has also prejudiced the former NSF forces at this level: The JMCC had clearly decided that SADF requirements for appointment and promotion would remain governed by Defence Act No. 44 of 1957, and this was subsequently included in the eventual SPP.[62]

BMATT, for its part, has tended to favor an elastic interpretation of standard procedures according to the dictates of a unique situation but has also tended to be sympathetic to the NDF-SADF on the nature of the standards themselves. Much like the NDF, it has stressed the importance of developing officer skills and culture to the maximum degree, particularly in cases where individuals are deployed to operate technology. The first batches of Air Force integrees at Langebaanweg had great difficulty because of their limited academic knowledge of mathematics and physics and, by September 1994, had been returned to Pretoria for remedial training.[63] The small handful of technically trained former MK personnel destined for the Air Force had no practical experience, and from the outset BMATT was privately skeptical that the greater majority of former NSF personnel could be trained up to the demanding, but necessary, specialist skill levels, least of all in the relatively short period of time allocated to bridging training. Bridging training, BMATT nevertheless insisted from its arrival, must conform to the international experience of professionalism, particularly in the SAMS, the SAN, and the SAAF, where "standards are often regulated by international law [and] internationally agreed Health and Safety standards that cannot be compromised."[64]

The NDF, it must be emphasized in all fairness, did not ride roughshod over the former NSFs in the complex business of matching manpower quality control with levels and skills. Bridging training, in NDF official perceptions, is in the spirit of integration and reconciliation in that it allows for an eventual leveling of the playing field once all constituencies have caught up to institutional requirements. JMCC recommendations that officers have a minimum standard-10 education for officership have been flexibly applied on several occasions.[65] Although educational qualifications remain a requirement for appointments to certain ranks, the introduction of potential testing within a mix of criteria for those behind has also been to the advantage of MK and APLA members without a demonstrable and formal education. At the beginning of integration, the NDF additionally accepted BMATT suggestions that placement be preceded by a prescreening process that would accelerate deliberations at placement boards and also work to the advantage of individuals. BMATT insistence that flexible seniority "notchings" within ranks be used to diffuse placement conflicts was also ultimately accepted, and Public Service Commission rules changed accordingly. Although labeled "reverse racism" in some circles, the later decision to allow two chances for bridging training candidates who faced testing has been an important safety net for guerrillas seeking career mobility in a conventional military environment.

Posting policy between bridging courses has also been adjusted to accelerate the elevation of former NSF members. These include shadow posts (where integrees have only partially completed corps and development training), so-called integration posts (specially created on a transition basis), and supernumerary positions where incumbents "are given gainful tasks and opportunities to gain experience" in the absence of other postings.[66] The mixture of assessment and appeal boards has finally been important in diluting standards-type conflicts and assisting the socialization of NSF forces. By mid-1995, BMATT noted, the various boards were "running smoothly and more frequently with appeals being dealt with promptly." They were, it added, "properly constituted, well organized and run and decisions are made with relevant documentary evidence." The assessment boards were encouraged to use their discretion with regard to individual cases and were "giving ex-NSF personnel the benefit of the doubt" on bridging training issues.[67]

Differences over standards, rankings, and promotions have nevertheless come together on practical issues of remuneration, and many of the provisions laid down by the Public Service Commission have had to be continuously reviewed by the military "in the spirit [and logic] of the integration process."[68] A portent of payment problems occurred in mid-1994 when, as BMATT noted, MK instructors appointed to assist in the AAs "refuse to work when they realised they would not be paid until after placement."[69] Since placement was sometimes slow, this became an ongoing problem with all cadres, particularly the so-called veterans and vulnerable (the old and particularly low-grade NSF personnel) who could not conform with the criteria laid down for potential tests. At the placement boards, NSF members often had difficulty understanding the ramifications of the contractual system associated with letters of appointment, especially the situation, noted above, where people of the same rank could receive different salaries according to their academic qualifications. Many MK personnel were under misunderstandings that their appointments were permanent and reacted angrily when it became apparent that it was NDF policy to offer only limited STSCs (which, apart from anything else, excluded medical benefits).

After placement itself, wrangles often occurred over the notching and size of salaries, but these were largely diffused after an agreement between the NDF and the Public Service Commission that adjusted notches and allowed for payments back to the point when personnel had registered at the AAs. Protests, spontaneous resignations, and declining morale on the part of former NSF members over the administration of salaries nevertheless continued. Many MK cadres with little experience in personal financial management had difficulty in coming to terms with the somewhat ponderous and often less than efficient administrative procedures that delayed payments and confused recipients. The inability of former NSF members to provide adequate background data wreaked havoc with a highly computerized (and necessarily indiscriminate) personnel system in which individuals were entered after accepting placement. The issue was again partially resolved when the NDF, acting on JMCC guidelines, agreed to pay all placed personnel the lowest notch on the civil service list prior to proof of qualification,[70] but this was not always helpful to the new integree with few, if any, papers on his or her background. Breakdowns in PMORD reflecting the Herculean demands on the military bureaucracy meant that rankings could not be confirmed quickly; thus in the earlier phases of integration payments were often late. This was especially demoralizing to former NSF members with families to support on nothing but their military incomes.[71] All live-in members of the military are subject to board and lodging deductions and, like other citizens, are subject to pay-as-you-earn taxation. Since neither the deductions system nor the benefits system was effectively communicated at the outset, some integrees were confirmed in their worst suspicions at the motives and procedures of the military apparatus.

Because of the initial refusal of the PAC to adhere to the CPR, it was not entitled to special ex gratia payments arranged for MK. Although this exclusion also applied to MK members who were late additions to the CPR, this became a source of double contention between APLA, MK, and the NDF. The docking of salaries of former NSF personnel who expressed their dissatisfaction with integration process by defecting from the AAs was another bone of contention, since upon return to camp it could take two months to reactivate payments. Those who went AWOL frequently found themselves unpaid for relatively long stretches.[72] Here again, however, the NDF took measures to address the situation with commanding officers being instructed to act "with highest priority."[73] These actions included changes in the salaries advice format and a communications campaign by the chief paymaster from mid-1995 to promote wider understanding of the payments system. To some extent, the benefits of this initiative were wiped out when in July 1996 the Public Service Commission itself introduced a new salary grading scheme under which operational allowances were effectively eliminated. By late 1996, when all parties were well into the learning curve, however, it could be justifiably stated that "pay problems associated with former NSF members have all but disappeared."[74]

Integration nonetheless posed a major administrative challenge to the standard procedures of the armed forces, particularly in its early stages, when personnel and systems were involved in what was then largely an experiment in uncharted waters. The various arms of service, for example, sometimes differed with each other as to the application of JMCC procedures as well as with Defence Headquarters (DHQ). Specification of rules governing ranking and seniority notching was a point of issue from the outset at the placement boards, with the Navy and DHQ insisting on a strict interpretation of organizational guidelines and the Air Force (and BMATT) somewhat more charitable in light of the new requirements.[75] Standard Army regulations disallowing leave (so-called walkouts) during the first eight weeks of basics became a major source of discontent during initial bridging training and also had to be subsequently amended. In a pointed display of alternative military culture, instructor trainees at Oudtschoorn protested standard restrictions governing the consumption of alcohol while on duty and, perhaps more reasonably, compulsory attendance at church services.[76]

An especially galling matter that arose shortly after the beginning of orientation training was the SAN's insistence that all senior former NSF personnel at its bases complete a security vetting document, part of which contained reference to previous Communist Party affiliations.[77] This display of bureaucratic zeal—no doubt motivated by the Soviet background of former MK officers—immediately created a furor, because similar procedures were not being followed in other services. In the Army, for example, newly appointed former MK generals had not been required to comply with security vetting apart from signing the Official

Secrets Act. MK was understandably outraged at this creative extension of JMCC provisions, the more so as the NDF now began to argue that security checks were essential preconditions for training in warfare.

From the outset of integration, then, communication skills on both sides were poor. Much of the rigidity displayed by the NDF at times had to do with the lack of consistent and articulate MK representation either at NDF headquarters or at field units involved in bridging training.[78] The absence of an MK representative at the School of Infantry to act as a nodal point for grievances was, for example, identified by an NDF assessment unit as a primary problem in activating training during late 1994.[79] Similar concerns were voiced both earlier and later in the process, at diverse units from Ladysmith to Gordons Bay. This meant that many MK concerns and policy positions simply went unheard by the NDF (although there were some instances of feigned deafness).

Lines of communication between the AAs and NDF headquarters were also sometimes poor and/or skewed. During late 1994, for example, the Integration Committee was being informed that developments at Wallmansthal were moving smoothly ahead—at the very time when the whole processing system was on the verge of collapse. Organization at this juncture was "no better and [in] some cases worse" than when the system was initiated. BMATT urged immediate action to streamline administrative arrangements, brief integrees, and track persistently mislaid documentation.[80] In this instance, the NDF, working through the commanding officer at Wallmansthal, quickly responded.

In general, however, for a mixture of reasons related to politics and prestige, NDF leaders were mostly reluctant to seek advice from BMATT on the basis of its accumulated experience in other parts of the subcontinent.[81] PMORD, the NDF's personnel administrative system, was initially confounded by the massive influx of integrees, many without documentation of any sort, even verifiable proof of South African citizenship. MK must share part of the blame for the resulting organizational chaos through its poor internal communications, which largely failed to brief integrees on the nature of the process, particularly admission requirements. Some NSF members were reluctant to provide background details for fear such would be used against them by SADF operatives in Military Intelligence.[82] Either way, there were often interminable delays at the AAs as individuals arrived but their documents did not, documents arrived without individuals, or personnel wrangled over minor details.[83] "Simple organizational errors" plagued placement procedures at the SAMS, leading BMATT representatives to ruefully admit that the process "is more complex than originally envisaged."[84]

The Army, the target for most integrees and TBVC personnel, was especially labored at Wallmansthal by the continued throughput of persons from induction to bridging training. According to one report, this "is stretching Director Army Training HQ to the limit."[85] At the Infantry School, an assessment team noted toward the end of 1994, the whole bridging initiative was endangered by the speed of training relative to student skills, a general lack of identification with the training program, and a host of associated problems from pay to lack of instructors.[86] Plans to make greater use of Navy and Air Force instructors did not materialize.[87] Although the strain was less intense in the other arms of service, the coordination of the various phases of bridging training also placed heavy demands on command and control as integrees were dispersed to facilities throughout the country. At least a portion of the breakdown of discipline and morale stemmed from sheer idleness as people waited in camps while the organizational apparatus moved slowly.

Parliamentary observers had predicted this as a problem requiring urgent attention,[88] particularly as organizational problems began to sour relations at the placement boards. By October 1994, the NDF was moving to effectively redesign administrative structures.[89] By February 1996, BMATT could report that "the assembly areas have been very well run and administered." "We have been impressed," it added, "by the effective Command, Control and Coordination in the AA's and the positive attitude and goodwill displayed at Placement Boards."[90] Part of this change is attributable to the decision of the NDF in its administrative overhaul to limit the number of integrees to 1,500 per intake following the initial chaos. This eliminated delays in processing and speeded up throughput. The subsequent decision by the constituent parties to centralize all intakes at Wallmansthal after the beginning of 1996 was also helpful in reducing costs and resources. In mid-1996, with bridging training now up and running, a thorough investigation was undertaken when it became clear that courses, particularly for officers, were falling behind schedule. Recommendations included the shortening of courses, rescheduling, and a new procedure for tracking the progress of individuals. BMATT, on this basis, could predict that bridging training for former NSF officers would be largely completed by the end of 1997.[91]

The sheer scale of the exercise and its compacting into a tight time frame by the political logic of transition undoubtedly were a major source of difficulties. Because of its unprecedented character, integration also strained established rules and procedures, both in the military and in the wider state bureaucracy, which have had to be adapted ad hoc to meet unexpected contingencies and problems. The relative inflexibility of public service requirements for pay and promotion, for example, was misaligned with NSF demands and expectations at the outset of integration and had to be altered accordingly. When the first NSF personnel arrived in June 1994, it was also feared that the NDF lacked the human resources required for an exercise of this scale and intensity, and to a degree this was prophetic. The idea was mooted by importing 250 additional instructors from "other Western nations," but this eventually came to nothing. Subsequently, in July, a program was initiated at Oudtschoorn to train select MK personnel as instructional assistants.

Although there were few instances when training of new recruits was canceled due to lack of instructors, there were frequent interminable delays as the NDF juggled its members.[92] Former NSFs were often not in the right place at the appropriate time, and the standards of courses varied substantially, particularly in the field units.[93] Naval instructors at Gordons Bay and SAS Saldanha were initially unmotivated about their new training responsibilities, which they regarded as an irritating part-time extension of their normal line duties.[94] The condescending attitude of senior SAN personnel was that naval integration had long since taken place, causing observers to suggest that the Navy was "in danger of drowning in its own propaganda."[95] Instructors, in these circumstances, were not inclined to make a special effort, and it was only after sharp words between BMATT and the Navy toward the end of 1994 concerning the latter's "less than focussed approach to integration" that the situation was effectively remedied.[96]

Former NSF reactions to training have differed quite substantially from service to service and place to place. The quality of infantry trainees at Ladysmith, for example, was poor, and they were unmotivated. At SAS Saldanha, however, BMATT was "pleasantly surprised by the enthusiasm, dedication and professional approach" shown by former MK students.[97] Many former SADF instructors in all service arms accustomed to a certain type of white student have, however, been seriously challenged by bridging training, particularly when classes have been unenthusiastic, undisciplined, and generally unmanageable. It was at this level—in the crucible of training—perhaps more than anywhere else in the integration process that the contrasting cultures of the SADF and MK-APLA came up hard against each other—with inevitable friction on both sides.

At the Infantry School, for example, instructors were allegedly aggressive and abusive irrespective of the age and rank of trainees. Older trainees at the end of 1994 were experiencing great difficulty in coping with the physical demands of standard programs designed for adolescents, while both instructors and trainees were locked into a mutually reinforcing spiral of frustration and hostility through the inability of instructors to communicate in adequate English.[98] At Ladysmith, in contrast, former NSF personnel clearly took advantage of the youth and inexperience of instructors to provoke unseemly behavior. One inevitable consequence of this situation was the progressive resignation of instructors once bridging training gathered momentum. Between January and August 1995, 482 instructors, mainly officers and NCOs, resigned from the Army alone. As a contemporary report grimly noted, "This figure only includes personnel directly involved with the mechanics of instruction and not supporting or command staff."[99] A vicious and mutually reinforcing spiral was then set in motion: Instructor-student relations worsened with each perceived mala vides on the part of the other, the quality of instruction inevitably fell, and all-around frustration accelerated.[100] Given the underlying suspicion between the constituent forces, training failures were widely interpreted by MK leaders as part of a subtle process to weed out former NSF members, particularly in the early stages of integration when distrust was at its height.

The NDF, as a means of management and conflict resolution, sought to fast-track instructors from the NSFs. Yet this was only partially successful in the short term. Many MK personnel were reluctant to be mentored as assistant instructors and become, in effect, extensions of former SADF power and control. Most MK personnel could not in any case be trained up to the accepted level with the immediacy that the situation demanded. Of the forty-six first-batch potential MK assistant instructors sent to Oudtschoorn for training, less than half could comply with their course requirements a month after admission.[101] Neither was there particular enthusiasm among former cadres for instruction by former TBVC instructors, upon whom the NDF was forced to periodically rely as a contingency measure.

Physical conditions in the AAs also reinforced negative first experiences for former cadres—although here, too, conditions improved markedly as the integration process built upon its own experiences. Conditions at De Brug were generally far superior to those in the hastily erected site at Wallmansthal. At the latter, the sudden huge infusions of repatriated soldiers during the first intakes of 1994 seriously strained the most basic facilities. Some of the cadres arriving from camps north of the border were in poor health, and many had little more than the inadequate clothes they were wearing. SADF planners had seriously underestimated the scale of the problem or, as MK still alleges, had consciously avoided making adequate plans as a disincentive to join the new NDF. It is a measure of the level of mutual suspicion that some MK leaders believed that the Wallmansthal AA was a concentration camp where they were to be cordoned prior to an SADF military onslaught. Either way, confusion was rife and living conditions were, at least at the outset, sufficiently poor to justify some of the worst MK suspicions. Adequate tents, bedding, and clothing were in short supply for much of 1994, and each delay tended to confirm NSF suspicions. Food was initially poor and unvaried, except for that provided to SADF personnel. This fueled conflict until the NDF eventually provided a common catering system contracted out to a civilian company.

Ablution facilities were initially poor, overcrowded, and a danger to public health. Medical examination of MK cadres revealed several cases of tuberculosis, persons requiring antimalarial treatment, and some cases of hepatitis B. MK medical personnel did not initially understand the bureaucratic procedures involved in accessing drugs and medicines from the SAMS, which also became a source of short-term frustration. Psychometric testing, introduced belatedly by the NDF in September 1994, became a point of conflict for suspicious former NSF personnel, particularly MK, who saw no necessity for these apparently strange procedures outside the terms of the JMCC agreements and subsequently instructed its members at Wallmansthal not to submit as a condition of preselection or placement.[102] This was irritated by BMATT's refusing to endorse the methodology and underlying assumptions of these tests, designed by the SAMS's Directorate of Psychological Services, on the grounds of cultural bias.[103] Ultimately, if not without protest, SAMS's test package was adapted to meet what BMATT considered international standards, and the whole exercise was repackaged as "potential tests" to meet MK fear of hidden SADF agendas.

Language differences, with their deeper cultural meaning, have additionally complicated the overall integration program. In principle, the NDF has been committed to the view articulated by the JPSCD that "oral and written instruction [in all bridging courses] should be conducted in the language best understood by most members."[104] This has not been a problem among the more senior former NSF officers, virtually all of whom are highly proficient in English, which is widely used in advanced instruction in such higher institutions of military learning as the South African Army College and the Army Battle School. Communication lower down the hierarchy has, however, been more problematic, either because SADF instructors are largely versed in Afrikaans, because NSF personnel do not (or will not) speak Afrikaans as the language of oppression, because their English is often poor, or because instructors (even integrees) know little in the way of indigenous African languages.

Language has thus become another political and organizational issue. In specialist service bridging training such as that in the SAMS, some former NSF personnel have been prejudiced—or seen themselves prejudiced—by Afrikaans-medium instruction. At the Nursing College, for example, assessment boards have found "difficulties in understanding the language of instruction [Afrikaans] to be a significant factor in [examination] failures," as well as the failure of students to complete designated courses.[105] The Nursing College has subsequently streamlined its nursing bridging course and office formative course into an English and Afrikaans component, although much of the literature and workshop discussions continue to reflect the entrenched Afrikaner culture of the armed forces. Despite interventions to monitor language discrimination by BMATT, the Parliamentary Integration Oversight Committee (PIOC), and the SADF Integration Working Group (IWG), many Army instructors are naturally uncomfortable in English and tend to revert back to their home language whenever the opportunity arises. Outside of the Special Forces, whose instruction and manuals are entirely in English because of the international flavor of their operations, most NDF documentation was, until very recently, still issued in Afrikaans.

BMATT has waged an ongoing and somewhat successful campaign to ensure that administrative instructions, communications, and orders are not disempowering or confusing because of their Afrikaans formulation. Yet the NDF leadership has tended to drag its heels on this issue, which it sees as linked to the history and organizational autonomy of the military. To complicate matters, the English-language skills of some former NSF personnel are far from perfect, not only in the lower ranks but also on technical matters. The earliest integrees to the Air Force, British observers noted, were having difficulty with specialist English,[106] which has reinforced the NDF view that "the use of English is not necessarily the solution,"[107] even while setting up special English classes for both former SADF instructors and their former NSF students. Generally speaking, English has tended to emerge as the normal teaching medium, and the whole language controversy is far less explosive today than in the heady, emotional atmosphere of early integration.[108] Some training courses and group exercises nevertheless fell between instruction in poor English or in fluent Afrikaans, something that is resented by all participants. Military base life and the working environment outside the classroom are also largely continuous with Afrikaans tradition and language in a manner that reinforces social distance between the various cultural groupings.

Many of these problems (particularly the physical problems) were simple (albeit serious) teething issues particular to Wallmansthal as a hastily constructed AA. Where existing facilities were available for integrees (e.g., the SAMS training center at Voortrekkerhoogte and the barracks at Wonderboom), standards were far better. At De Brug, where APLA was assembled following the departure of the NPKF in August 1994, conditions were, as we have noted, markedly better than those at Wallmansthal. Despite being sometimes seen as the poor cousin of its larger counterpart, the De Brug AA was far superior in organization, and in general the integration process for APLA went far better because of good forward planning by NDF staff, the layout of the area, which facilitated administration, and higher levels of discipline, command, and control among APLA forces compared to MK.[109] Most APLA members, for example, appeared with all the necessary personal documentation and detailed curricula vitae that facilitated the administrative process.[110] By mid-1995, many of the initial problems at Wallmansthal had in fact been treated and facilities made reasonable. Within the context of its time, however, the formative days at Wallmansthal and De Brug were important in shaping subsequent MK and APLA attitudes toward the NDF within the wider context of the tripartite relationship between the three constituent forces. Despite having less combat experience, the APLA leader group arriving at De Brug in August 1994 was labeled by BMATT as "smarter, better disciplined and more political-oriented" than MK. Very few of its members were rejected by the NDF, and then largely on medical grounds.[111] This did not go unnoticed by MK, which generally appeared to fit far less comfortably into NDF structures than did their PAC counterparts.

Securing the AAs was a more general problem given the mutual distrust between former SADF and former NSF forces. Security at Wallmansthal was originally the charge of SADF military police and 115 Battalion, whose very presence raised MK anxiety that they were being cordoned in an unarmed condition and thus highly vulnerable to attack. The failure of MK command-and-control structures to brief their cadres on integration—indeed, their emphasis that they remain alert—heightened the tension. In order to diffuse a potentially volatile situation, the JPSCD advocated that security be handled by the NSF itself.[112] NSF guards were subsequently appointed, but this did not entirely alleviate the problem, as the new sentries were also involved in bridging training and were available only on a part-time basis.[113] The speed with which integration (sometimes) worked also precluded them from effective training to resist peer pressure, and standards of discipline consequently suffered.

Drunkenness and associated problems were a pervasive source of conflict in the tedious conditions of the AAs, aggravated by administrative delays in the processing of integrees. This was perpetuated into bridging training, although in some units the existence or improvement of on-base recreational and club facilities raised the level of sobriety.[114] More intractable were walkouts and AWOLs, frequently initiated by pay problems but often triggered by individual or collective discontent on the slightest pretext. While integrees tended to return for pay parades, summary trials, courts-martial, and other desperate attempts to uphold the MDC became the order of the day in Wallmansthal during late 1994 and early 1995. During mid-1995, for example, over a thousand summary trials were being held for offenses ranging from drunkenness to going AWOL to disobedience.[115]

Toward the end of 1994, much administration at Wallmansthal was absorbed with the punishment of those who had violated military law in one form or another. Sentences ranged from discharge in very serious cases to more common admonitions and fines (most of which could not be collected as cadres rallied around offenders in resisting the system). In February 1996, some forty persons were still awaiting courts-martial at Wallmansthal, none of which could proceed because the offenders refused legal representation provided by the NDF but could not produce their own lawyers.[116] This led to the masterly understatement at the time that "there appears to be a lack of willingness by some former NSF members to accept the [MDC] which to a large extent is founded on self-discipline, pride and teamwork."[117]

Part of the problem clearly lay in the fundamentally different military cultures that were brought into the nexus of the AAs and then transmitted to bridging training. Problems of command and control were inevitable in these circumstances. Yet some responsibility lay with the NDF, whose various unit commanders often failed to effectively brief integrees on the nature of the process or to develop forward plans on such personal issues as pay and leave—certainly in the early and highly experimental first months of integration.[118] In many cases, lack of communication through the NDF hierarchy made this NDF heirarchy impossible even when grassroots personnel were sincere and motivated. While all players—including BMATT, the JPSCD, NSF leaders, and the NDF—adhered to the view that "every member of the Force must commit himself or herself to observe strict discipline and at all times adhere to the military code of conduct,"[119] the inflexibility of the NDF sometimes tended to fuel conflict that could have been avoided with a little more empathy, leniency, compromise, or cooperation (especially from the former NSF leaders).

Part of the blame also ironically lies in the NDF's insistence that integration be entirely nonracial. All statistics governing military law were entirely integrated once cadres left the AAs, and this made it impossible for the NDF to isolate violations by NSF personnel on the road to remedial action.[120] Hence, we see the plaintive suggestion by BMATT that "it would be helpful to all those involved in integration if the Attorney-General's Department could publish statistics with an objective analysis on disciplinary cases which would allow commanders to take appropriate and timely remedial action on prevalent cases."[121] The failure of the SAP to keep records on arrests for criminal offences also hindered monitoring, although the gravity of some offenses sometimes broke the surface.

These included the arrests of two Air Force NCOs for murder and robbery during early 1996.

Ultimately, discipline did improve as one moved farther away from the chaotic days of late 1994. Tension was reduced, for example, once the NDF initiated a policy of fully clearing each intake at the AA before admitting another. This procedure inhibited "old" integrees from "negatively influencing" their successors "with respect to past grievances."[122] The NDF also encouraged former NSF personnel to make full use of standard grievance procedures: formal letters to commanding officers, Commanders Communication Periods, monthly forums with commanders that could lead up to the arms of service and even NDF Headquarters (for collective grievances), and (in individual cases) representations to immediate supervisors leading up the chain of command to the president if necessary.[123] At 8 Infantry Battalion, for example, the commander (or his second in command), had made it established practice to personally address the troops on a weekly basis.[124] Yet well into the process NSF personnel have distrusted these established channels in preference for direct appeals to political leaders from the ANC, BMATT, their own commissar, or the MK's own Integration Committee. It was in fact only after commissars were brought into closer contact with their NDF counterparts, and disillusion had set in with civilian leaders in the ANC, that the cadres began to seriously consider using the structures that had been emplaced by the NDF from the outset.

The NDF was sharply opposed to BMATT intervention at this level, and when special student committees were created at units during bridging training, BMATT was specifically targeted for exclusion. In order to route complaints into official institutional channels outside the political arena, the NDF also established several special grievance programs and procedures for the specific purposes of integration. Leader group personnel from all services and constituent forces, for example, were sent to several fast-track training programs aimed at improving communications skills in a multicultural environment. By the beginning of 1995, about a hundred students had completed this specialized education.[125] The JPSCD and other players had suggested special mechanisms at integration points to facilitate the speedy identification of problems,[126] and a complaints office partially manned by former NSF members was subsequently established at Wallmansthal.[127] This was supplemented by a formal divisional structure to link statutory and NSF members who were to be deployed back to the AAs in command-and-control positions upon the completion of bridging training.[128]

After serious unrest at Wallmansthal in October 1994, both the Integration Committee and the minister of defense were encouraged to visit the site more regularly, and thereafter Modise appeared on an almost biweekly basis for a short period. This produced a mixed reaction from the MK audience, many of whom had already come to see their senior leaders as uncaring. Few in this constituency were especially impressed by the sudden and belated appearance of a chief who, in their opinion, had become all too cozy with former SADF generals. (Similar feelings were expressed at the time in regard to the new CSANDF, General Nyanda.) When President Mandela himself visited the AA in October 1994, the reception was somewhat more positive, at until he endorsed the official line that standards of discipline must be maintained irrespective of grievances.

The success of these initiatives, like other aspects of integration, varied from place to place. Generally speaking, the plan to use former NSF personnel in a conflict-management capacity did not come on line with the speed anticipated because of the often slow pace of bridging training. NSF personnel, wary of manipulation by the NDF, continued to drift toward their own commissars, although some of these personnel also eventually became targets of suspicion when they were unsuccessful in fighting their way through the administrative maze and confusion in dealing with complaints from their own people. As late as mid-1997, some of the democratically elected communications committees at various units still did not function properly because former NSF personnel did not entirely trust their own representatives.[129] The populist culture of MK also often asserted itself as integrees resorted to mass action in preference to the committee system established by NDF authorities. This happened during 1994–1995, for example, at 4 Artillery Regiment at Potchefstroom, as well as among women integrees at 5 Signals Regiment at Wonderboom, before commanders were able to intervene to diffuse the situation.[130]

Discipline nevertheless gradually improved by 1996 as intakes became smaller and more manageable, as common institutional loyalties were built during bridging training, and as the various committees and forums legitimated their existence by supplementing their control function with the ability to convey opinion and constructive suggestions up the chain of command.[131] Unfortunately, demoralization had by this time infected the former SADF itself, particularly those in assembly and training. We have already referred to the toll taken on instructors, and by early 1996 concern was being expressed at "the decline in morale in the SANDF which is particularly prevalent in middle management [i.e., former SADF] levels." A "pro-active, comprehensive and widespread communications plan," the report recommended, "is essential to reduce uncertainty and retain a well-motivated workforce."[132] Many former NSF members who had joined the armed forces with the sole intention of securing a gratuity welcomed demobilization as it began to loom over the whole process by late 1994. Their white counterparts, however, viewed rationalization as a distinctive threat. Uncertainty, prospects of limited career mobility, and the demands of implementing integration subsequently combined to aggravate the morale problem and accelerate resignations.[133]

Various institutional mechanisms (including the Integration Committee and workgroup composed of the various armed formations, the PIOC, and BMATT) were emplaced to assist the ongoing process.[134] And by early 1996, approximately two years after its initiation, many (but by no means all) of the difficult problems dogging the entire initiative—poor discipline, instructor shortages, and so on—had evoked some form of remedial action. Accommodations, training facilities, equipment, uniforms, and, to a lesser degree, instruction had all been enhanced. Later intakes at Wallmansthal tended to be younger, more cooperative, and perhaps less politicized than their predecessors, who had arrived direct from the MK and APLA camps north of the border. The result was that command and control noticeably improved, and it became possible to streamline the whole assembly and placement system in a climate where the time taken to process integrees had been effectively cut by 75 percent.[135] The twelve months between June 1995 and mid-1996 witnessed the greatest influx of former cadres (15,317), but with the termination of this first flood it became administratively easier to control the human input. By September 1996, a total of 20,761 former NSF personnel had been processed and sent to bridging training. As in the case of the TBVC forces, the overwhelming majority (89.1 percent) were steered into the Army, with very small numbers gravitating toward the other three service arms.

A good part of the remaining problems stemmed from the CPR (the list of those members of the liberation armies seeking membership of the NDF), which has been, in retrospect, was very much a mixed blessing for the armed forces throughout integration. On the positive side, integration as defined by CPR arithmetic has been vastly assisted by the singular failure of substantial numbers of NSF personnel to materialize for their military duty. The CPR as originally conceived made provision for 34,888 individuals to be incorporated into the new NDF, yet by September 1996, as we noted above, only 21,761 persons had in fact been assembled. This "loss factor," which has substantially eased integration, is attributable to many other factors. The South African Police Services (SAPS), for example, eased the burden on the armed forces in the incorporative project by recruiting from the CPR. Desertion (i.e., AWOL for more than thirty days), as well as resignations and discharges with ministerial approval, have also taken their toll. By late 1996, some 1,300 persons had been rerouted from the CPR out of military service through these channels. Many of those listed on the CPR never seriously considered a military career in the NDF, and when confronted with the rigors of military existence they opted for voluntary demobilization. Of 5,103 NDF losses in April 1996, 3,795 persons fell into this category. A small proportion of personnel were deceased, had been excluded from service following arrests for serious criminal charges, or had been steered into the Service Corps following very low estimates of potential in psychometric testing.[136]

Either way, after an initial surge of interest that threw the assembly areas (particularly Wallmansthal) into a state of chaos, the persons on the CPR materialized on a spasmodic basis far below initial projections. While 10,000 cadres descended on Hoedspruit and Wallmansthal between the April 1994 elections and July, the numbers (be they MK or APLA) tapered off with each successive intake. Military planners had, as we have noted, expected some 1,500 integrees per intake, and this figure was substantially exceeded, with all its negative spin-offs, in the first few months. Intake 6 by August 1995, however, had deteriorated to 992 persons, and thereafter each official assessment of the progress of integration bemoaned, not without some relief, the widening gap between anticipated and actual numbers. Documentation from March 1996 noted, for example, that only 308 CPR nominees reported to De Brug, which had geared up for the admission of 1,620 males, 300 females, and an additional 300 MK women.[137] Although this was attributable in APLA's case to its ambiguous constitutional situation, a virtually parallel intake of MK personnel produced only 240 reporting for duty. Only 13–16 percent of those designated for assembly on the CPR actually appeared during 1996,[138] although this was less true of the SAMS, where intakes tended to be much higher (in the region of 50 percent). Even then, many of those who did appear at the AAs during all stages of integration were not admitted due to what was colloquially referred to as "problems in their personal administration."[139] This involved individuals without appropriate documentation, such as proof of South African citizenship, persons under twenty-one without parental permission to integrate, individuals with no documents whatsoever, and, inevitably, opportunists and persons unlisted on the CPR who perceived integration as a channel for employment.

Conceived in these terms, the progressive reluctance of NSF personnel to integrate on the basis of the CPR undoubtedly alleviated a proportion of the administrative stress encountered by management structures in the initial stages of the process and thereafter, when administrative experience had accumulated but the number of integrees had dwindled. The ability of the NDF to at least partially resolve the problem of the instructor shortage in bridging training was at least partly due to the trickling of NSF members to the AAs and then into the training phase. Diminishing numbers also allowed for economies in an otherwise costly exercise. During the 1994–1995 financial year, for example, the integration budget was actually underspent by almost 50 percent. Although this was roundly criticized as financial mismanagement by the military, the situation is partially attributable to the gap between those expected to appear from the CPR and the actual number. On a less positive note, however, substantial human, administrative, and financial resources were indeed misallocated in the prevailing organizational confusion at least until mid-1995, when the NDF and BMATT came to the realization that the numbers to be processed were considerably less than anticipated.

In the last analysis, however, the CPR has been problematic and a significant contributor to the mutual suspicion and tension between the statutory and nonstatutory forces. Following JMCC deliberations, the CPR was intended by all parties to provide a clear specification of the balance of forces in the new NDF. By its own logic, this meant that the CPR became a sensitive and volatile political issue in the relatively adversarial climate within which integration was initiated.

While it was in the institutional interests of the former SADF that the CPR be as limited as possible, MK's minority status relative to the overall size of the SADF required quite the opposite. There are no exact figures as to the size of MK or APLA on the eve of the April 1994 elections, when the CPR was officially constituted. MK numbers had nevertheless miraculously swelled with the unbanning of the ANC, which reduced personal risk for those in its military wing, in particular during the run-up months to elections, when all manner of people were attracted to MK by the prospect of a demobilization payout or long-term career prospects in the armed forces. Neither MK nor APLA understandably exerted themselves to stem the flow of new recruits, some of whom claimed to have worked underground on the internal front for years. Even had MK desired to carefully sift through its ranks for those jumping belatedly onto its bandwagon, it lacked the personnel and administrative capacity to do so in the confused and excited environment of expatriates returning en masse from camps north of the border. MK compiled and recompiled its list to eventually come up with no less than four lists containing 83,000 names.[140] The Personnel Workgroup of the JMCC then proceeded to carefully define and scrutinize the criteria that had been used to calculate this unacceptably large tally and, following various meetings with regional commanders on all sides, came up with a consolidated but embarrassingly smaller short list of 27,801 that was finally approved by MK's chief of staff almost a year after elections.[141]

Either way, the official CPR was very much a haphazard affair, with inaccuracies and inconsistencies that have fueled political and administrative tensions from the first days to the present day. Many genuine but low-visibility members of MK who appeared at the AAs found themselves unlisted on the CPR and were turned away in a manner than confirmed suspicions that the former SADF intended to integrate as few NSF personnel as possible. Internal tensions within MK were also fueled by the simultaneous appearance at the assembly points of persons who were demonstrably not regular members of MK but had somehow managed to secure a listing for integration. In June 1994, the various service commands of BMATT noted the ongoing difficulty of MK in compiling lists of CPR personnel to be put forward even to senior placement boards. In June 1995, a year later, the minister of defense approved the inclusion of an additional 1,087 names on a "nonformal" CPR, but further investigation showed that a good percentage of the nominees was not genuine.[142] Even today, MK continues to sporadically come forward with names of cadres, some of which have been audited as acceptable for inclusion on the CPR but others of which have proved to be obviously fallacious.[143] Almost two years after April 1994, official statements decried the fact that "the MK CPR is still not correct!" Twenty-seven months after the beginning of integration, "the name list situation of the former MK and APLA armed forces has not yet stabilised."[144]

The ongoing tentative nature of the CPR has unnecessarily complicated each successive intake to some degree or another. Since the CPR provides that all on its listing are constitutionally eligible for inclusion in the NDF,[145] it has ultimately precluded the end of integration with all its attendant costs, including, until recently, the maintenance of a fully staffed assembly area. Years after initiation, former NSF cadres still appear in dribbles to demand inclusion. Some, initially registered on the CPR in the enthusiastic climate of the culmination of the struggle, have only now turned to the military as an alternative career option, with the possibility of a quick demobilization package. Others, who were not members of the original CPR, are only now claiming their right of inclusion.

An amendment to the Interim Constitution in May 1996 allowed for additional listings to the CPR, and 1,447 names were added by the PIOC in the form of an additional list.[146] In February 1997, however, concern was already being expressed that with progressively smaller intakes a "considerable residue of names" on the CPR would extend the integration process.[147] The NDF subsequently embarked on a major and costly communications initiative—"the most extensive communication and advertising campaign since the start of the integration process"[148]—to ensure that that all outstanding NSF personnel received notification of future callups through local and national media, regional commands, as well as ANC and PAC channels.[149] This included a toll-free phone number that to the frustration of the NDF was largely inundated by unemployed persons seeking positions, not genuine CPR nominees.[150] The eleventh Wallmansthal intake, it was emphasized, would be the *last mass intake*.[151] Yet those who arrived were largely from PIOC's additional list, so authorities were obliged to ruefully admit that "not much progress was made with members outstanding from the original CPRs."[152] Following the eleventh Wallmansthal intake in September 1996, over 13,000 integrees were still outstanding. By early 1997, integration was still going on—albeit with plans to deal with those who had not yet come forward on a simple ad hoc basis. A scaled-down version of integration structures would remain in place to work with regional offices of MK and APLA to deal with the thousands of cadres who, many years later, still remain outside the integration framework.[153] In 1999, five years after integration was supposed to be completed according to the original designs of the JMCC, some former MK and former APLA applicants for admission to the NDF still waited outside its gates.

A Balance Sheet: Has Integration Worked?

Has integration—the heart of the "military pact"—succeeded in attaining its objectives in a manner compatible with civil-military relations in a working democracy? Years after the initiation of the process, this was a virtually impossible question to answer, because even now we lack the luxury of historic retrospect that allows us to make an evaluation within the wider context of South Africa's political transition. As South Africa crosses into the new millennium, it is still in a state of political experimentation in which all the stakeholders, both in the military and civil society, remain involved in the mammoth project of building institutions to restructure human relations in the wake of the damage wreaked by apartheid.

The success and failure of integration are also colored by the expectations and criteria brought by participants and observers. The integration of the military is a microcosm of the larger political debates and struggles, with their various implications for the reallocation of social power with continued transition. If one, for example, conceives integration as a basic and visible administrative exercise involving the concentration of a diversity of military personnel in a single organizational space, then one inevitably comes to a different set of conclusions than if one uses a different battery of assessment criteria.

When questioned on the outcome of integration five to six years down the line, former NSF and former SADF personnel seldom concurred on whether, how, and to what extent integration has worked, because the perspectives of each are largely (if not entirely) rooted in different historic experiences, expectations, and universes of social and military worldviews that directly mirror their institutional origins. From the perspective of former SADF planners steeped in bureaucratic values, integration has been a large-scale exercise in strategic planning, and its achievements (or inconsistencies) are rooted in an essentially managerial understanding of what integration means for combat capacity and the overall maintenance of professional military standards. To some extent, as we have noted, the former NSFs have been ideologically incorporated into this technicist vision as part of the overall package determined during the course of transitional negotiations. Yet the spirit and meaning of integration is still different in the deeper subconsciousness of even the most professional MK and APLA personnel, for whom integration is still, in the end, what it was: the military manifestation of an intrinsically political process whose ultimate goal remains the creation of a legitimate and representative defense force as a facet of democratic society.

The debate over integration also turns on the issue of whether the non-SADF component have been truly integrated or simply absorbed. This reflects the fact that integration is, in many respects, an intrinsically psychological process that involves not only the emplacement of transformative structures but also more general changes to human consciousness. This implies, in turn, not only the blending of the various ethnic cross-currents that reflect the diversity of South Africa in its armed forces but also the intermingling of professionalism and politics in some virtually impossible organizational recipe that nevertheless succeeds in bridging the gaps between military cultures. At this deeper level, the real benchmark of integration is an organizational ethos that represents the realization of a "we" feeling that links persons—men as well as women—into an indissoluble and emotional bond that goes far beyond the daily routine tasks dictated to soldiers. Ultimately, a truly "national" defense force is a sentimental notion that presupposes a reasonably *single identity* that transcends the segmental affiliations of the various armed components both on and off the field of battle.

With due regard to these fine conceptual distinctions, integration has nonetheless been noticeably successful as an administrative exercise. Notwithstanding the problems inherent in the CPR, contradictions among military cultures, and different agendas, substantial numbers of soldiers have indeed been processed, rearmed, and (in many instances) retrained according to the requirements of a single and regular military.

While the great majority of nonstatutory personnel has been incorporated into the Army, many other former cadres appeared to have partially surmounted the barriers of specialist exclusion inherent in the Air Force, the Navy and the SAMS to obtain positions of potentially important leadership. In February 1996, for example, the first two MK pilots completed their conversion courses and received their wings from the

SAAF[154]—one among innumerable instances that have, since 1994, perplexed the skeptics in their belief that guerrilla warriors are undesirable human material for the complex technological environment of a modern military. No doubt the qualities associated with professional military service will be developed further through the administrative network created by the NDF to support bridging training, corps, and career and development programs into the indefinite future.[155] Since the emplacement of the first appropriate logistic management system for integration at its official launch in June 1994, some eighty-five projects have in fact been implemented and, with the exception of fifteen as of mid-1997, successfully completed.

The resources of all arms of service (especially the Army) have been mobilized to support this cluster of projects, ranging from relatively minor initiatives, such as changing uniforms and insignia, to obtaining parliamentary approval for counterintelligence policy, to the financial integration of the former NSFs and other major exercises across the military spectrum. Given the nature of integration, the logistics and personnel commands have been especially strategic to the success of many ventures. Seventeen assemblies and intakes of nonstatutory members had been implemented successfully since mid-1994, and the administrative expertise of the NDF has been honed with each successive exercise of this nature. With the last mass intake at Wallmansthal in April 1997, the management of the process was vastly superior to that at the outset three years earlier, when organizational systems groaned under the weight of time and numbers. Since the beginning of 1995, the speed and efficiency of intake and placement had improved markedly, notwithstanding the fact that the management of integration was assisted by the declining size of the groups who presented themselves at the AAs.

The outstanding issues on the administrative agenda are now also in the process of being addressed, and there was every reason to believe that integration as a technical exercise would be fully complete as scheduled with the official disestablishment of MK and APLA on December 31, 1999. The formulation of an interminably delayed affirmative-action plan was geared for completion by the end of 1997, and various supplementary projects designed to give practical content and institutional muscle to equal opportunities were in the process of implementation. With complete parliamentary and executive approval of the Defence Review, many of the technical obstacles to the development of a new Defence Act and MDC were cleared away. Both these instruments, at the center of military life, were well on their way to redefinition in 2000. Wallmansthal, the key AA, was officially closed during mid-1997, and the disestablishment of various other facilities associated with integration began as rationalization progressed. Rationalization, as we shall discuss below, is a process with enormous consequences for the armed forces and civil society. Yet the task of newly contracting personnel into the NDF as an accompaniment to rationalization was already initiated in September 1996, and "rightsizing," "downsizing" or the more brutal "channeling out" of all personnel over the required force structure should be fully complete by the end of 2001.

During late 1996, the beginnings of a culture and posture policy, with particular emphasis on civic education for soldiers, was begun, and the design of this important initiative to transform military culture was completed shortly. In the wake of the conclusion of the Defence Review, the long-awaited military ombudsman is likely to make his or her appearance on the civil-military scene. Meanwhile, new uniforms symbolize the new NDF. Viewed within its own terms, the NDF's Integration Committee and its working group has every reason to feel proud of a project that not only testifies to the spirit of reconciliation at work within South Africa's once diverse armed forces; it also is a universally recognized prototype for management and organizational restructuring in other large-scale public institutions faced with the challenge of adaptation and change in complex and diverse social conditions.[156]

The leadership of the former SADF, with its concern for the material process of bringing together various military fractions under a single organizational umbrella, are to a large extent satisfied with the administrative landscape of integration. Unfortunately, this well-warranted sense of satisfaction is not always shared by some of their former MK and APLA counterparts, many of whom, with their different value base for institutional and social change, clearly believed that integration has gone neither far nor fast enough. In July 1994, for example, General Nyanda, then newly appointed chief of staff of the NDF, went to great pains at the Air Force Gymnasium to emphasize to assembled MK cadres that in seeking admission to the SAAF they should recognize that they now fell firmly under NDF, not MK, authority. According to British observers, this met with "somewhat less than enthusiasm,"[157] and four years later MK (and APLA) still maintained their own systems of authority within the overall command structure of the military. While the Integration Committee has seen a progressive growth in the membership of black officers who function under NDF aegis, MK, APLA, and the TDF continued to have their own representatives in an arrangement that would technically continue until December 31, 1999. Until that point, when integration legally ended with the disestablishment of MK and APLA, both organizations continued to magnetize identification and loyalty away from the NDF as an umbrella organization. At the deep psychological level, then, integration may not even have started. In March 1997, this was alleged by several former NSF integrees who insinuated that this was attributable to the co-option of their own leaders. In reality, this is a misperception. The newly created Military Command Council (MCC) had co-opted no members of the former NSFs (with the exception of Lieutenant General Nyanda, then deputy chief of the SANDF); neither had the successor body to the DCC—the Plenary Defence Staff Council (PDSC)—virtually all of whose functional bodies (the main functional agencies of the armed forces) remain dominated by former SADF personnel. In effect, only five of twenty-seven members of the PDSC were discernibly linked with any institution other than the old SADF.

As in civil society, many aspirations of black South Africans in the military will remain unfulfilled in the short term at least. This is likely to remain the case until after 2000, when it was widely anticipated the ruling ANC will move more aggressively to address the unrepresentative character of state institutions, including the armed forces. By early 1998, there were already powerful forces at work to accelerate General Nyanda, the former MK chief of staff, into the position of chief of the NDF, particularly in the intelligence community, which had remained a bastion for former SADF influences. These were leading to the progressive institutional sidelining of General Meiring, with Nyanda as a clear successor-designate. The consequent exit of General Meiring and other senior personnel has, in turn, created space (or a "drag effect") through the hierarchy of the officer corps to elevate other upwardly mobile former MK and APLA personnel currently hovering in mid- to upper-level appointments. As of 1998, however, much of the old guard continued to maintain a firm grip, if not a stranglehold, over power relations with the armed forces. (General Meiring was displaced as CSANDF by Nyanda during the course of 1998 following the circulation of false rumors of a coup attempt against the government of President Mandela.)

Major changes have already, however, taken place in command structures that reflect the pressures of the new political dispensation. By June 1995, one year into integration, 417 NSF personnel had been appointed senior officers above the rank of major, and by the beginning of 1997 the number had risen to 467, including two lieutenants general, six major generals, and nineteen brigadiers. Lieutenant General Siphiwe Nyanda, previously chief of staff and chairperson of the Integration Committee, had recently been designated deputy chief of the NDF, and several integrees had moved into top positions in the regional commands. These included Major General Gilbert Ramano, previously head of the IWG, Northern Cape commander, and then designated as deputy chief of the Army. The Eastern Transvaal Command was under the authority of a former NSF member, while the chiefs of staff of Northwestern, Natal, Western Province, and Northern Transvaal Commands were also drawn from outside the ranks of the old SADF. Major General Thamba Masuka had been appointed head of the SAMS. The middle and noncommissioned ranks of the officer corps have also witnessed a substantial expansion of black officers. By the beginning of 1997, there were almost 900 so-called nonwhite captains and 3,616 warrant officers, sergeants, and corporals from MK or APLA backgrounds. Desegregation of the officer corps has also spilled over to the advantage of the former TBVCs, albeit to a lesser extent than the substantially larger NSF forces. TDF General George Matanzima was placed at the head of Eastern Province Command and there were, at the end of 1997, 193 former TBVC senior officers including a major general and eight brigadiers.

In disaggregating the statistics, however, the upward mobility of black officers from MK, APLA, or TBVCs is far less positive. At the beginning of 1998, for example, former NSF personnel made up 23 percent (15,539) of the 67,859 men and women in the uniformed ranks of the NDF. Yet only 11 percent of senior officers above the rank of major came from either MK or APLA. There were eleven lieutenant generals and forty-six major generals in the somewhat top-heavy NDF, but only eight of these officers originate in the nonstatutory armies. Of the 156 brigadiers who constituted the pool for possible general officers of the future, only nineteen were from the NSFs: of the 2,297 colonels and lieutenant colonels, only 164 were from MK or APLA. At the opposite end of the scale, among NCOs the situation was roughly equivalent. Only 3,616 of 30,749 personnel with the rank of warrant officer, sergeant, or corporal (12 percent) were of NSF background. This imbalance is reflected at unit level, for example, at 8 Infantry Battalion at Eersterus, where 98 percent of personnel are nonwhite (mainly colored), but where former NSF members make up only 29 percent of officers and 25 percent of NCOs.[158] The middle-management ranks of the armed forces were, however, relatively more representative, with 20 percent of all captains, lieutenants, and second lieutenants drawn from MK or APLA. This stands in contrast to the former TBVC members, who were proportionately better represented at noncommissioned and middle-officer level but relatively unrepresented among senior officers, where they make up only 5 percent of all officers above the rank of major.

Representivity in the functional divisions and the more specialist Air Force, Navy, and Medical Services is particularly problematic, because the greater majority of cadres have not been equipped with the standards skills necessary for combat as well as for the management of the complex organization that is the NDF. The various directorates for finance, logistics, and personnel typify the complex problem of trading representivity for accumulated experience, and all three divisions will suffer seriously if and when their upper and middle leadership takes advantage of the opportunities for voluntary retrenchment. This reflects the fact that the strategic and commanding heights of all three organizations are still, of necessity, dominated by members of the old SADF. Operations and to a lesser extent intelligence also remain largely unpenetrated by members of the former NSFs, partially because there are very few former MK, APLA, and TBVC personnel to staff the more technical appointments in those agencies, partially because they are elite divisions at the center of the military network. While new senior appointments have been made in Military Intelligence, for example, much of the specialist human infrastructure required to translate the people in these positions into wielders of institutional power and influence remains reserved for officers inherited from the old order.

Similar patterns are manifest in the branches other than the Army. While the SAMS emerged from integration as one of the more progressive services through its ability to offer midlevel technical appointments to new personnel, the long-lead nature of high-tech service in the Air Force and Navy makes it difficult to fast-track appropriately trained top personnel for the short term. Few members of the NSFs (and to a lesser extent the TBVCs) have come to either institution with the appropriate training (let alone practical experience) required for the higher musterings in the SAAF and SAN, both of which have remained understandably strong proponents of the modern standards upon which their organizational viability depends. For the most part, newly integrated persons who have measured up to these criteria have been appropriately awarded following quick conversion training. Otherwise, as statistics reveal, representivity remains an illusive goal in both organizations. In the Navy, for example, former NSF personnel make up a small proportion of overall numbers (approximately 9 percent), but less than 3 percent had acquired officer rank by mid-1998. Of the 396 former NSF members, there were only fourteen officers among the complement of 527 officers in the range sublieutenant to captain. There were only seven former NSF commanders or lieutenant commanders among the swollen numbers at this level drawn from the previous SAN. Naval NCOs were almost exclusively from statutory ranks, and former NSF personnel have made only a small mark in the rankings from leading seaman downward. The Air Force, despite its role as a progressive arm of service, also remains top-heavy with its preintegration old guard.

Given the relatively short duration of integration, its achievements in changing the composition of the officer corps are, however, substantial. With due respect to the NDF, it should also be noted that existing statistics tend to reflect "substantive," or actual, appointments. Many former NSF officers who were still on training courses had not yet been included in these figures, so that once these courses were completed the configuration of the command structure surely changed. There is nevertheless considerable unevenness. A more representative officer corps requires considerably more former MK and APLA senior personnel, particularly in the lieutenant colonel to brigadier range and among senior NCOs in the Army. This also applies, possibly to a greater degree, to the former TBVC armies, which appear to have benefited least from integration. There is also clearly room for considerably more representation in the functional directorates and arms of service other than (but not excluding) the Army.

In interpreting power networks within the officer corps, it is also important to look behind the statistics of integration and examine the various attitudes and social processes at work to shape relations within the officer corps.

The small proportion of former MK officers with advanced training in places such as India, Cuba, and Egypt generally did not pose placement problems, and most took staff courses to align their skills with NDF requirements. In many instances, however, black officership has gravitated between aggressive independence and compliance, not dissimilar to the psychology of black appointees rapidly elevated into new positions of power in the state bureaucracy at central, regional, and local levels. Some senior black officers feel genuinely authentic in their new roles and have eased into their musterings with a sense of professionalism and self-confidence. Many others, however, faced with the complex and intimidating scale of the military establishment within which MK and APLA are still second-level players, have not adjusted with the same sense of balance and composure.

Relations between officers of comparable rank but different sociopolitical backgrounds are frequently tentative and brittle. Senior white officers of SADF background necessarily cluster in their working and informal relations so that their MK, APLA, and even TBVC counterparts find themselves on the margins of various networks that make up the military establishment. Although familiarity and subtle cultural connections rather than overt discrimination are at the root of this separation, many black officers experience a sense of frustrating exclusion that underwrites feelings of disempowerment—however successful the objective character of the integration process. This encourages counterclustering that detracts from esprit de corps or, in many cases, overdetermination with regard to the ubiquitous but indefinable standards that white leadership in the NDF is geared to uphold. Many black officers who have graduated into middle and senior ranks are prime candidates psychologically for absorption into the preestablished culture of the armed forces, particularly if they are members of military minorities such as the former TBVC forces or even APLA.

Since officership is a relatively strange quality in the populist military culture of the NSFs, this process is also significant for the development of class cleavage among the former cadres, despite the commitment of most black officers to the task of carrying the ranks. Many in the lower ranks have detected these incipient signs of differentiation that undercut the solidarity of erstwhile comrades. As integration proceeded, with its various social and administrative problems, grassroots criticism tended to expand and, in the case of MK and to a lesser extent APLA, turn inward. The result is a fairly significant proportion of black integrees who have become openly critical of their former commanders, not excluding the new chief of the SANDF and the two ministers of defence (since 1994 Joe Modise and, since 1999, his successor, Patrick Lekota).

Within the military as well as outside it, there are still widespread perceptions that the armed forces are modulated apartheid structures. Given the limited lead time of integration, many of the characteristic problems of daily military existence surfaced as racial and political issues mirrored continuity with the old cultures and relations of apartheid. Some former MK cadres, for example, resent commands by former APLA personnel, and members of both former NSFs in the ranks periodically complain of discriminatory treatment that appears to work to the advantage of the old homeland armies. As of 1998, MK maintained its own Integration Committee, which became a focal point for integrees who had difficulties in resolving their problems through interaction with the system. It is a measure of the volume and character of the problems presented to the Integration Committee that its then chairperson, Brigadier Johannes Mudimu, circulated to all senior MK personnel (including its new generals) a document entitled "Back to the Drawing Board" alleging perpetuated discrimination by NDF leadership based on the view that all former NSF personnel are intrinsically inferior. Since a document of this nature could not conceivably have been produced without higher authority, its contents no doubt mirrored sentiments among MK generals regarding the slow pace of integration.

Faced with this type of high-power coalition, the various psychological integration programs designed by MK, BMATT, and NDF leaders to promote understanding of multicultural diversity among the officer corps have tended to be palliative. The implementation of most of these programs are problematic because of the general reluctance of anyone—whether black or white officers—to openly concede that it would be unnatural were there *not* racial conflicts in prevailing conditions. Racial prejudice at the leadership level is not overt, as British observers noted from the outset of integration. Racism has officially and miraculously vanished, yet most behaviors and institutional transactions contain subtle racial subtexts that pervade the whole military network. Black officers are reticent in publicly articulating feelings for fear of being accused of fomenting racism and undermining esprit de corp. For their part, whites have not been especially enthusiastic players in diversity management programs where participation is to admit to the existence of a problem. Although programs of this type are now built into normal training, a feigned historic amnesia has led to many workshops being canceled or scaled down for lack of popular demand.

Both MK and APLA maintained their own structures—which they were legally entitled to do until December 31, 1999—and both continue to attract allegations about discrimination from former NSF personnel, many of whom prefer to communicate with their own commanders rather than through the established grievance system.[159] Given the nature of South African society, most of these allegations—an immeasurable proportion of which is doubtlessly valid—have a racial connotation. Racism on both sides is, in fact, far from dead and particularly pronounced, it seems, the farther one moves down the organizational hierarchy and away from the proverbial glass house of DHQ on the outskirts of Pretoria.

On unit terrain, among lower members of the officer corps, and in the ranks, conflict often assumes bizarre manifestation. Trainee officers at the Army Gymnasium at Heidelberg, for example, have clashed over differing notions of personal hygiene,[160] and many white Air Force instructors have been horrified as former guerrillas have elaborated their uniforms with tribal regalia.[161] In some units, black officers are often frustrated by the token nature of their authority and the tendency of white counterparts to circumvent them in the daily tasks of base management. While most of these issues have been resolved through negotiation, racial relations are still edgy. There are multiple instances where interpersonal relations have transcended the trauma, yet generally there is little social interaction among different races apart from that demanded by role requirements. Since 1993, for example, most white personnel have migrated from Voortrekkerhoogte, one of South Africa's most eminent military towns near Pretoria. Today, there appears to be little social interaction among those who remain and the new black residents who now occupy about 80 percent of the 1,500 houses in the area. From all accounts, the community divisions are not specifically racial but reflect the difficulty former SADF soldiers have in fraternizing with neighbors drawn from the enemy.[162]

To some immeasurable extent, entrenched views have yielded in the face of the common business of soldiering, particularly when small groups from different races are trained together. Many newly integrated units, such as 151 Infantry, patrolling the Lesotho border and composed of a mixture of former SADF, MK, BDF, and APLA personnel, apparently work well in their professional tasks in a way that transcends historic affiliations.[163] There are also many middle- and senior-level white officers "who have shown they are positive about transformation," according to former Deputy Minister of Defence Ronnie Kasrils.[164] Yet positive feelings are not always unequivocal at the corporate level, where, the NDF itself readily concedes, there continues to exist " complex . . . old animosities and mutual mistrust."[165] In all fairness, a great many of the old SADF components of the armed forces are deeply concerned about the changing character of the military. Many of their former MK counterparts are equally disconcerted given that the new armed forces do not appear to be transforming into the restructured organization they once anticipated. Virtually all parties are satisfied that the joining of forces has taken place with relatively little conflict. But basic, grassroots race relations are still, in the last analysis, somewhat cold, formal, and largely lacking in camaraderie. Behind the official pronouncements about the new "national" defense force, many important stakeholders are far from happy. Impending rationalization, as we shall see at a later point, vastly compounds these feelings.

Integration has in many ways wound down as military leaders turned their attention to long-term organizational restructuring (see Chapter 3). Wallmansthal Intakes 15 and 16 in early 1997 were efficient and "in the spirit of integration,"[166] With the closure of the base in June 1997 following its seventeenth intake that April, the era of gargantuan intakes of NSF personnel effectively ended. All future admissions to the NDF, should they take place at all, will consist of either small groups or individuals whose names are put forward by MK and APLA from the CPR. Even these are likely to cease in their entirety, barring exceptional circumstances, once the armed forces muscle fully down to the business of rightsizing.[167] Internal relations in the armed forces, if imperfect, have improved markedly, particularly because of the increased use of former NSF junior officers to communicate and steer the integration process on the ground. The IWG visiting Air Force Base Louis Trichardt during mid-1997, for example, could detect "no problems,"[168] and in many units there are indications that the collective difficulties of early post-transitional military existence have given way to individual complaints. No doubt, much of this has to do with the tendency of rigorous joint training to forge a group spirit and common dedication to soldiering that transcends origins in the different constituent formations.

Various surveys of the collective psychology of the new military conducted by the Military Psychological Institute or the SAMS (through its Psychological Integration Program [PIP]) indicate the current state of mind in the NDF and predicts the future. These are not entirely negative, particularly when viewed against the historic and racial backdrop of pre-democratic South Africa. The great majority of soldiers, we are told,, see service conditions as bearable, satisfactory, or improving.[169] Only about a sixth of all NDF personnel appear to attribute internal conflict within the military to primordial and irresolvable cultural and ethnic tensions,[170] and a disproportionately high percentage in this category are upper-level former SADF officers, most of whom will soon leave the armed forces anyway. For the rest, conflict stems from bad management, personality factors, differences in military style, and lack of communication—problems amenable to organizational intervention.

PIP research also reveals that some among the lower ranks of the former MK and APLA (corporals and lieutenant corporals) are far from satisfied,[171] and this must be cause for concern. Nonetheless, by far the greater majority of NDF personnel has "accepted the new government" whatever their past affiliations. This bodes well for civil-military relations on a continent characterized by recurrent military intervention in its contemporary history.[172] While many upwardly mobile soldiers are still uncertain "that the government will look after my needs,"[173] most are still "positive about the future of the country."[174] It is indicative of the extraordinary reconciliatory capacity of South Africa that the majority of soldiers in the germinal NDF is "hopeful that all differences between former defence force members will [ultimately] be solved."[175] Generational factors necessarily come into play at this level. There are visibly pronounced differences between progressive younger former SADF officers and their older peers on issues of institutional change, and this is encouraging given the fact that the former must appropriate the future. As retrenchment and the natural progress of time takes its toll on the current batch of senior former SADF leaders, one can anticipate far less rigidity and more dynamism in implementing the actual project of transformation. Similar considerations also apply to personnel of the former NSFs, many of whom have been deeply scarred, psychologically if not physically, by apartheid and the trauma of integration.

Despite the odds, former NSF soldiers—the eventual inheritors of the armed forces—are far more positive about the future.[176] It is they who will remain the drivers of organizational change precisely because of their current feelings of disempowerment. This relatively small group of leading-edge officers, schooled in the rough politics of international exile, have already brought a political maturity to integration that complements (and sometimes defies) the technomanagerial expertise of their former SADF counterparts. Therein lies the recipe for the various successes registered by integration to date. In time, they, too, will be swept into history, making way for a new generation of soldiers, both black and white, free from the mutually destructive myths and prejudicial mindsets of the recent past. In time, new corporate concepts and understandings of military service will emerge and, one hopes, consolidate South African democracy.

Notes

1. British Military Advisory and Training Team (BMATT), Medical/201, July 15, 1994.

2. South African National Defence Force (SANDF), Integration Progress Report to the Parliamentary Integration Oversight Committee, April 11, 1996.

3. BMATT/SA/710/2, Commanders Weekly Conference: Record of Discussions, July 15, 1994.

4. SANDF, Description of Integration Process, Appendix A to SANDF Reply to the Draft Report on Bridging Course Training to the Joint Parliamentary Standing Defence Committee, November 23, 1995.

5. Joint Parliamentary Standing Defence Committee (JPSDC), Report of the JPSDC, June 9, 1994.

6. SANDF, Reply to the Draft Report on Bridging Course Training as Prepared by the JPSDC, November 23, 1995.

7. BMATT, Report 1/96 on SANDF Transformation for the Parliamentary Integration Oversight Committee, BM/SA/150/2, February 22, 1996.

8. SANDF, Description of Integration Process.

9. BMATT/Medical/201, September 22, 1994.

10. BMATT/Medical/201, August 26, 1994.

11. SANDF, Description of Integration Process.

12. TBVC Forces Integrated with the New National Defence Force, SANDF, Internal Communications Bulletin 40, CSANDF, September 1, 1994.

13. This excludes Bophutatswana Defence Force units previously based in the splinters of the homeland, e.g., the Thaba Nchu and Odey Independent Coys, who now fall under North-Western Command.

14. *The Star* (Johannesburg), April 16, 1994.

15. Tom Lodge, "The Post-Apartheid Army: Political Considerations." Paper presented to the conference entitled "Taking the South African Army into the Future," University of South Africa, Pretoria, November 13, 1993.

16. Greg Mills, "Armed Forces in Post-Apartheid South Africa," *Survival* 35(3) (Autumn 1993).

17. Ibid.

18. SANDF, Description of Integration Process.

19. SANDF, Integration of Forces into the South African National Defence Force, Appendix A to Integration Progress Report to the Parliamentary Integration Oversight Committee, September 16, 1996.

20. Parliamentary Integration Oversight Committee (PIOC), General Progress with Integration of the South African National Defence Force, 1994–1996, Appendix A to the PIOC Report to the JPSDC, September 16, 1996.

21. SANDF, Integration Progress Report to the JPSDC, August 22, 1995.

22. SANDF, Integration Progress Report to the Parliamentary Integration Oversight Committee, June 12, 1995.

23. Ibid.

24. SANDF, Description of Integration Process.

25. Ibid.

26. Ibid.

27. Integration Progress Report to the PIOC, April 11, 1996.
28. SANDF, Integration Progress Report to the JPSDC, March 19, 1996.
29. SANDF, Description of Integration Process.
30. Integration Progress Report to the JPSDC, August 22, 1995.
31. BMATT, Report on Bridging Training for the Parliamentary Integration Oversight Committee, Appendix C to the South African National Defence Force Progress Report to the PIOC, June 12, 1995.
32. BMATT/Navy/100/3, September 1, 1994.
33. BMATT/Army/101, July 8, 1994.
34. BMATT/Army/101, August 12, 1994.
35. BMATT/Royal Air Force, Report No.9, August 12, 1994.
36. BMATT/Royal Air Force, Report No 15, July 15, 1994.
37. BMATT/Royal Air Force, Report No 13, September 9, 1994.
38. BMATT/Army/710/2, June 24, 1994.
39. BMATT/Army/101, September 9, 1994.
40. BMATT, Report on Intelligence Corps and CIS Board, August 17, 1994, AMS/Int/5.
41. BMATT /Medical/201, August 5, 1994.
42. BMATT/Army Report of De Brug Assembly Area Team, July 11, 1994.
43. BMATT/Navy/100/3, June 23, 1994.
44. BMATT/Medical/201, July 1, 1994.
45. BMATT/Army/101, July 1, 1994.
46. BMATT/Medical/201, July 15, 1994.
47. BMATT, Commanders Weekly Conference: Record of Proceedings, August 5, 1994.
48. BMATT/Army/710/2, July 7, 1994.
49. BMATT/Navy Weekly Report 330/2, July 14, 1994.
50. BMATT/Navy/100/3, July 21, 1994.
51. BMATT/Navy /100/3, August 18, 1994.
52. BMATT/Navy /100/3, September 1, 1994.
53. BMATT/Navy, 100/3, September 15, 1994.
54. BMATT/Navy Weekly Report 330/2, July 14, 1994.
55. BMATT/Navy, August 4, 1994.
56. Integration Progress Report to the PIOC, June 12, 1995, ibid
57. *Salut*, January 1996.
58. BMATT, Report on South African National Defence Force Transformation to the PIOC, Appendix C to the South African National Defence Force Progress Report to the PIOC, February 26, 1996.
59. SANDF, Integration Progress Report to the JPSCD, March 19, 1996.
60. BMATT, Report on SANDF Transformation to PIOC, February 26, 1996.
61. Integration of Forces into the SANDF, September 16, 1996.
62. Ibid.
63. BMATT/Royal Air Force, Report No.9, August 12, 1994.
64. BMATT, Report on Bridging Training for PIOC, June 12, 1995.
65. Report of JPSDC, November 9, 1994.
66. SANDF, Integration Progress Report to the PIOC, February 26, 1996.
67. BMATT, Report on Bridging Training for PIOC, June 12, 1995.

68. SANDF, CSANDF Reply to the JPSCD Report of November 9, 1994, February 10, 1995.
69. BMATT/Medical/201, July 1, 1994.
70. Chief of South African National Defence Force, Reply to JPSDC, February 10, 1995.
71. SANDF/C/Army/D/TRG/C/504/1.
72. SANDF, Integration Progress Report to the PIOC, June 12, 1995.
73. Ibid
74. PIOC, Progress Report to the JPSCD, September 16, 1996.
75. BMATT, Commanders Weekly Conference: Record of Proceedings, July 29, 1994.
76. BMATT/Army/101, September 9, 1994.
77. BMATT/Navy/100/3, September 8, 1994.
78. BMATT/Medical/201, September 9, 1994.
79. SANDF/C/Army/D/TRG/504/1.
80. BMATT/Army/101, September 29, 1994.
81. BMATT/Medical/201, July 8, 1994.
82. BMÀTT, Report on Intelligence Corps and CIS Board, AMS/Int/5, August 17, 1994.
83. BMATT, Commanders Weekly Conference: Record of Proceedings, July 22, 1994.
84. BMATT/Medical/201, July 29, 1994.
85. BMATT, Report on Bridging Training for the PIOC, June 12, 1995.
86. SANDF/C/Army/D/TRG/C/504/1.
87. BMATT, Commanders Weekly Conference: Record of Proceedings, August 31, 1994.
88. Report of JPSDC, November 9, 1994.
89. CSANDF, Reply to the JPSCD, February 10, 1995.
90. BMATT, Report on SANDF Transformation for the PIOC, February 22, 1996.
91. SANDF, Integration Progress Report to the Parliamentary Integration Oversight Committee, September 16, 1996.
92. JPSDC, Draft Report on Bridging Course Training, November 23, 1995.
93. BMATT, Report on Bridging Training for the PIOC, June 12, 1995.
94. BMATT/Navy/100/3, September 8, 1994.
95. BMATT/Navy/100/3, September 15, 1994.
96. BMATT/Navy/100/3, September 8, 1994.
97. BMATT/Navy/100/3, September 22, 1994.
98. SANDF/C/Army/D/TRG/C/504/1.
99. SANDF, Integration Progress Report to the JPSCD, August 22, 1995.
100. BMATT, Report on Bridging Training for the PIOC, June 12, 1995.
101. BMATT/Army/101, August 4, 1994.
102. BMATT/Medical/201, September 9, 1994.
103. BMATT/Medical/201, August 5, 1994.
104. SANDF, Integration Progress Report to the PIOC, September 16, 1996.
105. BMATT/Medical/235, October 10, 1994.
106. BMATT/Royal Air Force, Report No. 9, August 12, 1994.

107. SANDF, Integration Progress Report to the PIOC, September 16, 1996.
108. Ibid.
109. BMATT/Army/101, September 7, 1994.
110. BMATT/Medical/201, September 9, 1994.
111. BMATT/Army/101, August 12, 1994.
112. Report of the JPSCD, November 9, 1994.
113. CSANDF, Reply to the JPSCD Report, February 10, 1995.
114. BMATT, Report on SANDF Transformation for PIOC, February 22, 1996.
115. SANDF, Integration Progress Report to PIOC, June 12, 1995.
116. SANDF, Integration Progress Report to PIOC, February 26, 1996.
117. BMATT, Report on Bridging Training for PIOC, June 12, 1995.
118. BMATT, Report on SANDF Transformation for PIOC, February 22, 1996.
119. Report of the JPSCD, November 9, 1994.
120. SANDF, Integration Progress Report to PIOC, February 26, 1996.
121. BMATT, Report on SANDF Transformation for PIOC, February 22, 1999.
122. CSANDF, Reply to the JPSCD Report, February 10, 1995.
123. BMATT, Report on SANDF Transformation for PIOC, February 22, 1996.
124. PIOC, Report of Visits to South African National Defence Force Units and Headquarters, September/October 1996, January 14, 1997.
125. CSANDF, Reply to the JPSCD Report, February 10, 1995.
126. JPSCD, Draft Report on Bridging Course Training, November 23, 1995.
127. SANDF, Reply to the Draft Report on Bridging Course Training, November 23, 1995.
128. CSANDF, Reply to the JPSCD Report, February 10, 1995..
129. PIOC, Report on Visits to SANDF Units and Headquarters, January 14, 1997.
130. SANDF, Integration Progress Report to PIOC, February 26, 1996.
131. Ibid
132. BMATT, Report on SANDF Transformation to PIOC, February 22, 1996.
133. SANDF, Integration Progress Report to the JPSCD, March 19, 1996.
134. For a detailed analysis of these organizations, see Philip Frankel, *Marching to the Millennium: The Birth, Development, and Transformation of the South African National Defence Force* (Pretoria: South African National Defence Force, Directorate Corporate Communications, 1998).
135. BMATT, Report on SANDF Transformation to the PIOC, February 22, 1996.
136. SANDF, Integration Progress Report to PIOC, April 11, 1996.
137. SANDF, Integration Progress Report to the JPSCD, March 19, 1996.
138. SANDF, Integration Progress Report to PIOC, September 16, 1996.
139. Ibid.
140. SANDF, Briefing to the 11th COD Regarding the CPR Situation by Vice-Admiral Loedolff, Appendix to the PIOC Report, September 16, 1996, HSP/DIR/C/101?9/2, September 4, 1996.
141. Ibid.
142. Ibid.
143. Ibid.
144. Ibid.

145. See Interim Constitution, 224(2), and Transitional Executive Council Act, Section 16 (3b).

146. PIOC Report to the JPSCD, September 16, 1996.

147. SANDF, Integration Progress Report to PIOC, February 26, 1996.

148. Briefing to the 11th COD Regarding the CPR Situation, September 4, 1996.

149. Ibid.

150. Ibid.

151. Ibid.

152. Ibid.

153. Ibid.

154. *The Star* (Johannesburg), February 20, 1996.

155. See Major General Deon Mortimer, "Integration, Rationalisation, and Demobilisation." Paper presented at conference emtitled "Taking the Army into the Future," University of South Africa, Pretoria, November 13, 1993.

156. A team from the SANDF led by Major General Marius Oelschig, chief director of transformation, won the Franz Edelman International Award in management sciences and operations research for its "Project Optimum, Guns or Butter: Decision Support for Determining the Size and Shape of the SANDF in May 1996." See *The Star* (Johannesburg), May 8, 1996.

157. BMATT/Royal Air Force, Report No. 8, July 1994.

158. PIOC, Report on Visits to SANDF Units and Headquarters, January 14, 1997.

159. BMATT/Army/101, September 9, 1994.

160. *Sunday Independent* (Johannesburg), February 11, 1996); *The Star* (Johannesburg), October 9, 1995.

161. *The Star* (Johannesburg), October 6, 1995.

162. *Sunday Times* (Johannesburg), May 12, 1996.

163. *The Star* (Johannesburg), August 11, 1995; *Sunday Times* (Johannesburg), October 6, 1995.

164. *Mail and Guardian* (Johannesburg), April 4, 1997.

165. SANDF, "Problems and Solutions Regarding the Integration Process," Internal Communications Bulletin No. 55, October 17, 1994.

166. BMATT/Army/101, March 19, 1997.

167. Integration Work Group, Minutes of Session 303, August 6, 1997; Minutes of Session 305, August 20, 1997.

168. Minutes of the Eightieth Session of the Integration Committee.

169. SANDF, Military Psychological Institute (MPI), Evaluation Research/Final Report on the Psychological Integration Program (PIP), Appendix F9, 1996.

170. Ibid., Appendix F4; SANDF, MPI PIP, Analysis of Questionnaire, para. 78.

171. PIP, Analysis of Questionairre., para 106.

172. Ibid., para 105.

173. Ibid., para 107.

174. Ibid., para 108.

175. Ibid., para 76.

176. MPI, Evaluation Research/Final Report on PIP, p. 19.

3

Smoke and Mirrors: Transforming the Armed Forces

Cedant arma togae *(Let the soldier give way to the civilian).*

—Cicero, **Orationes Philippicae** *(ca. 60* B.C.*)*

The only thing harder than getting a new idea into the military mind is to get an old one out.

—B.H. Liddell Hart, **Thoughts on War,** *vol. 5 (1944)*

From the beginning of negotiations over the military pact, all the military formations agreed (in principle, if not in detail) that if the new SANDF were to become a functional component of the new political dispensation it would have to be reengineered on different social foundations. The membership and internal power relations of the new armed forces, the participants concurred, would have to represent the multicultural diversity of the Republic, and civil-military relations would have to be appropriate to a democratic system with the military under firm civilian control. Although professionalism and combat efficiency were primary imperatives, particularly for the SADF, MK representatives were insistent that these organizational values coexist alongside a commitment to respect human rights by a military under strict subordination to a legally constituted politically authority.

SADF delegates essentially agreed with this, but the mechanics and game plan for instituting a new system of civil-military relations alongside a cost-effective military were a bone of contention. Hence, as we have seen, many of the debates in the Joint Military Coordinating Council governing short-term amalgamation of the various armed formations were actually complicated, if not obstructed, by longer-term transformative questions that had to be factored into the Strategic Planning Program governing the indefinite future. The SPP nevertheless clearly underwrote the view that major structural and cultural changes would have to be implemented if the military were to remain relevant into the twenty-first century. Years into democracy and the millenium having arrived, most SPP prescriptions for institutional change continue to dominate internal debates within the military and at its intersection with the civilian realm.

Institutional Reengineering: The Agenda

It is essential, in the words of the chief of the Air Force, that the SANDF transform itself into a "machine capable of facing the twenty-first century with confidence"[1]—and this mirrors not only political agendas, be they former SADF or former MK, but also deeper structural tendencies in the armed forces. At present, the armed forces are "hollow" in the sense of a profound imbalance between capital equipment and manpower, with numbers having been inflated by over a third as a direct result of integration.[2] This necessarily undermines combat capacity.[3] Faced by increasingly restricted budgets initiated before the onset of democratization (but reinforced by it), the once-massive force potential of the military has eroded away with the dissipation of it raison d'être and driving strategic principle—the traditional "threat from the North." The current force design is neither doctrine sustainable nor affordable given that the military establishment has less than half the finances it enjoyed in the last days of apartheid. It is not valid for security purposes that demand, inter alia, a reassessment of institutional systems, not excluding the overall relationship between doctrine, manpower, and technology. Hence, we saw the controversial decision of the Defence Review to restructure from a large conscript organization into a small and highly professional "core force" with the appropriate reorganization of training and weapons systems.

The client base for the military has also changed discernibly, not only on the internal front, where political developments now demand a realignment of organizational norms to meet such values as legitimacy and representivity, but also in the international arena, where South Africa has become a newly welcomed member of an interdependent global community.

With the Republic's reacceptance into the community of nations concomitant with transition, South Africa is expected to take a leading role in international peace operations on the African continent. Here, once again, is an imperative for organizational change to meet new missions, tasks, and role requirements. Within the Republic itself, moves to redesign the military are reinforced by a powerful interest-group network, including the ruling ANC, which, armed with new and more inclusive concepts of national security, is working to reshape the governmental machinery in the wake of apartheid. Part of its agenda involves ensuring that the military adheres to international conventions governing the acceptable behavior of armed forces, that it subordinates itself to civilian control, and that it ultimately aligns its institutional interests with wider movements toward social reconstruction and development. This presumes not only ongoing diminution in the defense budget, with its profound ramifications throughout the military establishment, but also the incorporation of previously marginalized ideas and groups into the mainstream of military activity. Acting under the populist influence of the liberation armies and the principles of the new Constitution, the ANC since 1994 has tried to redefine, upgrade, and democratize the military through, for example, enhancing the role of women and trade unions. With the conclusion of the Defence Review, changes to the Defence Act and the MDC were imminent.

Although these developments do not rest easily with some of the senior leaders trained in the conservative ethos of the old SADF, the armed forces have largely bowed to demands for change to enhance public credibility and organizational efficiency. The result is a new ambiance of transformation in official pronouncements and new institutions within the SANDF network. Official military documentation and changes in nomenclature reflect the new atmosphere of heightened transparency and managerialism. The old Communications Service, for example, has now become an upgraded Corporate Communications Directorate with new tasks, including the development of equal opportunities for all NDF members irrespective of race or gender. The annual reports of the armed forces, once closely guarded, are now freely available and conveniently repackaged to reflect the new environment. Hence, the 1994–1995 report, "The National Defence Force in Transition," followed by "New Era Defence" (1995–1996), were based on the principles of an affordable, adequate, accountable, and appropriate defense force.[4] During 1995, three important new structures were established: the Integration Committee, a Force Development Steering Committee (under the CSANDF and the Chiefs of the Arms of Service tasked to streamline capital funds acquisitions projects), and a Directorate for Transformation in the Operations Division, with the purpose to utilize a combination of staff from the various branches and the newly established Department of Defence (DOD) to steer restructuring projects.[5] The creation of the Directorate for Transformation immediately set off vigorous competition between interest groups within the civilian and military sectors to establish hegemony over the new organization, reflecting the competitive struggles that dominate the overall transformation process. The appointment of the controversial General Marius Oelschig (commander of the Ciskei forces responsible for the Bisho massacre of ANC supporters during the run-up to the elections) was the beginning of a two-year struggle over the role, mission, and leadership of the Directorate among the NDF, its component formations, the DOD, and the Joint Standing Parliamentary Committee of Defence (JPSCD).

Despite the power struggles, a major consulting firm, Deloitte and Touche, was appointed to advise on organizational change, and the Directorate has forged ahead to translate principles derived from transitional negotiations to the drawing board. Plans to decentralize authority to the arms of service while maintaining jointness in the new NDF have been developed, and these will in all probability do away with the current Chiefs of the Army, Air Force, Navy, and Medical Services in the near future. Cross-service support programs and the use of shared agencies are simultaneously being investigated in line with the goal of optimizing existing support structures in a cost-cutting environment. The SAMS is also destined for disestablishment as a separate arm of service in a new milieu dominated by a new spirit of rationalization.

As integration moves out of the spotlight, the Directorate is likely to become a far more visible and prominent organization within an overall military network whose restructuring is, in the last analysis, constitutionally obligated. Provisions to present personal abuse and collective or individual discrimination in the new Bill of Rights, for example, present a direct challenge to some of the entrenched norms and organizational practices inherited from the old SADF. Such responsibilities demand changes not only in structures but also in organizational culture. Given that the force designs of *all* the constituent formations have been invalidated by major changes in the both the domestic and foreign strategic environments, the mission of building a relevant and inclusive military culture may be the most important challenge facing the NDF.

Bureaucratic Control: DOD, MOD, and the Defence Secretariat

National security, the Constitution emphasizes, must be pursued in compliance with the rule of law and subject to parliamentary and presidential prerorative. This is also echoed in the seminal White Paper on Defence (1996)—arguably the clearest articulation to date of the principles of "defense in democracy." Here the task at hand, as in other instruments, is to reverse the system of power relations developed under apartheid by creating strong civil institutions for military management, such as a Ministry of Defence and Defence Secretariat to determine the role of the armed forces in public policy. This in turn mirrors the fact that under apartheid the armed forces essentially appropriated the MOD, indirectly in the first instance through a close patron-client relationship with then Defence Minister P.W. Botha; then more ostentatiously through the appointment of General Magnus Malan as minister of defense following what was, in essence, a quid pro quo, where the SADF supported the succession of Botha to the prime ministership in the wake of the so-called information scandal. Building upon the Defence Act of 1957, which conveniently ignores civilian control (with the exception of cursory administrative provisions in Chapter 10), the securocrats thereafter utilized its various provisions (sections 73–87) equipping the minister with virtually unrestricted powers to ensure national security—before eventually emasculating the MOD as an authentic instrument of public policy within a framework of civilian oversight.

Under General Malan, the MOD became a one-man hegemony, and this situation pertained until de Klerk decided to end the National Security Management System (NSMS) and the demotion of Malan to the Ministry of Water Affairs in the face of public reaction to evidence of covert SADF funding to Inkatha (i.e., the Inkatha Freedom Party, since 1994 part of the Government of National Unity). Even then, the appointment of the *verligte* (enlightened) Roelf Meyer to the MOD did little to reinvigorate the office, which remained overshadowed by the National Co-ordinating Mechanism, the successor to the NSMS, from whose ranks the small staff of the MOD was recruited. This ensured that the MOD remained firmly under the control of the old-style, total-strategy securocrats, most of whom (as we have noted) were inclined to regard Meyer as a young, sinecure appointment by de Klerk with little experience in or identification with military affairs.

Transformation requires a complete reversal of this undesirable situation. Hence, following the April 1994 elections, the new Government of National Unity moved swiftly to address the problem by introducing various measures to reinvigorate the MOD as part of the democracy-building process. As indicated in the White Paper, the leaders of the NDF supported initiatives to build a truly democratic system of civil-military relations, reflected today in constitutional provisions requiring that the armed forces be fully responsible to the general electorate. As in other constitutional democracies, for example, the executive (i.e., the state president) is now the commander in chief of the SANDF and confers and cancels all permanent commissions in the armed forces. He (or she) may declare a state of national defense involving the deployment of the SANDF to uphold territorial sovereignty, uphold internal order, or act in compliance with South Africa's international obligations—but only with the knowledge and consent of Parliament.

Prescriptions for civilian control are echoed and spelled out in the third chapter of the White Paper. The opening sections restate the constitutional provisions pertinent to the "hierarchy of authority between the executive, parliament and the armed forces, with civil supremacy as the point of departure."[6] Thereafter, a clear distinction is drawn between the authority and powers of the CSANDF, who enjoys "executive military command of the armed forces" subject to the direction of the minister of defence in times of peace, and the president under a "state of national defence" or time of war.[7] The new MOD (which consists of a minister, his deputy, and a personal staff with oversight powers regarding policy formulation) is accountable at all times to Parliament, which is vested with extensive powers over defense legislation and budget, as well as the right to review presidential decisions regarding deployment of the armed forces. The White Paper also provides for the powerful parliamentary Joint Parliamentary Standing Committee on Defence with capacity to investigate and make recommendations with regard to "such functions relating to parliamentary supervision as may be prescribed by law."[8]

Provision is made for the DOD under parliamentary jurisdiction, with strictly limited powers over matters of national security, subject to the overriding principle that "it has a positive duty to provide sufficient information to ensure adequate parliamentary and public scrutiny and debate on defence matters."[9] The DOD will, according to the White Paper, "support the creation" of a military ombudsperson (similar to the Swedish plenipotentiary for the military or the Bundestag's defence commissioner), whose role will be that of an independent official, acting under parliamentary authority, to monitor democratic civil-military relations on an ongoing basis.[10] Provision is also made for the personnel, logistics, and financial functions of the SADF to be "closely regulated and subject to independent audit on a continuous basis."[11] Amendments to the Defence Act in 1995 specify the restructured DOD, which comprises the SANDF and the civilian Defence Secretariat. According to the White Paper, the minister of defence "directs and controls performance of the defence function" through, inter alia, the statutory Council on Defence, which includes in its membership both the CSANDF and the new secretary of defense.[12] The latter, supported by the Defence Secretariat, is given responsibility for financial planning, research and development, procurement of weapons systems, and general administrative control over the daily activities of the armed forces.

Civilianization of the type envisioned in the White Paper must simultaneously cater to demands of diverse constituencies within the barracks, in civil society, and at the interface between civilian and soldier. As indicated in the comparative literature on civilianization, the institutionalization of military disengagement on a sustained basis is inherently difficult where armed forces have developed a strong sense of organizational autonomy. One inevitable by-product is that ministries of defense becomes sites of political and bureaucratic struggle as the actors rush to defend (or extend) their power and territory. Given its heritage of militarization, South Africa is no exception to the rule that relations between soldiers and civilian overseers are frequently punctuated by personal, jurisdictional, and policy conflicts.

This is particularly evident at the cutting edge between the SANDF and the newly created Defence Secretariat—arguably the key institution for binding the military with civil society. The formal aspects of this relationship (the demarcation of powers, functions, and responsibilities between the CSANDF and the defense secretary) are described in a variety of instruments, including the Constitution (Second Amendment, Section 120), the Defence Amendment Act of 1995, the White Paper, and the Defence Special Account Amendment Act of 1995 governing the financial relationship between the NDF and the Secretariat. Together these create a relationship that represents, in many respects, a reversion to the situation prior to the diminution of the MOD under the total strategy of apartheid.[13]

The new system is also reasonably continuous with the balanced approach to maintaining military disengagement and civilianization in many contemporary democracies through a fine-tuned system whereby the armed forces are subordinated to the state, with their autonomy protected from civilian intrusion. In principle, the military can no longer appropriate power from civil society or even develop hegemony over state policy. This is reflected throughout the various new instruments governing the reallocation of power and responsibility between the NDF, the MOD, and its Defence Secretariat. With an eye to the mission creep of the military in the last years of apartheid, the Secretariat is specifically configured to ensure that the armed forces work within the constitutional framework within which Parliament acts as an agent of organizational control. The balanced model, for example, implies the minister of defence is the primary means of communication between Parliament and the DOD and the armed forces: He is, as the first defense secretary, Pierre Steyn, has explained to the generals, responsible "for conveying the needs of the DOD to the elected government" while "conveying political guidelines and the national policy framework to the DOD."[14]

The Secretariat advises the MOD "on all aspects of defence policy, performs the financial accounting within the DOD," and "takes responsibility for inter-departmental and parliamentary liaison on behalf of the DOD."[15] Within this equation the CSANDF is confined (at least in theory) to "decision-making in those areas that relate directly to the execution of their brief" within the framework of inviolable civilian supremacy.[16] Although the military may contribute to policy formation on the basis of functional expertise, "civilians," the White Paper insists, "are responsible for the political dimensions of defence."[17] While the CSANDF retains executive power over professional matters as a matter of institutional autonomy, the translation of policy into strategy, administration, training, morale, and, above all, the planning and conduct of operations is ultimately vested in the minister (or the president in cases of national emergency)—at least in theory. The formation of defense policy, according to Secretary Steyn, is no longer "an end in itself and takes place within the broader ambit of national policy."[18] The Secretariat, as it is now conceived, also works to facilitate between the armed forces and civil society while acting to transform the armed forces by promoting reinstitutionalization and the reprofessionalization of military values as a hedge against future intervention. In return, the Secretariat ensures "regularity of defence expenditure" while maintaining political control over the military budget.[19].

The new system represents a major departure from the spirit and practice of civil-military organization in the recent past. Effective operation of the balanced model in South Africa or elsewhere does, however, require military compliance, and the Secretariat has taken considerable pains during its short history to market the new and unfamiliar arrangements governing power relations to the armed forces.

Secretariat officials have, for example, been fairly alert to the sentiment of military leaders that the total-strategy experience was ultimately injurious to corporate interests and have subsequently made much of the buffer function of the Secretariat to prevent "unwarranted intrusion and meddling of politically inclined instances in their daily affairs."[20] Since the Secretariat takes responsibility for interdepartmental and parliamentary liaison, so the logic goes, the military is freed to concentrate on the primary responsibility: to prepare and execute war. Appeals of this nature to the warrior element have been supplemented by managerial overtures pitched at military technocrats. Secretariat appropriation of many functions such as logistics, personnel, and auditing is ostensibly cost-effective, "prevents the growth of large and cumbersome staff structures within the Defence Force," and "saves money for the armed forces." Since virtually everyone in the NDF is concerned with internal deployment, financial restrictions, and the demands of social reconstruction and development, the Secretariat is committed to assisting the armed forces to secure budgetary support appropriate to the military's charge as well as to help the utilization of armed forces in nontraditional roles with due regard to "less publicly contentious alternatives."[21]

Yet the balanced model remained a site of conflict, partially because the Secretariat was insistent in defending its new prerogatives but, above all, because the notion of functional equality between the military and its civilian masters was relatively unfamiliar to the great majority of military leaders. As South Africa moved toward its second democratic elections, military leadership had no problem with the principle of civilianization, a matter of corporate self-interest. The first CSANDF, General Meiring, is highly regarded among his colleagues (and, to a lesser extent, civilian politicians), precisely because of his astute management of integration and commitment to restructuring; the officer corps under General Nyanda will doubtlessly take the process farther and faster. Nevertheless, many senior military leaders remain in the apartheid past, reared on total strategy, with its implications of vast autonomy for armed forces; many still have difficulty in internalizing the practical implications of civilian constraints on the military. While former MK elements are not about to give carte blanche to the Secretariat in reorganizing the hierarchy of institutional power, the proposed new civil-military interface—no matter how carefully marketed—represents a direct challenge to inherited codes, norms, and operational procedures. Today there is a general recognition of the need for organizational change to align the armed forces with the new political dispensation in these circles, which is constantly reflected in the public rhetoric of former MK officers and senior former SADF counterparts. Still, military leaders (former SADF, MK, or APLA) are not about to meekly surrender their accumulated prerogatives for the sake of democratic experimentation, and many remain less than comfortable with the institutional interdependence inherent in the balanced model.

The implementation of this model has bred bureaucratic struggles and frustration, particularly in the Secretariat, which sees itself as the vanguard of civilianization. In the first years idiosyncratic factors also entered the equation since the then–minister of defense, Joe Modise, was sometimes seen as insufficiently supportive of MOD in dealings with a military hierarchy. This inevitably conditioned relations between the MOD and the defense secretary and intruded on the sensitive relations between the Secretariat and the NDF, where Steyn was the proverbial ham in the sandwich. Generally speaking, MOD must be far more assertive on matters of political control and policy formation if it is to define the terrain between the military and civil society.

In the absence of ministerial willfulness to force through the civilianization project, much of the work has tended to devolve to lesser officials in the MOD and Secretariat, particularly the first deputy minister of defense, Ronnie Kasrils. Needless to say, his "progressive" views did not endear him to the senior former SADF hierarchy. Relations between CSANDF General Meiring and Secretary Steyn were also tenuous from the outset of the Secretariat, not only because of differences in management style but also because many senior officers then regarded Steyn as pretentious and ambitious. Moreover, Steyn, when he served as Chief of the Air Force, was the unofficial leader of the military liberals and was widely expected to become CSANDF in the wake of transition. Most senior officers still have difficulty in forgetting the close associations between Steyn and de Klerk that ultimately led to the Steyn Commission of inquiry into "third-force" activities and the subsequent forced resignation of twenty-three senior officers of the old SADF. Ultimately, Steyn resigned and was replaced by his deputy, Mamatho Netsianda, a black South African who at least the old guard considered less controversial and more pliable.

The capacity of the Secretariat to defend or extend its institutional turf is also impeded by the human logistics of a new, uncertain, and miniscule institution confronted by the entrenched behemoth of the NDF. Since its establishment, the Secretariat has tried to bolster its staff to meet the demands of servicing policy for the MOD, Parliament, and the NDF simultaneously. Despite public-recruitment campaigns, the great majority of its strategic managerial positions were empty two years after its establishment. By early 1996, for example, only ninety-nine posts (of a some 600) had been formally approved, and only ten had been filled on a permanent basis by persons whose responsibilities exceed individual capacities.[22] The Directorate of Defence Policy, for example, has been simultaneously tasked with coordinating departmental policy on regional security, "defence posture and doctrine, involvement of the Department in internal stability roles and the involvement of the armed forces in internal reconstruction and development activities."[23] However, there were only four persons working in the Chief Directorate of Defence Policy, where a total of thirty-one were designated to perform multiple complex tasks. Similarly, the Directorate of Human Resource Policy (designated to focus on a complex of issues including affirmative action, equal opportunities, rationalization and demobilization, integration, personnel procurement, the Service Corps, and the development of policy on military veterans) consisted of one person plus an assistant. In articulating institutional leverage to deal with a partially receptive military, the Secretariat, it would be fair to say, was a slow starter with only a thin and incomplete top management segment, virtually no middle management, and a mere handful of administrative personnel.

Part of the explanation lies in the financial constraints of the defense budget, which was forced to bow to investment in social development in the postapartheid reconstructionist agenda. Diminishing allocation hits not only the military but also ministerial institutions whose purpose is to drive civilianization. Building human muscle for these institutions also has to deal with the inheritance of recent militarization, one consequence of which has been to virtually strip society of defense management skills—except, significantly, in the mainstream ranks of the former SADF component of the military. Most of the highly technical skills necessary to formulating defense policy remain the monopoly of military bureaucrats from the major statutory defense forces, and most of these personnel, with due regard to the new political system, have been conditioned by years of total strategy to see civil society as overly intrusive in even the best of cases.

The commitment of the Secretariat to representivity compounded the problem, since the greater majority of potential candidates for posts tended to come from a white background—at least initially. Generally speaking, the new state bureaucracy has had great difficulty competing for skilled people with the private sector following transition. In these circumstances, the Secretariat has been forced to rely on seconded former SADF officers. By late 1996, these exceeded the number of civilian personnel in the Secretariat while commanding such strategic heights of Secretariat work as intelligence, logistics, and communications.

Despite these difficulties, the Secretariat has forged ahead to fulfill its charge to provide what Steyn has termed "good policy based on the needs and requirements of the Defence Force."[24] In attempting to do so, it has already played an important role in blending the demands of democratized public policy with managerial criteria for policy formation involving identification of policy issues, environmental analysis, and the detailed examination of policy proposals prior to submission to the MOD for final approval.[25] The Secretariat has firmly established itself in such diverse roles as providing advice on defense policy to the MOD, chairing the National Committee on Conventional Arms Control (NCCAC), and interacting with Parliament through its Chief Directorate of Efficiency Services. That directorate also played a role in negotiations between the NDF and communities regarding the ownership of military land, while its counterparts have ranged across a diversity of policy matters, from social reconstruction and the future of Armscor to Secretariat involvement in the relatively new National Crime Prevention Strategy (NCPS). The Directorate of Intelligence has also been active in reexamining the role of counterintelligence and in defining ways to limit military intelligence in the performance of its key functions.

Profound changes in the political environment stimulated demands within the military establishment for a thorough assessment of its role in and connection to civil society. Early in the democratization process, CSANDF Meiring expressed "a sincere desire to communicate more regularly and openly with stakeholders who also have legitimate interests in the defence and security of the country."[26] The Secretariat, for its part, sought to capitalize on these new attachments to democratic transparency in the process of legitimizing and extending its influence.

The Secretariat is empowered to take a primary coordinating role at the nexus of civil-military society in the making of defense policy; one consequence has been an all-encompassing Defence Review. The Secretariat has been at the cutting edge of developments since the establishment of the Defence Review Working Group in early 1995. Initiated on the heels of transition, the Defence Review has dealt with virtually every facet of civil-military relations to establish policy foundations that will eventually carry the country well into the twenty-first century. Since the Secretariat and the NDF are concerned with transforming the armed forces, considerable attention has been given to the institutional and social management of such issues as the nature and consequences of integration as well as rationalization, which, as we have noted, must inevitably (if illogically) follow. There is also concern about the internal deployment of the armed forces short of the "most exceptional circumstances" involving threats to the constitutional order.[27] The Defence Review has sharply focused on the alignment of primary and secondary missions, particularly on plans to incrementally phase out the SAA in the short- to medium-term from rear-area protection activities involving interoperability with the SAPS in the maintenance of law and order.

With a view to long-term planning, the Defence Review has considered strategic posture in accord with the new Constitution; force design appropriate to maintaining a capable and sustained deterrent to potential attack; the nature and reconstitution process for a "core" force; the technological and manpower contingencies upon which force planning must be based; and future policy for weapons procurement to service the needs of the military in the new millennium. The transformative momentum at work in the NDF has also motivated the Defence Review to give considerable attention to human-resource issues, particularly the development of policy for the part-time and territorial forces, in securing their representivity, enhancing service conditions, and maintaining combat readiness. The end of the Republic's isolation and new concerns with collective security have additionally raised questions in the Defence Review process concerning the deployment of the armed forces in stabilizing and rejuvenating the southern African region through military cooperation. This has necessarily spilled over into an ongoing dialogue over the responsibility and capacity of the NDF for the prevention, management, and resolution of regional conflicts. Finally, South Africa's controversial arms industry has also come under scrutiny from the Directorate of Logistics of the Secretariat(chairing the Defence Review Arms Industry Sub-Committee).

The military is especially concerned with developing its legitimacy in the new political order as a matter of corporate and national interest. As Secretary Steyn has reminded the generals, "without legitimacy in the eyes of the citizenry, the Army [and the other service arms] will quite literally, not work."[28] This requires not only representivity in military institutions but also visible participation of the armed forces in the ongoing process of social reconstruction and public debate over defense issues. One consequence is that the local Defence Review has a distinct social and transformative quality that is, in many respects, quite different from similar exercises to audit the armed forces in other countries. As in these other cases, the Defense Review constitutes a periodic and authoritative analysis of the current and future condition of the military establishment. Yet the South African military is in itself in a process of organizational transformation, and this means that the Defense Review has also been concerned with a number of nontraditional features of civil-military existence. Hence, the Secretariat believes that "a very consistent policy needs to be worked out" with regard to the general Reconstruction and Development Program (RDP) of national government, albeit with due regard to the costs and risks of involvement for the armed forces.[29]

The Defence Review also constitutes a local revolution in the making of defense policy when seen against the background of its previously specialist and then secretive and exclusive character under apartheid.[30] To the contrary, the Secretariat is committed to ensuring that the widest possible range of stakeholders in the public sector and civil society be involved in the policymaking process in order to produce the "rich and varied mix of inputs [as] ingredients for the formulation of good policy anywhere in the world."[31] Since its creation, the Secretariat has been explicitly committed to "ongoing, meaningful and instructive dialogue between the defence community and political society," with its multiple lobbies and competitive interest groups.[32] This stake in social engagement and civic participation has meant consistent interaction throughout the Defense Review, including workshops and meetings on defense matters conducted in the public eye at regional and local levels. Regional governments and territorial commands have been integrated into these efforts to make defense policy more accessible to grassroots opinion.[33]

In generating popular involvement and consensus around defense debates, the original Defence Review Working Group kicked off with a consultative conference in Cape Town during 1995, followed by two conferences that cross-fertilized efforts to produce a draft and subsequent final defense White Paper. Both White Papers have been extensively criticized, especially by members of the NDF, as inarticulate and vague. Yet they reflect the consultative spirit of the Defence Review in emphasizing broad strategic principles intelligible to the man in the street rather than detailed technical issues.[34] Both White Papers also articulate the essential principles of civilianization incorporated in the balanced model of the Secretariat, emphasizing constitutional control of the armed forces, parliamentary oversight, Secretariat control over policy, program, and budget, and the development of a sustainable professional military ethos. The final results of the first phase of the eventually concluded Defense

Review dealt with hard issues such as posture, roles, mission (in its first report), followed by a second report on softer matters such as human resources, the defense industries, and civil-military relations.

The Defense Review has not been without its critics in civil society who, in the heady climate of new democracy, have questioned its representative and consultative nature. Civil society has, however, also provided support through such organizations as the Institute for Defence Policy (now the Institute for Security Studies) and the Institute for a Democratic South Africa (IDASA), so that the Defense Review has, in general, largely realized its original aim to "provide well-motivated and objective planning forecasts over the medium to long-term which can provide the basis for the 'master plan' upon which defence resource and budgetary requirements [can] be based in the future."[35]

There can be also be little doubt that the Defence Review has been a major learning experience essential to the democratization of defense policy despite initial fears in some quarters that it would be "carried out largely behind closed doors by military officers or Defence Secretariat committees."[36] While the culmination of the Defense Review was persistently delayed by various organizational and conceptual difficulties, the exercise has been of great importance in inculcating a tripartite relationship between the Secretariat, the NDF, and civil society. The result is a document, unprecedented in local military history, that is "owned" by all parties. As befits new procedures for policymaking in a tentative democratic society where the lines of power, institutional responsibility, and social control remain highly inarticulate, however, the Defense Review has not fully circumvented the bureaucratic struggles arising between civil and military authorities.

Years after democratic elections, the "synergetic relationship" that Defence Secretary Steyn saw as a precondition to good relations between soldier and civilian remains largely unrealized. While the military has weighed the incentives and disadvantages of civilianization and has subsequently endorsed the proposition of restructuring under a revamped MOD, the existing (and largely white) officer corps is by no means unanimous or unambiguous in its support.

Generally speaking, the policy culture of the Secretariat and its embracing ministry are closer to that of political democracy than that of the military hierarchy. This, if nothing else, breeds caution—if not suspicion. There are hardly any senior officers (whether of statutory or nonstatutory origin) who have not, for example, welcomed the Defence Review as a professional sales program at a time of weapons obsolescence and financial constraints. Yet there are many who have privately express reservations about a "populist" character arising out of the grist of public opinion. Without necessarily reverting to the covert nature of defense policy, many officers would have preferred a more tight and, by definition, less inclusive defense-management process more conducive to military control over decisions that impinge on its corporate self-interests. The commitment of the Secretariat to ongoing consultation with civil society during and after the conclusion of the Defense Review is of some concern to NDF leadership, not because civilian inputs are unappreciated but rather because this is unfamiliar to an institution that emphasizes speed, unilateralism, and centralization of opinion in articulating defense policy, particularly on hard national and institutional issues.

Concern with the unashamed penchant of the Secretariat for accelerated transformation remains an irritant for many senior officers (especially those of SADF background) who would prefer a much more modulated approach to change driven by more pliant and controllable civilian elements. Although the newly appointed black officer corps has a personal, political, and professional stake in accelerated transformation, it is also cautious about a vigorous Secretariat. Conservative views, however, are most pronounced in the SAA, which is the largest arm of service, with the least exposure to democratic concepts of transparency and public accountability and the least tolerance for displaying its internal affairs to civil society.[37] Many senior SAA officers are not entirely happy with the pace of Secretariat activity; neither are they especially receptive to positions on such contentious policy issues as affirmative action or, until recently, participation in the Truth and Reconciliation Commission. In these circles, the 1992 Steyn report to de Klerk still rankles in a way that carries over into more general perceptions of the Secretariat as a wildly progressive organization in the overall network of civil-military institutions.[38]

The NDF hierarchy has sometimes tried to circumvent the proposed new system of civil-military relations under the DOD. From the outset, the Secretariat has had to deal with the military's vacillation in granting security clearances to its civilian staff. This reflects ongoing power struggles within Military Intelligence, where control of information is perceived by both the old and new guard as an important source of political leverage. The NDF has also not been active in implementing the constitutionally prescribed transfer of control over military finances from the NDF to the DOD, with the result that it was delayed persistently. And the generals have not been energetic in assisting the Secretariat with manpower problems, which it sees as best resolved in an arrangement whereby civilian staff remain "understudies" of military personnel for the foreseeable future.[39] On the contrary, they have proposed being integrated into the functional ranks of the NDF. This will no doubt save money, but it will also—conveniently for the generals—effectively undermine the capacity of the Secretariat for independent action.

This reflects the ongoing fault line between the Secretariat and the mainstream military establishment, with the former SADF component still largely at the core. Both actors differ over policy in a new system of civilianization, which necessarily inhibits the mutual confidence and trust necessary for an effective working relationship. This in turn reflects the wider fact that there is still a lack of clarity as to the national interest and the protective role of the armed forces. Today, even though the Secretariat has objective (i.e., constitutional and legislative) control over military leadership, it needs to establish the subjective control associated with a full-fledged and stable system of civil-military relations. Many senior officers still have difficulty in comprehending the delicate link between civilianization and military autonomy in a democratic society. Despite the efforts of the Secretariat to display the positive features of its existence to soldiers, there are still mixed feelings within the officer corps over such a policing agency.

Relations between the Secretariat and the NDF are not irredeemable given the logic, demands, and interest-group competition arising out of transition. For the foreseeable future, one can anticipate a more coherent link between institutional prescriptions and personal agendas that binds the Secretariat and the NDF into a more stable set of policy transactions. Both the Secretariat and the NDF desire to maintain the physical security of South Africa, generate economic growth, and promote internal and regional stability; the operational requirements simply have to be worked out. As of 1996, the Secretariat is in the process of meeting its objective to fill 80 percent of its allocated posts in the near future,[40] and if it can do so in the face of financial constraints, shortages of appropriate personnel in civil society, and antipathy in the NDF, it will become an important locus for specialist military knowledge and civil opinion.

Various defense-management programs now address the shortage of specialist defense-management skills among the black community. These can assist the Secretariat to realize its objective of representivity and, in doing so, will enhance its leverage within military circles. Further civilianization will also be assisted when (and if) the relatively large presence of military personnel now in the Secretariat move back, as they appear to be doing, across the military boundary. The displacement of Steyn will also have important ramifications should he be succeeded in the long term by some person or persons with strong and decisively transformative ANC-MK associations.

Despite the tentative nature of civilian control, the DOD and its minister have a strong power base in civil society and the ranks of the ruling ANC. At both levels, there are strong commitments to a democratic agenda that includes civilianization of the armed forces. The acceptance of a similar set of commitments by military leadership is an important lever for institutionalizing a more coherent and stable system of civil-military relations appropriate to consolidated democracy. Civil society, with the DOD at the leading edge, has worked persistently, if erratically, to exploit this opportunity, with important payoffs. By 1996, for example, the difficulties involved in the balanced model were already becoming recognized in certain circles, and during the course of the year a series of discussions was initiated at ministerial level to accelerate transformation by outflanking the principle of functional equivalence in Secretariat-CSANDF relations. Against a background of mounting pressure on the military for its involvement in dubious schemes and human-rights abuses under apartheid, these eventually resulted in the decision to oblige General Meiring to surrender his position as official head of the DOD to Secretary Steyn, who was simultaneously vested with the function of chief accounting officer for the armed forces.[41] This long-delayed action decisively shifted the balance to the advantage of the DOD, where the Secretariat now has the technical power to command the military purse in carrying forward the transformative agenda. The DOD, and especially Deputy Minister Kasrils, were resolved at the time to extract control of the transformation process from the former SADF elements in the military as far as is politically and practically feasible.[42] Now, with greater power for the Secretariat to monitor financial directives, the coalition for civilianization has moved to flex its muscle. General Marius Oelschig, the original and controversial NDF appointee to head the Directorate Transformation, has long since been replaced with a senior black officer after several years of political wrangles between the armed forces, the MOD, and the JPSCD. Since substantial numbers of white officers constituting the old guard are similarly and most likely to end their association with the armed forces in the face of attractive severance packages, this will substantially reduce the leverage of the obstructionist elements.

Parliamentary Oversight: The JPSCD

In the meantime, the institutionalization of reliable civilian control depends heavily, as in other democracies, on effective oversight by the parliamentary committee system, in the South African case in three bodies enshrined in the new Constitution: the Select Committee on Security and Justice (SCSJ) in the new National Council of Provinces (previously the Senate), the Defence Portfolio Committee in the National Assembly, and the bicameral Joint Parliamentary Standing Committee on Defence.

Since the 13-member SCSJ is largely concerned with linking the country's nine new regions into the defense debate, while the Portfolio Committee is an instrument for the drafting of legislation and meets relatively infrequently, much of the burden for linking the popular will the public policy rests with the JPSCD. Modeled on the Committee on Defence of the German Bundestag and armed with extensive constitutional powers to investigate the functioning, finance, armaments, and preparedness of the NDF, the JPSCD has considered many issues at the civil-military interface and subsequently diversified into several subcommittees for legislation, budget and policy, military transformation, and defense-industry oversight following a February 1996 meeting on Robben Island to review its own activities. Since 1994, the thirty-six-member committee, with its various permanent and alternative personnel, has been frequently briefed by the MOD and its Secretariat on most of the pertinent issues of integration and transformation, including rationalization, demobilization, affirmative action, and budgetary implications of organizational restructuring. Supplementary presentations have been made by the various arms of service, many of which have touched directly on the reorganization of military culture, the role of gender, religion in the armed forces, and civic education for military personnel as a component of the maintenance and development of professional norms. In March 1996, for example, the Ministerial Task Group for Civic Education served the JPSCD with an extensive report dealing with the place of the defense function within the Constitution, the role of international law in military behavior, and the general task of building legitimacy for the NDF as a facet of defense in democracy.

Issues pertaining to the role and future of defense industries also dot the JPSCD agenda. The JPSCD has met with Armscor and the minister for public enterprises, to discuss the reorganization of Denel with a view to black empowerment. South Africa's arms-sales policies have fallen under the JPSCD spotlight with Kader Asmal, chairperson of the NCCAC, explaining both the workings of his organization as well as the Republic's more contentious transactions with other African and Middle East countries. Ultimately, and perhaps most important, the JPSCD has been a driving force in the formation of the draft and final White Papers, each of which has provided the conceptual and policy framework for the focal point of JPSCD activity since 1997. By April 1997, the JPSCD already had considered the first two final reports of the Defence Review dealing with such issues as defense posture and doctrine, cooperation between the military and police in the maintenance of internal order, force-design options, international peace operations, the structure of the DOD, human resource issues, and the future of part-time forces.

There is still, however, very little in the way of systematic documentation, apart from some scattered notes on proceedings, to assist researchers in evaluating the organizational capability of the JPSCD. The JPSCD is nevertheless representative of many of the structural and idiosyncratic problems confronting parliamentary control by committee of defense matters in nascent democracies, particularly where, as in South Africa, the military has a strong and recent tradition of corporate independence. Despite its strategic role in the Defence Review process, its busy schedule, and reputation as one of the most frequently convened of parliamentary committees, the JPSCD has still to come up to full strength as an instrument in the institutional network for civilian control. Composed largely of party bureaucrats who have risen through the ranks, the JPSCD is, politically speaking, a heavyweight. ANC members have included strategic party organizers at local and regional levels, a former national chairperson of the South African National Civics Organisation and high-level former members of the National Youth League. High-ranking ANC women have also been evident in the delegation, including a previous deputy president and secretary-general of the Women's League. This tends to confer a degree of prominence on the workings and decisions of the JPSCD that places it near the forefront of the entire parliamentary system.

As a specific instrument for the evaluation of defense policy with experience to confront the High Command of the NDF along a constellation of complex technical issues, however, the JPSCD is considerably less impressive. Only a few of its members over the years have had any specific military background, and although it is sometimes asserted that the JPSCD encapsulates "the cream of MK," only a single member, a graduate of the military school in Odessa, has a military education. Insofar as other members have actively participated in the liberation struggle, it has been in the area of unconventional warfare. The simple consequence is that most of the ANC majority on the JPSCD are still not especially well versed in the more technical and specialized aspects of operating a modern, complex, and high-tech organization such as the NDF along the lines of conventional defense management.

The national government has consequently invested substantial energy to empower JPSCD membership. This has included overseas tours for all members to directly observe defense-committee procedures in Britain and Germany, as well as visits to local defense industries, units in the various arms of service, the AAs, and the various sites for bridging training. Strategic coalitions with officials in other state organizations, notably the Defence Secretariat, are also important in building intellectual muscle. Yet the strength of the JPSCD was still largely confined to its scrutiny of the more general political issues actively projected by former NSF integrates at the grassroots (i.e., service contracts, the conditions surrounding integration and bridging, the demobilization policies of the NDF, pensions, and other human-resource aspects). At this level, the JPSCD is noticeably energetic, self-confident, inquisitive, and pointed. But it is less so when it comes to the more difficult, abstract, and technical matters of defense policy routinely put forward in the characteristically complex technocratic language of NDF planners.

The difficulty experienced by most JPSCD members in matters of strategy, posture, and force design is partially a reflection of universal differences in specialist and policy skills that reside on different sides of the civil-military divide. In many countries, parliamentary defense committees are disempowered by an inability to penetrate the dense technicist, self-protective communications of soldiers. South Africa is no exception. The situation is rendered more difficult by the fact that the parliamentary system is still in the process of establishing its own logic and identity, part of which involved an almost obsessive insistence on public accountability and transparency. One physical and visible consequence is a vast network of committees with little purpose other than to provide outlets for parliamentarians to publicly wax lyrical; most are poorly resourced, as is the JPSCD.

Since parliamentarians are thinly spread across the dense committee network, time constraints compound maladministration to adversely affect participation and performance, particularly in the case of the smaller parties, all of whose members have to combine JPSCD work with competing obligations and responsibilities to other committees, some of whose work either coincides or overlaps with that of the JPSCD itself. Attendance problems have consequently dogged the JPSCD, and some meetings dealing with important matters of policy have had to be delayed or even abandoned for lack of a quorum. Many JPSCD members have a broad interest in security policy, which leads them to sit on the Safety and Security, Correctional Services, and Justice Committees—some of which still meet on the same days as the JPSCD despite the commitment of the parliamentary bureaucracy to improve scheduling.

The compulsion to scatter scarce resources is especially intense when many JPSCD personnel are obliged to sit in on budget debates. JPSCD members are not especially inclined to upgrade their oversight and investigative capacity by independent research into esoteric military matters, and most tend to rely on the scattered information provided by the various party study groups. This is particularly important when relatively inexperienced members are required to be almost entirely self-reliant given the weak administrative support. Public inputs are largely ineffective, despite the fact that the JPSCD receives submissions from interest groups, including defense industries, trade unions, religious, and cultural organizations. With notable exceptions, however, public participation is lacking in quality , meaning JPSCD members do not receive data, ideas, and policy guidelines to compete with the networks of the military establishment. The problems facing the JPSCD do not eliminate its ability to conduct relatively probing examinations. Most of this, however, tends to operate within the context of a system that clearly favor the better-informed and more highly skilled.

Within the JPSCD itself, some ANC members as well as Nationalist and Democratic Party representatives tend to shape proceedings behind the appearance of a solidified JPSCD on the one side and the military on the other. Prior to the 1999 elections, two or three among the small Nationalist Party contingent with some specific military background, including a former commander in the Venda Defence Force, clearly enjoyed a firmer grasp than most on defense issues—although this was frequently wasted on marginal issues with potential for political capital. Since there is substantial overlap between membership of the three parliamentary defense committees, members of the JPSCD can also draw on the resources of sister organizations. Although the Democratic Party did not sit on the JPSCD, prior to 1999 its sole member on the Portfolio Committee was influential on defense debates out of all proportion to party representation by virtue of his experience as a seasoned parliamentarian with extensive knowledge of procedural and legislative matters. The Democratic Party Senator, on the Committee on Security and Justice, has specialist knowledge to support party positions. Former SADF Chief General Constandt Viljoen was also an alternative member of the Portfolio Committee at this point but seldom attended meetings to bolster the Freedom Front in defense debates.

The situation also inevitably lends itself to penetration by organized lobbies and interest groups, including the defense industries (always active behind the scenes) and think-tanks. The Institute for Security Studies was reputed in ANC circles to be the major source for much of the information that enables the Democratic Party member to leverage the information gap and disproportionately steer many committee deliberations. Personnel from the Institute for Conflict Resolution at the University of Cape Town has also been important in translating complex defense debates into language intelligible to most JPSCD members. Needless to say, the armed forces utilize technicist terminology to leverage the committee as circumstances warrant.

The NDF, it must be emphasized, is now firmly committed to the principle of parliamentary control and the admonitions of documents such as the draft White Paper that "defence policy and military activities . . . be sufficiently transparent to enable meaningful parliamentary and public scrutiny."[43] Yet the military is still not acculturated to civilian intrusions. The ancestors of the JPSCD, the defense committees of the tricameral parliament, were, after all, largely rubber stamps; despite rhetoric accepting of the new political dispensation, the new armed forces are still coming to terms with parliamentary organizations armed with oversight and investigative powers. The inevitable result is that much of the early history of JPSCD-NDF relations has been tense, if not adversarial, as the JPSCD pushes for a more open, accountable, and transparent military.

Civil society as reflected in the JPSCD has registered a number of victories in the tussle over turf that mirrors the wider struggles to define civil-military relations in the new democracy. The JPSCD, despite its various liabilities, has established credentials in a manner that would have been inconceivable during the years of total strategy, and the armed forces have accepted that they are required to explain their behavior along a range of previously sacrosanct issues. Yet the current military leadership is still sentimentally attached to its independent past and (former MK personnel not excluded) remains automatically sensitive to intrusion. This leads to a system of relations that is neither confrontational nor entirely frank and amicable.

The generals, JPSCD members frequently complain, take every opportunity to short-circuit the ability of civil society to probe military matters, particularly strategy and doctrine, where the JPSCD is at a disadvantage. This feeling, originating in the period when General Meiring was chief of the NDF, following the 1994 elections, has not fully diminished with the appointment of his successor. Following South Africa's questionable intervention in Lesotho in late 1998, some JPSCD members felt that the armed forces were less than candid under interrogation. Military leadership is especially adept at disempowerment through overinformation, and techniques deployed so successfully during transitional negotiations frequently resurface in JPSCD deliberations. The military, so the argument goes, dutifully hangs out its internal laundry when pressed to do so. When it does, it also trots out complex charts and technical terminology specifically designed to confuse and force the demurral of uncomprehending civilians.

Internal committee dynamics reflect the wider political relations, interests, and agendas at work in Parliament: ANC members follow a fairly vigorous transformative agenda, the Democratic Party is the watchdog of liberal-democratic civil liberties, and the Nationalists and Freedom Front members appeal to constituencies on the right. With due respect to normal partisan competition, however, political relations within the JPSCD are generally positive and cooperative. The JPSCD at its outset appears to have taken a semiexplicit decision to elevate national security matters above party interests, and this has been subsequently reinforced by the consensual leadership style of the JPSCD chairperson for most of its history, the mercurial Tony Yengeni, now chief whip of the ANC in parliament. The result is that few ideas have actually come to vote, with the notable exception of debates over issues such as language and religion as facets of military culture. In this instance, none of the minority parties could avoid the temptation to confront the dominant ANC on a sensitive issue laden with political capital.

Internal relations along civil-military lines have been more problematic, although mutual suspicion and hostility have at least partially given way to a reciprocal learning experience in which JPSCD and NDF members became more familiar and comfortable with one another. Latent conflicts have nevertheless exploded to sour relations between citizens and soldiers. The JPSCD and NDF leaders have, for example, frequently locked horns over integration and, more generally, the transformation of the military into a reasonably democratic institution with a defined sphere of organizational autonomy. It is a measure of the jealousy with which the NDF guards its historically accumulated political powers that it consistently avoided, if not actually refused, to clarify the informing assumptions of its strategic management plan for transformation, Project Optimum, to the JPSCD. The effect at the time was to make it virtually impossible for the JPSCD to effectively audit transformation within the armed forces, even if its members were able to comprehend the extraordinarily complex computer procedures used by the NDF in guiding the process.

The procedures and leadership for military restructuring have also been a major bone of contention, with direct conflict coming over the exact boundaries between civil and military authority, particularly in the early days of the JPSCD. The original decision by the NDF to award its R49 million transformation tender to leading management consultant Deloitte and Touch stirred considerable opposition in the JPSCD, many of whose members saw this another failure of the armed forces to consult with civil society on matters of major public interest. The unilateral appointment of Major General Oelschig by the NDF to originally head its transformation directorate was also hotly contested at the outset, not only on the grounds of Oelschig's track record but also because it represented yet another unilateral NDF decision. Both sides dug in their heels, with the NDF arguing that corporate autonomy justified appointing its own transformation manager and the JPSCD alleging lack of transparency. Eventually, the matter was resolved by the belated decision of General Oelschig to retire altogether.

Still, the JPSCD remains deeply sensitive to violations, real or apparent, of its constitutionally sanctioned powers. Much of the debate over the controversial procurement of new corvette craft for the Navy was less about the cost of the acquisition than lack of consultation. The recent decision of the JPSCD to sanction the purchase is the result of many factors, not excluding the fact that the Navy has condescended to fully brief the JPSCD to its satisfaction with regard to the need, purpose, and costs of the weapons platforms. The Army and Air Force, however, remain more obstinate in JPSCD perceptions. The JPSCD, to its chagrin, was not initially informed of the decision by the NDF to purchase the first locally produced Rooivalk attack helicopters, while military circumvention and obstruction (disguised as control over internal affairs) is also generally regarded as the major reason for the persistent delay in the transfer of the accounting function from the NDF to the Secretariat—possibly the most significant lever for civilian control—until very recently.

The intense debates over language and religion in the armed forces are another instance where the corporate interests of the armed forces have come up hard against JPSCD agendas. The JPSCD, for example, was deeply offended by the NDF decision to hold a commemorative parade in May 1996 for the Namibian operations that resulted in the notorious Kassinga massacre. Minister Modise was subsequently obliged to offer apologies to Namibia at the insistence of JPSCD members concerned with the insensitivity of the armed forces. General Meiring, not known for his receptiveness to JPSCD invitations (except those emanating from the Freedom Front chairperson of the Portfolio Committee), was personally summoned to explain this act in a fashion that did little to improve his strained relations with Yengeni.

The NDF and the JPSCD, most participants concur, have reached a level of rapprochement. Nevertheless, the complex mixture of organizational and personal stakes holds out the prospect of ongoing conflict. With the 1999 elections now concluded, the ruling ANC will be more energetic in its demands for reorganizing the state bureaucracy, something that would inevitably filter down to the JPSCD. Yengeni, who has long been personally frustrated by the slow pace of reform in the armed forces, has already been redeployed in favor of a less controversial chairperson subject to the tight discipline of the new Thabo Mbeki cabinet.

Whether the committee has the will or capacity to impose more rigorous civilian control over the military remains linked to a variety of personal, administrative, and political factors. The replacement of Meiring by Nyanda could conceivably push the amicable-adversarial character of JPSCD-NDF relations into a distinctively more collaborative mode. Yet there is no particular reason to believe that mere changes in the racial composition of military leadership will automatically slow the bureaucratic momentum that drives NDF military leaders of all persuasions to define organizational autonomy as broadly as possible. Much also depends on the quality of human resources within the JPSCD, which unfortunately has lost strategic personnel with the genuine capability to contribute to defense debates. Certainly, the members of the JPSCD could do with considerably more specialist research backup, parliamentary services, and a more realistic schedule.

Ultimately, however, the posture of the JPSCD depends on the political climate, particularly the willingness of the ANC to engage in the dangerous business of tampering with major institutions of state security when democracy is yet far from full consolidation. The JPSCD, it has been suggested in some circles, is far less energetic in its pursuit of unambiguous military restructuring than at the outset of democracy. Already by mid-1998, there were some indications of distinct, if not necessarily disruptive, divisions of policy and style among its ANC members, not all of whom were entirely comfortable with the populism of Yengeni. The JPSCD, as an institution, has not entirely escaped the incrementalizing logic of daily governance that has eroded the initial political idealism throughout state structures in the first days of democratization. Former President Mandela, as we have noted, has also not hesitated to reign in the JPSCD when it stepped on the toes of the military culture on sensitive issues of religion and language. Executive power is likely to be further strengthened under President Mbeki. In these circumstances, there is no particular reason to believe that a tightly controlled ANC caucus will be any less cautious (or authoritarian) in allowing the JPSCD to independently exercise its prerogatives against the military establishment.

Constitutional Prescription: Human Rights and Military Law

Military and civil society always represent two reasonably distinct worlds of values, with tension waning and waxing as human rights are internalized in erstwhile authoritarian institutions. In South Africa, civil-military tensions stem from the disjunction between the Defence Act and the MDC, on the one hand, and the Constitution on the other. The Interim Constitution provides that the SANDF be a balanced, modern, and technologically advanced military force in the spirit of the MDC and current defense legislation. Yet current legislation centered on the Defence Act of 1957 is largely anachronistic in light of the realities of the new South Africa reflected in the Constitution (now the ultimate body of rules for the military), which outlaws discrimination, enshrines fundamental rights, and emphasizes transparency, civil control, and governmental accountability. These issues entirely escape both the MDC and the Defence Act inherited from apartheid, substantial aspects of which refer to a political universe now swept away into historic redundancy. Portions of the Defence Act dealing with the reserve system of cadets and conscription, for example, make no sense whatsoever in the new political dispensation. South Africa has also long subscribed to major international instruments such as the Hague Conventions and the Geneva Conventions and

Protocols. Yet these have not previously been incorporated into municipal law, and the Defence Act is in most respects out of line with the realities of modern public international law.[44] Whether this justifies extended amendment or the development of an entirely new legislative and administrative basis for the armed forces, involving a codification of all current defense provisions together with the repeal of all security legislation in the Republic and the former homelands, as suggested by some commentators, including the drafters of the current White Paper, is a debatable point.[45] In the meantime, the inherent incompatibility between legislation and its new political environment generates a series of issues that strikes to the very heart of reacculturating the military to internalize overall constitutional sovereignty and universal conceptions of human rights more generally.

Civilian personnel in the South African military are, for example, in an anomalous position. Technically they may participate in collective bargaining and join trade unions in accord with international conventions, but because they provide an "essential service" they are prohibited from striking by the restrictions of the Public Servants Relations Act of 1993. Uniformed personnel may neither participate in strikes nor join unions other than ministerially approved associations, in sharp contrast to many European states moving toward progressive labor practices for soldiers. The Bundeswehr, for example, has a union, unit personnel councils, an ombudsman, and a powerful Federal Armed Force Association, all of which improve working conditions for career members of the armed forces through ongoing consultation with the Ministry of Defence.

In the experimental democratic climate of civil South Africa, similar ideas have spilled into the military as a result of the emergence of independent unions in the police, the incorporation of people from the liberation armies infused with a populist spirit, the anxiety of military personnel over their future in the face of impending rationalization, and constitutional provisions that recognize the right to freedom of association, the right to fair labor practices, and the right to strike. Challenges to the underdeveloped vocational structures in the NDF are also the result of the shift toward an all-volunteer force, which will further erode civil-military boundaries by increasing the already substantial proportion of civilians in the ranks.

Article 109 of the Constitution also provides for a Human Rights Commission with power to monitor and investigate as well as to take necessary steps to secure the observance of human rights. This commitment to the development of a human rights culture in the Republic in combination with various constitutional provisions regarding human rights immediately implies tension with local military law, which has, due to the peculiarities of apartheid, failed to keep pace with developments in the international community. The relationship between public international law, foreign case law, and domestic military law is generally problematic given, for example, Sections 37–38 of the Constitution, covering the rights of members of "all organs of state," natural and juristic persons to apply to a "competent court" where rights specified in the Bill of Rights are infringed or threatened.

Judicial proceedings in most military courts worldwide leave much to be desired, and the South African military court system, fed by the rigid authoritarian psychology of *total strategy*, is no exception. While procedures exist to protect the rights of defendants, proceedings in the NDF, as in other military institutions, heavily favor the prosecution. This is particularly evident in the summary-trial and court-martial systems, where trial officers tend to have minimal legal training apart from instruction in the application of the military code. Although summary-trial powers are fairly limited, democratization clearly requires an alteration of these procedures for dispensing justice, which touch directly on sensitive matters of hierarchical discipline and, ultimately, the jurisdictional and organizational autonomy of the military.

Constitutional provisions extending political rights to all persons of voting age in South Africa are also potential conflicts despite universal opinion that career soldiers should be precluded from engaging in party-political activity under the conditions of demilitarization. The shift toward part-time forces, however, raises problems in defining a "career soldier," and this remains to be more clearly articulated in the process of restructuring civil-military relations.

Section 36, the controversial section concerning the suspension of portions of the Bill of Rights under states of emergency, is also consequential for the ambiguous role of the military in conditions of so-called national defense. Soldiers are presumably entitled to some rights regarding freedom of expression enshrined in the Bill of Rights, and here, once again, there will have to be subtle adjustments to take into account the specific requirements of those with a military tasking. Section 31, which guarantees everyone the right of access to state information in the exercise and protection of their civil rights, is also problematic for the SANDF with its nonstatutory networks and culture of secrecy nurtured under total strategy.[46] Language policy, as we have already noted, is an additionally volatile and symbolically saturated issue in an Afrikaner-dominated military in a new nation with eleven official languages. While it is probable that English will eventually be introduced as the common language for military communications as part of the wider intention of the SANDF to dilute its racial and ethnic image, the matter clearly lends itself to a less functional and constitutional interpretation in line with sections governing the cultural rights of minorities.

The Politics of Gender

The twin tasks of realigning the organizational culture of the military with the human rights provisions of the Constitution and reconciling different normative foundations for military service in institutions such as the SADF and MK are also particularly evident and illuminating in the case of gender issues and the development of equal opportunity policies for women. The new South Africa adheres to such important international conventions as the Convention on the Elimination of All Forms of Discrimination Against Women, while the equality clauses its the Constitution are conducive to an enabling environment for women in all of the Republic's civil and military institutions. Yet the military, in line with militaries elsewhere, has always been a super-masculine institution whose codes and structures are inimical to women's advancement. Cultural tension associated with women's rights also arises from the fact that MK women have historically appeared to have played a far more substantial role than their white counterparts in the statutory forces. Whereas SADF women have always been confined to supportive activity justified by the normal disempowering ideologies at work to limit social participation by women in military activity, MK women have, in contrast, always been available, if not deployed, for combat and in some cases served as commissars in the antiapartheid struggle.

This long-standing history of military participation carried over into the spirit of the first talks between the SADF and MK, and many MK women were subsequently designated for incorporation in the proposed NDF alongside male comrades. The psychological traumas experienced by many returning exiles have been documented, and it appears that in the course of amalgamation women as a group suffered particular stress when directly confronted with the overwhelming masculine culture of the SADF.[47] The sheer absence of physical facilities at the assembly points in the first stages of amalgamation were particularly problematic for female MK members. At Wallmansthal, for example, administrative insensitivity on the part of the newly created NDF led to new integrees being bunched together in common quarters with all the attendant social problems. Women lacked basic privacy, were sexually harassed, and were forced to perform menial labor in a way that raised the level of tension within the camp. White women already serving in the armed forces failed to act as a cultural buffer because of their inability to identify with the particular psychological problems and historic experiences of their new MK colleagues, who eventually organized into a lobby that demanded (and achieved) separate facilities for women at the assembly points.

The JMCC network that oversaw the beginnings of organizational transformation also made provision for a special working group to ensure gender sensitivity in the new defense force, and this unit subsequently went on to produce a document that became, once accepted by the Defence Command Council, the keynote for current gender policy. It was during these discussions that the principle of women in combat roles was strongly articulated by MK representatives and, despite reservations, accepted by their SADF counterparts. Outside the barracks, women's rights in the NDF have been strongly supported since April 1994 by ANC, which has been active at many levels. Mandela and most senior ANC leaders have fully identified with the cause of women's liberation as a guiding principle of party policy, and the strong feminist parliamentary lobby has made a number of submissions to eradicate sexism to parliament's JPSCD within the context of wider project to extend women's rights throughout the state bureaucracy.[48] Some of these representations have subsequently been incorporated into the draft and final versions of the White Papers as well as the Defence Review.

Women have a long history of participation in the uniformed and civilian components of the South African military as well as in part-time forces and Commando units. White women were excluded from the conscription process that fed huge reserves of white manpower into the SADF during the sunset days of apartheid, but women were directly and indirectly incorporated into total strategy through actual service in the SADF, ideological support to legitimate its operations, or labor in the defense industries.[49] Democratic transition further propelled gender issues into a unprecedented place on the agenda for organizational transformation. British military observers of the early stages of integration process commented upon the "high inspiration of women in MK."[50] BMATT placement teams subsequently made a point of ensuring that its own women members were involved in the role allocation of MK women, despite severe reservations in the Army concerning the use of women in combat roles. In June 1994, this was, from the SADF perspective, "unacceptable based on the current interpretation of rules" and a major point of contention.[51] Yet women's emancipation within the framework of military service is now widely debated at all levels, and, perhaps more important, various principles and structures have been emplaced to fulfill the now official commitment of the NDF to policies of gender nondiscrimination.

Under the previous order, the SADF made various nominal gestures toward sexual equality by recruiting women into a wider range of roles involving medical and welfare work, telecommunications, signal work, and instruction; today, following democratization, it has further broken free—at least in principle—from policies of job reservation that traditionally hindered the career mobility of women. Hence, we see the unequivocal commitment of the NDF to the view that "women who meet the entry requirements of any particular mustering or appointment now compete on equal footing with their male counterparts."[52] According to a senior female officer who has ostensibly met these criteria, the involvement of women in every structure at all levels of command, including strategic planning and decisionmaking, is now integral to NDF policy.[53] Women remain segregated for basic leadership and junior training, but thereafter all specialist career and corps training is done jointly "with the same academic and physical requirements expected of both men and women."[54] Except where "inapplicable,"[55] differential training, development, and utilization has been scrapped, and the deployment of women is accepted in principle. In the Air Force, for example, a handful of women have been selected as potential pilots and have commenced training that complements their counterparts in more traditional roles such as air-traffic control, radar, and fire fighting. The Women's Advisory Group has been established to monitor and investigate gender discrimination in the Navy and to prepare women for service on combat vessels.[56] Salary scales, income-tax provisions, housing, medical aid, pensions, and group insurance benefits throughout the NDF have been fundamentally revised in accord with principles of equality. Pregnancy in unmarried women, previously grounds for dismissal under the MDC, has been written out of regulations, and pregnancy leave is recognized.[57]

The Directorate for Equal Opportunities, although concerned with wider issues, has highlighted the issue of gender, and Major General Jackie Sedibe, South Africa's first female general since October 1996, has been assigned a key role in the process that embraces all four of the service arms. Her accelerated career has made this a very controversial appointment in mainstream (i.e., male) defense circles, where it is quietly viewed as tokenism at its worst. Some of these views are shared by high-ranking white female career officers who resent political manipulation of the promotion system even while welcoming the emergence of a women in a position of such stature. The elevation of General Sedibe from the position of responsibility for "women's affairs" to more wide-ranging matters of equal opportunity is nevertheless an important symbolic step forward in institutionalizing gender equality in the armed forces.

The number of women in the armed forces has increased significantly from the late 1970s, when women made up about 7 percent of the SADF.[58] This is attributable to the desire of military leaders to make increased use of all available labor in the defense of apartheid and to the subsequent integration of MK female cadres into the new SANDF following the demise of South Africa's minority system. Today, women constitute a significant proportion of the part-time territorial forces and civilian personnel working in administrative positions in the NDF; there are 8,440 women in uniformed ranks. Of the approximately 17 percent of all NDF personnel who are female, a proportion has begun to emerge in high officership positions—although not as dramatically as General Sedibe herself. It is a measure of this progress that by the end of 1995 women constituted about a quarter of the 2,068 officers above the rank of major. Leadership of the state bureaucracy of the new South Africa is still, however, seriously unequal with regard to female appointments, and women, some commentators feel, "still do not have sufficient decision-making power to effect important changes."[59] Only five brigadiers out of a total of 150 in the NDF are women—and three of them were white personnel inherited from the former SADF. Of the total 654 colonels in the NDF, a mere twenty were women. Women who achieve senior officership tend to be heavily concentrated in the most junior of the service arms, that is, the SAMS, where military boundaries are most indistinct and which are still regarded as the "natural" emplacement area for female involvement in the armed forces.

Female representation in the officer corps of the Air Force and Navy is minuscule, although statistically speaking the Navy is the most representative on gender issues. In the Army (the dominant and most conservative service) women are clustered in the personnel, ordnance, and signals corps; tasks are routine, repetitive, and, in the opinion of military leadership, best suited to females. In this patriarchal climate, women are also seriously underrepresented at middle to upper officership levels. Many who have acquired positions of seniority still experience difficulty in exercising authority. Black women officers, who constitute a tiny minority, suffer double jeopardy in an organization whose ethos is still deeply white and male. Although overt discrimination is not often evident, members of this group are frequently treated as an aberration or a curiosity rather than accorded the status inherent in their rank. The great majority of women of all races is still in supportive roles of one sort or another, and most strategically placed women officers, both black and white, see female generalship as most unlikely in the foreseeable future—except possibly in the marginal ranks of the SAMS. This tends to be confirmed by feeder recruitment into the Military Academy, which, not unlike institutes for military education elsewhere, remains a male dominated bastion. At the end 1996, only 12 percent of its students were women, most the offspring of white families with traditions of military service and high officership. There was, at the time, only one black female student.[60]

The Air Force has recognized that its future composition "will inevitably require a new dimension with regard to the utilization of human resources."[61] Yet the physical resources available for women soldiers are still relatively underdeveloped outside of the premier training institution for women personnel: the South African Army Women's College at George. Lack of suitable, separate, and private accommodations has tended to hinder the deployment of women on a national basis and in combat roles in crisis areas such as Kwa-Zulu. The testing of females' combat skills is also hindered by ongoing shortages of physical facilities at the Lohatla battlefield. South Africa may well be "fortunate to have a government in power with the will to improve the conditions of women radically,"[62] but for all practical purposes the military remains a patriarchal institution with distinct racial cleavages. This is reflected in the fact that in its twenty-five-year history half of the commanding officers at the college have been male. The college, whose intake is from women volunteers with a commitment to a military career, still has few black recruits, partially because of its entry requirement that students have at least a matriculation certificate, partially because a uniformed military career is still not considered a serious option among the overwhelming majority of South African women, irrespective of race group. Many black women officers with experience in the MK camps north of South Africa during the antiapartheid years also clearly resent institutions such as the Women's College, not only because of its role as a breeding ground for white officers but also because of its emphasis on dealing with women as a special and peculiar entity within the military framework.

Similar sentiments are understandably not shared by white women officers, especially graduates of the Women's College who, although favorably disposed toward more equal opportunities, tend to recoil from the perceived aggression, or "anger," of their black counterparts. Irrespective of racial and social origins, many women officers concede privately to the continued existence of informal mechanisms of exclusion that work to their disadvantage despite the philosophical commitment of the new NDF to the view that women can embark on a military career of their own choosing. A few years into transition and organizational transformation of the armed forces, these networks of exfiltration remain powerful in emplacing women notwithstanding the laudable regulations about gender equality. Black women officers tend to emphasize gender equality in MK as a counterpoint to the SADF, yet a substantial proportion of new black officers clearly identify with the view of former SADF counterparts that military service is a male business. Identification with this common stereotype is in fact an important connecting point for bonding male officers, irrespective of race, into the distinctive social constellations that enhance gender distinctions in the process of reinforcing militarism in arch-patriarchal institutions.[63] Feminist critics of the military who functioned as either observers or participants in transitional negotiations concerning the proposed new NDF within the context of the JMCC noted, as early as 1993, that SADF and MK officers tended already to cohere in conceptualizing the process of institutional restructuring in disturbingly masculine terms; this, some commentators now suggest, may well be another index of the extent to which MK has been acculturated to conform with traditional SADF standards.

White officers are nevertheless more insensitive to gender issues, and this increases as one moves down in the ranks, where official pronouncements about equality have limited practical meaning to everyday behavior. From experiences at Wallmansthal, it appears that many of these views are shared by the young lions who make up 90 percent of MK despite the rhetorical insistence of their leaders on gender equality. Sexual harassment is technically punishable by military law, but matters of this type seldom, if ever, break the surface. When they do, as with race conflicts, they tend to be treated not as gender issues but as instances of poor discipline.

In the Army, the majority of officers has rhetorically identified with the notion of women as combatants but, like wider South African society, have yet to fully internalize these attitudes. Surveys on the state of public opinion regarding women in the military reveal that paternalistic perceptions of the role of women are deeply entrenched, particularly among the older white segments of the population on the right, where hostility toward social reconstruction for democracy is most intense.[64] Throughout the overall population, however, there is shared opposition to exposing women to physical risk because, in the words of one study, "women are revered to the extent that their role in society is seen as irreconcilable with that of a soldier or policeman constantly exposed to danger."[65]

Much of this is paternalism is deflected into the military, where the predominantly male, white officer corps is, at best, in a situation of suspension on a historically male-dominated terrain. Many have unconsciously or explicitly absorbed the principle that gender equality is a component part of the wider project of building social legitimacy for the military and consequently reject the consignment of women to positions of outright inferiority in the armed forces. There are also clear signs of a healthy new respect for women recruits as important contributors to the NDF, particularly among male officers in the higher musterings. Yet sexism and the ideology of gender roles remain rampant in the culture behind the institutional paraphernalia constructed to enhance women's mobility.

Most male officers, be they former SADF or MK, continue to adhere to the stereotype that women are neither physically nor emotionally equipped beyond their special capacity for work involving manual dexterity, repetition, or personal care; women assist a mutually reinforcing spiral for their own disempowerment by accepting this marginalizing logic. Notions of affirmative action stimulated by the integration process tend to focus on race rather than gender, and there are few senior leaders, whether former SADF or MK, who would like promotional criteria to be specifically influenced by gender background. Gender-sensitivity programs have been a part of military education prior to transition but have tended to focus on the display of good manners by gentleman officers rather than a considered interpretation of gender empowerment. No systematic effort has subsequently been made to alter course content since the advent of the new political order, and the occasional seminars to acclimatize officers to the new roles of women have not been especially well received, certainly less so than in the SAPS, where, arguably, more effort has been made to consciously increase gender representation.

The Defence Review reiterates formal commitments to gender equality, but "on a practical level, it will take far longer to remove the remaining obstacles that still exclude women from certain positions" beyond clerical, administrative, and service positions that conform to traditional constructs of femininity.[66] At a time of rationalization and overall budgetary limitations, it is unlikely that women will be singled out as a preferential group, either for protection or advancement. For the foreseeable future, the input of women into organizational transformation also appears fairly limited despite the intention of feminist lobbies in parliament and civil society to target the military as a particular example of patriarchy in the state sector. This has undoubtedly mobilized more women to participate in debates on defense, where they have made singular and original contributions. Black women in particular have defined activity of this nature as a natural consequence of extended arrangements for citizenship inherent in the new democratic order. Yet South African women, apart from the former MK personnel with their unusual military socialization, are not especially motivated by defense and military issues; neither are they particularly attracted to service in the armed forces, least of all outside their traditional roles.

The existence of strong personalities such as General Jackie Sedibe have been important in securing women a position as combatants, in deconstructing masculinity in the heartland of patriarchy, and in ultimately breaking down the division of labor. At the same time, there are still few women (other than MK) who actually perform combat roles, even in fighting formations. In some "teeth" infantry units, for example, women are still assigned—some would term "ghettoed"—in the more supportive positions. The ability and motivation of MK women to translate their status as liberated women into a power base for projecting new cultures into the NDF are also limited by their dispersal throughout the military network and by careerist commitments embedded in the "patchwork of overlapping race and class alliances" that shape postmodern conceptions of women's behavior.[67]

Despite the notion that female members of the former NSFs represent a new ethic of soldiering unfamiliar to South African military traditions, most MK women are apparently not in favor of absolute androgyny in the codes governing the treatment of women in the NDF. Most are also tied to the armed forces by the fact that they provide a source of security and employment in a harshly competitive economic environment. The capacity of MK women to assist ideological retooling in the armed forces is limited by their institutional dependency: Few are equipped with skills convertible to civilian roles, and a large proportion are single mothers, many of whom seek to place their older offspring in the NDF as a means of secure their future. The behavior of their white counterparts—the product of a different race and class experience but who nevertheless reflect the various mythologies at work to disempower women in society more generally—assists the restating of the traditional concept of women as "protected" and "defended" elements within the military framework.[68] The lack of representation of women in the officer corps is due less to the conscious policies of exclusion than to the fact that women in the military have to make difficult choices between marriage, mothering, and careers that are fundamentally different than those facing males.

The social universe of a newly postauthoritarian South Africa outside the NDF is not especially receptive to professionalized women at this point, and this is projected into the military, where few survive the continuous period of service necessary to advance upward through the institutional hierarchy. Senior officership demands years of uninterrupted service, long senior staff courses, and a general degree of ongoing commitment that few women are able to make. Service in the SAA is frequently seen by women recruits as especially philistine, yet the relatively small size of the Navy and Air Force means few musterings, and these are highly competitive. Placement policies also work to the advantage of men, who are more mobile when it comes to assuming vacant positions in various areas of the country. Women intent upon a military career generally tend to factor out in the region of captains and majorships. Women's rights are more of an issue than used to be the case, but few women—certainly white women—have anything approximating a politically driven gender agenda for changing social relations within the multidimensional military patriarchy. Most are subsequently content with being designated for routine and support work.

Reacculturation: Toward a new Civil-Military Relationship?

The issue of trade unions, collective bargaining, and the enforcement of discipline have also appeared on the reacculturation agenda in a climate where there is strong support in many circles for the view that "the MDC in its present form is [no longer] an effective and impartial channel for restitution."[69] The DOD has committed itself to examining "various approaches to the question of appropriate labour relations machinery"—bearing in mind that unionization is the exception in militaries in even in most democratic countries.[70] In these circumstances, labor-relations policy is less likely to gravitate toward active trade unions in the NDF rather than some sort of quasiprofessional association delineating civilian from permanent members in the settlement of internal disputes and a military ombudsman working in conjunction with the parliamentary defense committees and the still newly appointed Public Protector.[71] Internal discussions within the armed forces suggest arrangements along these or similar lines for mid-late 1999, if not sooner.

Whether this is adequate to manage an inherently dynamic and conflicting environment where there is little concurrence between soldiers as to what actually constitutes military discipline remains a debatable point. During integration, differences on this issue were a source of tension between the regular military and the populists from MK and APLA. A number of minor mutinies that circumvented official channels for the expression of grievances were then the order of the day, and it is perfectly reasonable to expect problems in institutionalizing mechanisms to manage organizational conflicts arising out of explosive issues such as affirmative action, human rights, gender, and rationalization. Military leadership continues to welcome transparency and "sincerely desires to communicate more regularly and more openly with stakeholders who also have legitimate interests in the defence and security of the country."[72] Yet the proverbial old guard in the officer corps continues to have mixed feelings about change that undermines their commitment to the entire project of transformation. Former SADF elements are not averse to display their sentiments or, from time to time, engage in visibly provocative behavior. Military reactions to past presidential interventions to defend the role of Afrikaans as the language of control and command have been openly self-satisfied, and there are numerous instances where white high-ranking officers have consciously embarrassed outgroup personnel by using Afrikaans in official communications with English-speaking MK officers or ANC parliamentarians. To the embarrassment of the JPSCD and then-Deputy Minister Kasrils, no one over the rank of brigadier attended the Defense Review conference held in Parliament in February 1996—arguably the most important meeting of its type regarding the restructuring of the armed forces to have been held since the 1960s.[73]

The absence of a deep consultative ethic in the armed forces underwrites a clear need for long-range military resocialization if the armed forces are to legitimize themselves through "overcoming the legacy of apartheid and ensuring that the SANDF, and it leadership in particular, is representative of the South African population."[74] Within this context, institutions and programs for military education, training, and leadership development, such as the Joint Staff Course at the Defence College in Pretoria, the four Service Staff Colleges, and the various specialist schools for maritime warfare, armor, artillery, and so forth, are absolutely crucial. Narrow combat training occupies (and should occupy) most of the formative syllabi in the specialist schools, but there is room (and should be room) for more civilian input into the annual courses (at the Staff Colleges in particular). The Defence College also offers a four-month program to the highest officers, and here as well there are opportunities for the transmission of new civil-democratic values into the military heartland—were the military is less cautious in exposing its top leadership to ostensibly subversive civilian influences. Finally, changes in syllabi, membership, and organizational style are on line at the Military Academy at Saldanha Bay, although here transformation has been punctuated and consistently delayed by bureaucratic power struggles and obduracy on the part of old guard elements.

Ultimately, the White Paper readily concedes that despite all the cultural and institutional changes initiated during democratization "the SANDF does not yet reflect the demographic composition of South Africa."[75] In the middle and lower ranks, the capacity of former MK and APLA soldiers to make a cultural input is circumscribed by their full-time involvement in bridging and training courses to qualify for full contractual acceptance into the military. Although many of the soldiers on STSCs receive excellent training that conforms to standards set by the BMATT, the emphasis is on function rather than military education. Behind appearances in the higher ranks of the officer corps, human dynamics circumvent the formal the chain of command and ensure that decisionmaking power lies where it always was: among the white officers, or, lately, white officers and a thin coterie of overdetermined black personnel. There can be little doubt that a large proportion of new officers from the liberation armies and the former statutory homeland armies is less than self-confident in the unfamiliar, relatively huge, and consciously intimidating high-tech environment of the NDF. Inhibitions are compounded in many cases by a lack of personal expertise that creates space for the older, more experienced, and inevitably white officers to exercise influence disproportionate to rank. Some new commanders are little but commanders in name, and in these circumstances their capability to encourage cultural change from within the organization is fairly limited. General Nyanda, the highest among the new guard, was conspicuous in his absence from the round of Defense Review conferences geared to reconfiguring civil-military relations, and he and most of his colleagues in the higher ranks of the officer corps appear to represent the military equivalent of the new political class, slipping quickly and comfortably into positions of privilege within the new South Africa. Some of these new officers from the former NSF armies may eventually attend institutions such as the Military Academy, where they are more than likely, some critics suspect, to fit into the old power networks of the armed forces than work for real organizational adaptation. This stands in sharp contrast to the heady climate of negotiations in the early 1990s, when most of these officers were vigorously committed to the objective of restructuring the armed forces.

Supporters and critics of organizational change in the armed forces also operate on the presumption that there exists a specific and definable culture that requires reshaping. Closer examination, however, reveals that apart from a vague ethos derived from apartheid and a collection of populist notions transmitted through MK there is no such value system in the SANDF. Democratic transitions are logically disruptive, and the South African military, despite its self-confident references to a coherent "new" National Defence Force, has been seriously buffeted by the winds of change at the institutional and cultural levels. Perhaps the greatest challenge facing the armed forces is not adaptation (which presupposes something to adapt) but rather what one astute commentator has deemed a "vacuum in corporate ideology"—a nonculture, as it where, that disorganizes and ultimately threatens the psycho-institutional cohesion of the armed forces.

In contrast to the apartheid years, when total strategy provided officers with a finite enemy in the form of the ANC and global communism, many officers are now uncertain of their role absent the combination of black, red, and yellow perils. Military leadership itself is unclear about the mission orientation of the military apart from vague postulations about border duty, and some generals of all persuasions, it has been alleged, would prefer that the military remained unarticulated in order to protect the diminishing defense budget. Military sociologists have repeatedly emphasized the importance of a motivated officer corps, yet in the SANDF there is no official, meaningful, and widespread institutional dialogue of the rationale for service that interconnects with the realities of the postapartheid dispensation.

This situation, in a sense, facilitates intervention by civil society to reacculturate the military through lead-in information that both guides and shapes discourse in a democratic direction. On the downside, however, many career officers now find themselves in a demoralizing, suspended situation without an enemy or any discernible function. Organizational culture will inevitably change but, one suspects, at the cost of many experienced professionals driven from the military simply because of the sense that they have nothing meaningful to do. A great many of these former SADF officers today remain only in anticipation of an alternative career or a generous severance package upon rationalization in 2000. Perhaps even more serious is the fact that the new SANDF has some difficulty in attracting motivated and career-minded personnel to offset the losses. There is no doubt a pool of appropriate and recruitable human resources committed to military service and transcending race divisions can be built in time. Alternatively, the military must change as this pool darkens and there are fewer numbers of whites who contemplate a military career. In the intervening period, however, the majority of recruits from MK, APLA, the former homeland armies, and civil society more generally tends to approach the armed forces less with transformative impulses than purely instrumental and self-interested reasons. This constraint on cultural transformation will no doubt continue for as long as the country is unable to develop sustainable mechanisms for job creation.

Military socialization procedures can arguably reshape recruits into genuine civil servants. This, however, depends on the existence of progressive personnel management procedures related to democratic education and training—procedures to which the SANDF is still not especially susceptible in a situation of ongoing residual tension between the civil and military sectors. The universal experience, however, clearly indicates that institutional failures of this type almost inevitably generate problems of political control that sweep the polite issues of civilianization off the agenda. It is for this reason that the current problems of corporate ideology, manpower maintenance, and recruitment are very disturbing, despite the conventional portrayal of the military as easing effectively into a new system of democratic civil-military relations.

As legions of theorists have also pointed out, military institutions have their own peculiar characteristics that are always resistant to civilianization. Neither is it desirable that the militaries be civilianized beyond a certain indefinable level where it becomes impossible to efficiently perform their social role in defining state interests. Pinpointing that level is the intellectual heartland of civil-military relations, with due respect for the different historic traditions and cultural experiences of military organizations and their wider social environments. Having said that, however, cultural reorganization in the SANDF in any significant and lasting sense appears to require far more internal and external reinforcement than is the case at present. Time will inevitably erode the current military culture as the old guard is displaced by a new generation of officers nurtured in a democratic climate and more in synch with its values. Although the present culture, with its lingering associations to apartheid, will inevitably run into reproductive problems with natural attrition and changing recruitment patterns, acceleration toward that critical level where soldiers automatically appreciate and internalize the civil-political context of their actions—the apogee of subjective military control—clearly requires far more energy and support from within the military and civil society in the shorter term.

Effective parliamentary control over the defense budget, one of the most powerful mechanisms of civilianization, has already been achieved, but other mechanisms need to be emplaced or upgraded to diminish military leverage over society. The new Constitution is, in many respects, far less articulate on many defense provisions than was the Interim Constitution, and Parliament has been left to fill in the details governing the behavior of state institutions through enabling legislation.[76] The institutional framework for civilianization, involving such organizations as the Defence Secretariat and the JPSCD, is still experimental and tentative. Civilianization ultimately requires a strong civil society working through institutional channels, and there is still room for civil empowerment. Constitutional provisions governing fundamental human rights and their limitation in cases of national emergency will certainly have to be more carefully defined prior to the formulation of a new Defence Act more in tune with the new political dispensation. A new Defence Act will, in turn, constitute a critical threshold in this process of clarifying the new constitutional democracy—not only in the sense of refining and testing the strategic mechanisms already emplaced but also in establishing guidelines to steer the organizational culture.

As with democracy-building in general, much depends on the extent to which civil leadership regards demilitarization and civilianization as political imperatives in the vast constellation of public policy issues. The tight intersection of the Afrikaner military and political class characteristic of apartheid has been broken, yet macrosocial reconstruction is always dangerous and unpredictable in a way that encourages political leaders, especially new leaders, to fall back upon the armed forces as a source of capital. In South Africa, there are already some indications of this syndrome in the existence of the United Democratic Movement and the Freedom Front, two political parties at polar ends of the political spectrum that are led by former generals (albeit in military dress). In these circumstances, it remains an open issue whether it will be practical or possible to forge the type of value-oriented military necessary for democracy. As theorists of organizational change persistently point out, the road from entrenched hierarchy to an ethic of consultative behavior is a matter of years rather than months, and it is entirely natural for bureaucratic and institutional resistance to be encountered all along the way. The "new" SANDF is sometimes characterized as the "old" SADF without the dirty tricks and with a scattering of black officers. This is unjustified. Equally misleading, however, is the view that the armed forces have become a rainbow institution that has broken with its white, male, Christian, Afrikaner origins. In the last analysis, what is important is that the first tentative steps to transformation have been taken under the aegis of a newly empowered civil society.

"Much works well," a fairly recent intelligence report noted hopefully, but leadership, the sine qua non of effective military organization, is exceptionally difficult to exercise in circumstances where "indiscipline has become the enemy of the Defence Force."[77] The Psychological Integration Program established to, inter alia, monitor institutional change noted that privates and some lower-order personnel often revealed more positive attitudes to change than did their own officers,[78] but among the officer corps there are substantial problems of leadership at all levels. The planned exit of many senior leaders of the former SADF, not unwelcomed by the constituency seeking accelerated transformation, fuels demoralization throughout the NDF, particularly at the middle-management level, where many officers labor without adequate administrative backup. Many, according to the surveys, now experience "sinking ship syndrome."[79] Disillusion is fueled by the obsolescence of equipment and an awareness of limited funds to the point where many midlevel personnel in the officer corps wonder "if it is not time for them to find another means of living" like their seniors.[80] The anticipated departure of senior leaders will in any case remove, at one fell stroke, the primary source of mentorship for upwardly mobile former NSF members who may have completed the necessary staff courses but inevitably lack the hands-on experience of conventional defense management.

Junior leadership is relatively unsocialized (if it comes form the former NSFs) and often deeply frustrated (if it derives from the former SADF and has been involved in the daily battle for integration). Many seasoned commanders in middle management have experienced disorientation when confronted by the magnitude and unfamiliarity of an integration process followed by transformation. Pressed by bridging and retraining schedules, they see themselves as prisoners between senior military planners, with limited conceptions of what occurs on the ground, and ground staff that is equally confused and, in some instances, noncompliant. Unit commanders need to cross-pollinate their experiences to come up with lessons that can be translated from integration to the broader process of transformation. This is because they "are senior enough to understand the implications of orders, but junior enough to struggle with privates and their misperceptions, attitudes and daily problems."[81] All available research points to the fact that a high proportion of white middle management now doubts its ability to manage institutional continuity, least of all institutional change. Leadership involves the enforcement of discipline, which the former NSFs are quick to label race discrimination. Many former NSF personnel are modern enough to understand that personal or institutional instances of racism can now be pursued under South Africa's new Bill of Rights, so that "the situation has now moved from the parade ground to the court."[82] This emasculates the whole system of military justice and, in the opinion former SADF officers, impugns their professional and corporate dignity. When military personnel with ten to fifteen years experience question the value of the entire system, "this is a danger to be heeded."[83]

Transformation remains the primary item on the military agenda. Yet there is little consensus as to what this means or implies. In the military (as elsewhere in the public service), the politics of identity necessarily generates conflict as both old and new guards seek to protect their turf and brand transformation with their own set of meanings. The military contains many elements, most of whom originate in MK or APLA, who are frustrated by the slow pace of change, who believe that the process of integration has hardly begun, and who utterly reject the technicist and intrinsically conservative notion that transformation requires little adaptation within the existing structural dispensation.

Others—the colloquial old guard, with its largely white former SADF component—see the forces at work to change the substance and spirit of the military as dangerous, corrosive, and ultimately subversive of combat capability. It is out of the interaction between the two formations, with their often diametrically opposed conceptions of military existence under the new political dispensation, that a discernibly new defense force will conceivably emerge.

Notes

1. Speech by Lieutenant General W.H. Hechter, Chief of the South African Air Force, on Behalf of the Chief of the South African National Defence Force, Conference on the South African National Defence Force and Transformation, University of South Africa, Pretoria, October 15, 1996.

2. Captain Fanie Uys, "The SANDF Transformation Process," paper presented to Conference on the South African National Defence Force and Transformation, University of South Africa, Pretoria, October 15, 1996.

3. Ibid.

4. See South African National Defence Force (SANDF), The National Defence Force in Transition: Annual Report, Financial Year 1994/95; Department of Defence, New Era Defence, Annual Report, Financial Year 1995/96.

5. Annual Report, 1995/96, p. 20

6. Republic of South Africa, *Defence in Democracy: White Paper on Defence for the Republic of South Africa*, May 1996, p. 10.

7. Ibid., p. 10, sec. 2.7.

8. Ibid., p. 11. sec. 4.

9. Ibid., p. 12. sec. 8.
10. Ibid., p. 12. sec. 9.
11. Ibid., p. 12. sec. 10.
12. Ibid., p. 13. sec. 21.
13. Pierre Steyn, "The Defence Secretariat and the South African Army," *African Security Review* 5(1) (1996); Pierre Steyn, "The Defence Industry and the Role of the Defence Secretariat," *African Security Review* 5(6) (1996).
14. Steyn, "The Defence Secretariat and the South African Army," *African Security Review* 5(1) (1996).
15. Pierre Steyn, "The Defence Secretariat and the South African Army," paper presented to the Conference on Preparing the South African Army for the Twenty-first Century, Council for Scientific and Industrial Research Centre (CSIR), Pretoria, October 19, 1995
16. Quoted in Philip Frankel, *Marching to the Millenium: The Birth, Development, and Transformation of the South African National Defence Force* (Pretoria: South African National Defence Force, Directorateof Corporate Communications, 1998), p. 159.
17. Ibid.
18. Ibid.
19. Ibid.
20. Ibid.
21. Ibid.
22. Annual Report, 1995/96; New Era Defence, pp. 11–12
23. Ibid., p. 13.
24. Frankel, *Marching to the Millenium*, p. 161.
25. Annual Report, 1995/96.
26. *The Star* (Johannesburg), June 27, 1995.
27. For a more detailed discussion of the dilemmas that this creates for the armed forces, see Chapter 4, on social reconstruction.
28. Steyn, "The Defence Secretariat," CSIR conference paper; also quoted in Frankel, *Marching to the Millenium*, p. 163.
29. Ibid.
30. Rocklyn Williams, "Overview and Backdrop to the Defence Review." Presentation to the Defence Review Workshop, Jan Smuts House, University of the Witwatersrand, Johannesburg, July 29, 1996. See also Williams, "From the Defence Review into the Future."
31. Frankel, *Marching to the Millenium*, p. 163
32. Ibid.
33. See Philip Frankel, "Report on Proceedings," Defence Review Workshop, Jan Smuts House, University of the Witwatersrand, Johannesburg, July 1996 (presented to Defence Secretariat July 1996).
34. Frankel, *Marching to the Millenium*, p. 164
35. Ibid.
36. Institute for Democracy in South Africa, *Democracy in Action* 9(6) (October 1995).
37. The transparency of the armed forces must now also be seen against the background on new legislation—the so-called Open Democracy Act—which will

make it extremely difficult to veil its actions and internal developments from public scrutiny, except in cases of obvious national interest.

38. Frankel, *Marching to the Millenium*, p. 165.

39. *The Star* (Johannesburg), November 22, 1995.

40. Annual Report, 1995/96.

41. *Sunday Independent* (Johannesburg), February 16, 1997.

42. *The Star* (Johannesburg), October 27, 1996.

43. *White Paper*, p. 7, sec. 11.

44. N. Botha, "The Role of Public International Law in the South African Interim Constitution Act 100 of 1983 and its Effect on the South African Defence Act 44 of 1957 in Revision of South African Defence Legislation" (Midrand: Institute for Defence Policy, September 1994, p.1.

45. *White Paper* 12(8), p. 6.

46. Walters and Partners, "Law Relating to the Australian Defence Force," p. 113.

47. Detailed studies of the role of women in MK still need to be compiled. There is nonetheless substantial evidence to suggest that gender equality was not normally the order of the day. Clear indications of this emerged early in the integration process with substantial conflict between male and female cadres at the Wallmansthal Assembly Area.

48. *The Star* (Johannesburg), November 19, 1995.

49. On the role of women in the defense industries under apartheid, see, e.g., Simon Ratcliffe, "Forced Relations: The State, Crisis, and the Rise of Militarism in South Africa." Unpubl. Thesis, University of the Witwatersrand, 1983.

50. British Military Advisory and Training Team (BMATT), BMATT/Navy/100/3, June 23, 1994.

51. BMATT/Army/101/1, July 1, 1994.

52. SANDF, The National Defence Force in Transition, p. 70.

53. Ellen Molekane, "The Role of Women in the South African National Defence Force," *African Security Review* 5(5) (1996): 2326.

54. Ibid.

55. SANDF, The National Defence Force in Transition, p. 70.

56. Ibid., p. 99.

57. Ibid., p. 70.

58. South African Institute of Race Relations, Annual Survey, 1980 (Johannesburg: SAIRR, 1981).

59. Molekane, "The Role of Women."

60. Military Academy, "Student Numbers for B. Mil Degree, 1995," Unpubl. paper, Military Academy, Saldanha Bay. 1995.

61. SANDF, The National Defence Force in Transition, p 84.

62. Molekane, "The Role of Women."

63. On this point, see Cynthia Enloe, *Does Khaki Become You? The Militarisation of Women's Lives* (Boston: South End Press, 1983).

64. See Jakkie Cilliers et al., "Public Opinion on Defence and Security Issues," in *About Turn: The Transformations of the South African Military and Intelligence*, ed. Jakkie Cilliers and Markus Reichardt (Midrand: Institute for Defence Policy, 1996), pp, 223–250

65. Ibid.

66. Ibid.

67. On this point, see Diana Coole, *Women in Political Theory: From Ancient Misogyny to Contemporary Feminism* (Hemel Hempstead: Harvester Wheatsheaf, 1993), p. 187.

68. The notion of women as a protected element in the military is very strong, in particular among older, white, former SADF, gentleman officers in the higher rankings.

69. Heinecken, *Social Trends*, p. 85.

70. *White Paper*, chap. 6, p. 34.

71. Heinecken *Social Trends*; Mark Malan, "The Implications of Unionisation for the Combat Effectiveness of the Armed Forces," paper presented to Symposium on Labour Relations, Pretoria, March 2, 1994.

72. *The Star* (Johannesburg), June 27, 1995.

73. *The Star* (Johannesburg), February 19, 1996.

74. *White Paper*, chap. 6, p.33.

75. Ibid.

76. *Mail and Guardian* (Johannesburg), February 9, 1996.

77. Ibid.

78. SANDF, Military Psychological Institute (MPI), Evaluation Research/Final Report on the Psychological Integration Program (PIP), p. 15.

79. Houdings en Meningopnames: Konsolidasie-Verslag van Fokusgroepopnames, Directorate of Intelligence for Effect Analysis, Pretoria, 1997.

80. Ibid.

81. Ibid.

82. Ibid.

83. Ibid.

4

Guns and Butter: Social Reconstruction and Rearmament

We can do without butter, but despite all our love for peace, not without arms. One cannot shoot with butter.

—*Joseph Goebbels,* **Speech in Berlin** *(January 17, 1936).*

It is not big armies that win battles: it is the good ones.

—*Maurice de Saxe,* **Mes Revenes** *(1732).*

It is customary in democratic countries to deplore expenditure on armaments as conflicting with the requirements of social services. There is a tendency to forget that the most important social service than a government can do for its people is to keep them alive and free.

—*Sir John Slessor,* **Strategy for the West** *(1954).*

Shifts in power across the civil-military boundary to the armed forces have major consequences for society, and for as long as analysts have pondered militaries they have debated the consequences of militarization. Following World War II, for example, considerable literature emerged on the relationship between militaries and modernization. This ultimately led to a widespread consensus in the late 1950s and early 1960s that militaries could well be the only social group in underdeveloped states capable of establishing political stability and promoting socioeconomic growth in the face of structurally weak and institutionally enfeebled civil society. Infused by a mixture of Eurocentric notions of social development and a fear of revolutionary insurgency under Cold War conditions, even the founders of modern military sociology were given to waxing lyrical about the supremacy of military "virtues," the penchant of the military for Western democratic institutions, and the possibility of replicating the "progressive" experiences of places such as early-twentieth-century Turkey on a universal basis.[1]

Two and a half decades later, in the wake of accumulated evidence of military misrule, incompetence, and corruption in many countries, analysts are somewhat more sanguine about the so-called Ataturk model, with its presumption that "the military coup is crucial for the continuation and acceleration of nation-building in Asia and Africa."[2] In light of the recent track records of militaries to persistently seize power from civil society, to stimulate internal warfare, distort political life, and stifle economic growth through massive and unnecessary arms purchases, there is consensus that militaries can rule rather than govern. Even then, they are essentially consumers of social resources—human, financial, and administrative—and ultimately contribute very little to socioeconomic development. Sobered by the successive failure of military regimes to deliver on their development agendas in meeting popular demands (when such agendas exist at all), most contemporary commentators see the social reform trickled down from military rule working largely to the benefit of privileged social interests with membership in dominant civil-military coalitions.[3]

Horrified by abuses of human rights in countless cases, most have concluded that military-driven development has more costs than benefits—and the costs may damage the fabric of civil society long after the soldiers have returned to the barracks. This is true in Africa, where one military enthusiast noted the armed forces "cannot build legitimate political institutions through the use of force. . . . They cannot transplant their organisational style to the civilian realm, they are not equipped to bring stability, modernisation or political participation." In conclusion, he added that they "lack sufficient flexibility and innovativeness to govern effectively."[4]

Out of Pocket: The Defense Budget

South Africa is fortunate in having escaped an unambiguous military coup as a facet of its history, with its attendant sociopolitical and economic ravages. This reflects many factors, such as the durability of the British civil-military tradition even during the years of total strategy, when military leaders were consorting with counterparts in pariah states such as Taiwan, Chile, and Israel; the conscript character of the military for much of its history; and the close tutelage of P.W. Botha, which spared the armed forces the necessity of a formal coup while allowing them access to the pinnacles of state power. All this conspired to maintain civilian predominance over the political process, albeit precariously so under total strategy. From the late 1970s, moreover, as the Nationalist government proved increasingly inadequate to the task of maintaining control in the face of mass mobilization, the military was nevertheless able to accumulate considerable political leverage; as civilian institutions weakened, the military emerged as a major, if not the predominant, player in the public policy process allocating social resources. The consequences of this development have not yet been systematically measured and may never be done so. Even at the arithmetic level of expended finance, we will probably remain uncertain as to what apartheid invested in militarization given such factors as the existence of the Special Defence Account (SDA), which obscured the amount of money flowing into the armed forces under apartheid, consciously unusual accounting practices, and the often veiled transfer of resources between state departments to obfuscate figures for defense spending. If South Africa follows the universal trend—where militarization has resulted in massive misallocations of resources in Third World economies—then there are grounds for believing that the rise of the military in the last years of apartheid, the onset of the garrison state, and the subsequent vast expansion of the defense economy was inimical to economic productivity and social modernization.

Certainly, the military under total strategy was a major consumer of public finances expressed in the annual defense budget. For much of the forty-five years of Nationalist rule, the modernization of the armed forces was a priority for a state under increasing pressure, and from 1948 the defense budget increased progressively, if not dramatically. As late as 1958–1959, for example, a mere R36 million was allocated for defense purposes; by 1982–1983, however, when militarization had taken firm hold, this had risen to almost R3 billion. Contained within this trajectory were two major accelerations in the defense budget, both relating to the heightened security concerns of an increasingly isolated ruling class. During the early 1960s, for example, the military underwent a major expansion program hot on the heels of domestic disturbances (resulting in the Sharpeville massacre), a national state of emergency, and the movement of the ANC and PAC into underground struggle. Similarly, a second expensive modernization program was initiated by an overlapping white military and political elite in the mid-1970s following the 1976 rebellion, the deterioration of South Africa's strategic position following Portuguese withdrawal from the subcontinent, the emergence of Zimbabwe, and the appearance of Cuban troops in Angola.

Thereafter, with the full articulation of total strategy by a military obsessed with creeping communism emanating from the north, the defense budget ratcheted upward. Although the drain on the national economy was not exceptional relative to some other Western countries likewise engaged in the Cold War, it was significant within the domestic context, where most members of the white minority shared the view of the armed forces that it was essential to maintain a favorable balance of military power in order to head off the imminent twin threats of communism and black nationalism. In 1960–1961, only 0.9 percent of gross national product (GNP) and 6.6 percent of state expenditures were "officially" moving in a defense direction. By 1978–1979, however, 5 percent of GNP and 14.3 percent of state expenditures went to the military; by the mid-1980s, nearly 20 percent of government funds were being regularly invested in the defense establishment.[5]

By the mid-1980s, official defense spending had already increased tenfold relative to a dozen years earlier—excluding figures in the Special Defence Account, which had by then been elevated to a second unofficial defense budget (public revelation of its contents was deemed inimical to the national interest). Originally established in 1952 as a small fund to facilitate arms purchases on the global market, the Special Defence Account is widely regarded as the benchmark for military spending under exclusive executive control outside the purview of the state audit in the later years of apartheid. In 1976–1977, we know that approximately R11.8 million was already being diverted from civil-society development through this channel. By 1980, the SDA had swelled to over R1 billion at a time when the entire official defense budget was just short of twice that amount. By this time, there was also speculation, eventually culminating in the so-called information scandal, that the fund was being deployed to assist the ruling Nationalist Party in various covert operations to maintain power.[6]

The onset of democratization has produced a reassessment of military spending, as in many countries after the end of the Cold War. Newly democratic South Africa also faces major challenges of social reconstruction to address the legacy of apartheid. Even prior to coming to power, President Nelson Mandela pledged to cut defense spending within the context of civilianization,[7] and since 1994 he and his ANC leaders continued to identify with this goal (at least until recently). The philosophy of transforming swords to plough shares as a central facet of national reconciliation has subsequently spawned a vigorous and ongoing debate over the role of defense in democratic South Africa involving various advocates of the Reconstruction and Development Program (the RDP, now reorganized as the Growth, Employment, and Redistribution Program, or GEAR) on the one side, and a military establishment accustomed to a reasonably comfortable lifestyle on the other.

In this running battle over demilitarization, the military is seriously disadvantaged by the hostile conditions of transition. In the first place, the NDF is still not a focal point for patriotism, and it does not have a strong domestic constituency to back up its own views of its appropriate size, structure, and core missions. Unlike the American public, whose esteem for the military can be leveraged to secure public appropriations and defend institutional interests, most South Africans do not spiritually identify with the new NDF or its various service arms as national institutions. Short of further efforts at nation-building, the military is still associated with the excesses of apartheid, including prominent members of the ANC in the Cabinet and the upper reaches of the state bureaucracy. The recent revelations of the Truth and Reconciliation Commission have doubtlessly crystallized the view among blacks and whites that the military is both an evil and wasteful institution, even though public opinion on defense issues remains inarticulate and uncertain despite the efforts of such organizations as the new Defence Secretariat to create what it terms a "national consensus" on defense.[8] What little evidence exists suggests that several years into transition most people are "doves" in identifying with the emphasis of RDP-GEAR on the subjugation of defense expenditures to broader social imperatives. This is particularly true of the ruling ANC's main constituency within the context of a "revolution of rising expectations" attendant on democratization—the millions of socially disadvantaged persons aspiring to employment, education, and housing to whom military pronouncements about national security and acceptable defense capability ring both abstract and hollow. If the new NDF is to effectively sell itself, it will have to inspire public confidence in itself as a national institution and thereby address diminishing social appetites for military spending.

In the meantime, its bargaining capacity is also undercut by the lack of a discernable conventional threat to national security. To the consternation of some members of the military establishment, chapter 4.8 of the draft White Paper on Defence states explicitly that South Africa "is not confronted by an immediate conventional threat and does not anticipate military aggression in the short-term future." South Africa, it appears, has moved miraculously from "total onslaught" to "no onslaught," and this has fundamentally changed the policy framework. Unlike the precarious apartheid years, when money flowed almost automatically into military coffers, the NDF is now reduced to asking for funds on the basis of a problematic "natural" level of spending, which is determined by political negotiations between development lobbies and soldiers. In the words of one commentator, soldiers today are forced "to fight tooth and nail for money to finance important new acquisitions for the continent's most powerful defence force."[9]

The discomfort of the armed forces is compounded by the emergence of a peace movement among human rights organizations within civil society that promote the notion of butter versus guns and, to the exasperation of soldiers, projects the view that any defense spending is "unnatural" given the pressing urgency of reconstruction and development. The South African Council of Churches, for example, has called on the MOD to dismantle the local arms industry and to commit most of the existing defense budget, the biggest in the region, to the RDP. Ultimately, many new antimilitarist organizations such as Ceasefire and Gun-Free South Africa—generically the "churches" in the words of then–Deputy Minister of Defence Ronnie Kasrils—have questioned whether South Africa needs any formal defense structures whatsoever.[10]

The combination of changes in the international environment along with the elevation of democratization and development goals to the center of public policy have effectively eroded the paradigm or previous justifications for massive defense spending. As in many countries where defense is a soft target for saving money, the new South African government has lighted upon its armed forces, all the more vulnerable because of their inability to clearly define their role in the new order; this is likely to continue in annual budgets battles.[11] In the meantime, the climate of austerity is reflected in the provisions of the White Papers that have guided defense policy since 1994, as well as in the new Constitution, which explicitly calls for an "affordable" defense force (generally taken to mean one that consumes no more than 2 percent of GNP in accord with criteria laid down by the International Monetary Fund and the World Bank). As before, it remains difficult to gauge current defense spending given differences as to what to include or exclude, interoperability between the NDF and other state departments, and collateral utility and support for RDP-type social development.[12] Nevertheless, defense spending has declined an estimated 44 percent in real terms since 1989—the second highest decline in the world after Russia—and may be as high as 65 percent depending on how one computes the arithmetic.[13] Claiming 15.7 percent of government expenditures even after the conclusion of the Angolan and Namibian wars, the defense budget now constitutes a mere 8.2 percent of all expenditures.[14] The sacred SDA, still in place, has been decreased by half, and further reductions, if not elimination in the interests of transparency, were expected as a consequence of the Defence Review. Between 1994–1995 and 1995–1996, the total official budget dropped from R12.1 billion to an estimated R10.5 billion, representing 2.1–2.94 percent of gross domestic product (GDP).

Either way, the international threshold (2 percent of GDP) is being achieved within a short period. Within this framework, 72 percent of the budget is deployed for operational costs such as salaries, pensions, uniforms, rations, equipment maintenance, and the like. This leaves relatively little for the purchase of new equipment in contrast to the 1980s, when almost half the budget was devoted to weapons procurement in the face of international embargoes and a commitment to rapid and extensive modernization.[15] Additional budget pressure stemmed from the abortive National Peace-Keeping Force, created to stem violence during the 1994 elections at an estimated cost of R384 million and personnel costs of several million rand related to the integration of the old SADF with the TBVC and nonstatutory armies. Although these latter expenses (an estimated R2 billion in 1996–1997) have gone by the boards with gradual completion of the process, they are likely to be replicated, even superceded, by the costs of demobilization and rationalization, which the swollen NDF must now tackle.

None of this has, however, satisfied antimilitarist and development lobbies, who continue to press for an even larger "peace dividend" based on demilitarization. Most are of the opinion that further cuts in the capital and procurement budgets are desirable and possible. The continued existence of the SDA is a particularly visible target for critics, as is the tendency of the military to roll over funds from one financial year to another even following the 1994 elections. This tends to minimize the apparent size of the budget so that defense, the critics argue, actually receives far more on an annual basis than what appears in the official statistics. The Finance Committee of Parliament has subsequently been directed to examine the continuation of this procedure.[16] Parliament is generally hostile to the continuation of the SDA in a newly transparent democracy and that is widely regarded as an unacceptable hangover from apartheid that allows the executive to allocate defense expenditures in a manner subversive of legislative sovereignty. Generally speaking, parliamentarians continue to believe that the budget could be better planned, rationalized, and projected at a time when policy is so sharply focused on economic reconstruction and the alleviation of social distress.

Within the military itself, there is understandable concern over financial constraints, widely seen as dangerous to the sense of purpose vital to the effective functioning of any military organization. Although partially recognizing the existence of a new policy framework in which the military must now compete for resources on a level playing field, military leaders in all three major service arms are less than happy with budgetary tendencies that undermine combat capability. There is a feeling among officers that radical budgetary cuts are dangerous and unacceptable to national security in the long term. As bases have closed and units disestablished in the last five years, NDF spokesmen pointed to the fact that South Africa largely conforms to international recommendations on defense expenditures as a proportion of GDP. Current expenditures, they argue, are proportionately far less than the double-digit figures of many adjacent African countries (including Angola, Mozambique, Tanzania, and Zimbabwe) and compare favorably to the 2.6 percent of GDP threshold in the subcontinent. Both Namibia and Lesotho proportionately spend more on defense, they point out, although the South African armed forces bear the added burden of integration.[17] There is a widespread feeling that further cuts in the defense budget are unacceptable if South Africa is to maintain the modern and technologically developed capability.

Interservice rivalries will inevitably emerge with additional financial restrictions, which could prove dangerous to the corporate solidarity and political stability of South Africa. Although optimization of existing resources for command and control, training, personnel management, logistical support, and general administration can assist in blunting budgetary constraints, there is some threshold, so the logic goes, when threats to organizational functionality can no longer be managed. The NDF, according to its former chief, General Meiring, has already fallen below the point of a properly equipped "core" capacity necessary for the maintenance of national security.[18] Similar sentiments have been voiced by then–Minister of Defence Joe Modise—a newly converted advocate of a strong military establishment—who has warned Parliament that South Africa will be reduced to a "second-rate" military force should further reductions be contemplated.[19]

Although conceding the absence of any immediate threat, military leaders are anxious that this situation excludes development and procurement funding, both of which are driven by long-term lead-in factors. The core capacity referred to by General Meiring is already running into equipment difficulties due to lack of funding in the region of R1.1 billion per annum, and most security analysts reject the possibility of compensatory cuts in operational expenses for border protection and support for the SAPS, which would simply shift costs to the SAPS budget. Finding economies in training, research, and development is also questionable. Reduced training costs are difficult as the NDF works to upgrade former NSF members to the technical standards of a modern, conventional military; cheaper training will, once again, erode combat capacity. Maintaining minimum strategic technological levels, NDF leaders argue, will place South Africa at a comparative disadvantage in a world military system where technological development and diversification is at a premium, and cutting technology poses difficult and expensive problems of reactivation should South Africa experience some conventional military threat in the indefinite future. These considerations are particularly pertinent to the high-tech service arms, the Air Force and the Navy, both of which already face serious problems of weapons redundancy.

Internal Deployment: The Service Corps and Collateral Utility

As a prophylactic against the acquisitive claims of the RDP-GEAR, the peace lobbies in civil society, and developmental imperatives more generally, the military establishment has sought to identify more closely with the reconstructionist agenda of the new government, hoping to enhance its leverage over the public purse. By 1996 Modise was announcing that the armed forces were following a zero-based budgeting process "to reprioritize defence activities and improve the balance between capital and operating expenditure in the spirit of the RDP imperative."[20]Other military leaders have sought to pinpoint activities whereby the military can make positive developmental inputs without necessarily sacrificing their role and capability. This has led to the long-standing notion that the armed forces can become a "school for the nation" as in other Third World countries where militaries played a role in national liberation and integration. Hence, we hear frequently that the mainstream NDF, the part-time forces, or the reserves have enormous potential to bridge the deep racial and class divisions in society; without that, neither democracy nor development is possible.

Given the role of the military as a client force for the ruling oligarchy under apartheid, it is doubtful whether the NDF can project itself as the defender of national traditions, patriotism, and a glorious past. In the United States, the military is, in the words of one analyst, "an important source of continuity in national affairs, lending warmth and life to the abstractions contained in the historic documents and bloodless monuments."[21] In South Africa, such would require amnesia in the public memory that allowed the majority of black South Africans to identify with the armed forces as a national institution; at a lower level, it would require the NDF to resolve the outstanding problems of integration on the agenda. With regard to the former, the findings of the Truth and Reconciliation Commission have been unhelpful. Still, military institutions of all sorts can be "an inculcative force for nationhood" through their unique capacity to socialize people from diverse class and ethnic backgrounds.[22] With this in mind, the armed forces have moved in the wake of transition to create new institutions that connect them more fully to nation-building. Integration has indeed led to an unprecedented expansion of the numbers of personnel in the armed forces; rationalization is on the cards; and it is imperative, in the corporate interests of the military as well as the wider interests of society, that mechanisms be emplaced to manage the massive movement of soldiers out of the barracks and into the social mainstream.

During the course of negotiations under the aegis of the JMCC, for example, the idea of a Service Brigade to allow the armed forces to contribute to human-resource development compatible with the reconstructionist goals of postapartheid society was suggested by both SADF and MK negotiators. Differences emerged as to the nature of the Service Brigade, its constituency, its role, and the long-term responsibility of the military for its finance and administration. Nevertheless, the concept survived in the form of the Service Corps, which has become a centerpiece for the NDF in demobilization and rationalization. The Service Corps is also a useful barometer for measuring the problems and responses of the military to the unfamiliar demands of development.

The Service Corps has generally not been an unqualified success in bridging the gap among the subsegments of civil and military society. Based loosely on the principles of the Special Service Battalion established in the 1930s to provide opportunities for white youths dislocated by the Depression, the purpose of the Service Corps in theory is to train volunteers from the ranks of the youth and unemployed in the long term and to equip demobilized and rationalized members of the NDF to participate in civilian life or "a career in the Supporting Services of the NDF."[23] From the outset, however, the conversion capability of the Service Corps, initially commanded by Lieutenant General Lambert Moloi of MK, has been dogged by a mixture of financial, organizational, and human problems. The Service Corps system envisions a network of subunits of linked to each of the service arms and the nine territorial commands; it has not materialized, nor is it likely to unless the organization is adequately funded. If the Service Corps is to provide vocational and life skills to service the RDP (or rationalization per se)—if it is to train 5,500 persons per annum—it will require, it is estimated, approximately R150 million per annum.[24] Given cuts in the defense budget, this amount is unlikely to come from the armed forces. The Service Corps has tended to rely on "external" funding. In effect, it survived initially only because of the generosity of the Taiwanese Government (which came forward with the R141 million necessary for the Service Corps to establish its first vocational training center).

There are also nonfinancial problems that are possibly more intractable. These include a very low motivation among the first intakes within the context of a curriculum that offers only "very basic training," overstates military discipline, and out of touch with the capacity, interests, and needs of participants.[25] The initial recruits were the so-called veterans and vulnerables from MK and APLA who were not, from any point of view, the most auspicious group with which to kick-start this important initiative. Even among this relatively old and uneducated component, however, there was little enthusiasm for an organization where six months of instruction would precede only six months of guaranteed employment in supporting services (taken to mean the tail end of the military network). Hence, many intakes soon requested transfers back into the military mainstream upon arrival at the Service Corps; they were then rerouted back to the Wallmansthal AA, where they had originated.[26]

The subsequent work of the Service Corps in reintegrating personnel into civil society has been equally unimpressive, partially because the NDF has little enthusiasm for an institution that draws on its own account to fund a social reconstruction program with little military participation. This view is transmitted to instructional personnel, many of whom, like students, see the whole Service Corps as nothing more than a dumping ground. Instructors have had difficulty linking programs to impart literacy, technical skills, and entrepreneurial skills to the profoundly disadvantaged with their own vocational experiences as career soldiers; they have been dispirited from the outset. This could have changed thanks to the Taiwan connection, which promised to make available at least a hundred new instructors and administrators at the single Dunnotar Centre east of Johannesburg.[27] Unfortunately, South Africa has broken relations with Taiwan in favor of diplomatic recognition of mainland China; further assistance is most unlikely.

Most senior NDF officers (including those of MK origin) have been concerned from its inception that the Service Corps could be the harbinger of another round of mission creep. In that circle, the Service Corps is marketable only if its caters solely to demobilized or rationalized members of the military, even then subject to the proviso that costs are transferred out of the tight defense budget. Involvement with any wider constituency—the youth or the unemployed—is regarded not only as a nonmilitary task but also as a contradiction of the mission to disengage the armed forces and reprofessionalize the barracks. Still, the NDF is caught between corporate claims on its coffers and its interest in servicing social development; this has led the Service Corps to reject, for example, overtures from civil society that it assist in the conversion training of black paramilitary formations spawned by the political conflicts of the early and mid-1990s. Negative responses to the ANC-aligned Self-Defense Units (SDUs) and the Self-Protection Units (SPUs) created by Inkatha reflect the view of the former Chief of the Army, Major General Reg Otto, that the Service Corps is an "inappropriate" institution for the armed forces.[28] Despite the fact that planned rationalization may displace some 25,000 personnel, most senior officers would concur and would welcome its being passed off to the state bureaucracy, perhaps the Department of Labour. This tendency to sideline the Service Corps is echoed by a large proportion of its own part-time graduates who, after a short taste of its work, have opted for one-time demobilization grants and returned to civil society to join the ranks of the destitute, the criminal, and the unemployed. Since white military personnel see the Service Corps as a rudimentary institution appropriate for training unskilled blacks, its capability as a conversion-management institution within the framework of rationalization is compounded. This suggests that the Service Corps may become a race-based transfer point between civil and military society within the rationalization project or, more likely, a purposeless quasimilitary institution with no prospects for social input whatsoever.

Fortunately, the NDF possesses collateral utility inherent in its organization, equipment, mobility, and dispersal throughout the country. These resources can be deployed as an alternative for purposes of reconstruction and development. The South African military, has, for example, a heritage of disaster management and calamity control; given that the majority of its personnel have neither the skills nor inclination to become economic managers or servants of civilian reconstruction and development projects, the primary role of the armed forces is most likely to be in providing this collateral utility.

The various arms of service are in the process of fulfilling and extending this very mission. SAMS, the Navy, and the Air Force offer programs that directly service the RDP or are compatible with its general purposes. The Army, a land force with secondary responsibilities, is involved in border protection—its importance increasing with the massive influx of illegal persons and resources in the wake of democratization—as well as area protection, which has been extended from defense in depth to the maintenance of law and order. With continued political violence, recurrent attacks on farming communities, and a nationwide spiral of violent crime, the responsibilities of the Army can be expected to increase in this context. Much the same applies to protecting South Africa's extensive but porous land borders, where twenty-three Army companies are now deployed on average throughout the year.

The Constitution also vests the Army with direct responsibility for maintaining overall law and order in collaboration with the SAPS. As we have seen, this underpinned the mechanics of state repression under apartheid. Today, however, interoperability between the military and police is essential if the police are incapable of maintaining internal stability at a basic level. Both the NDF and the SAPS worked closely in determining the security framework for the April 1994 national and 1995 local elections and continued to do so for the 1999 elections, when approximately 20 percent of all security forces were deployed to the still volatile Kwa-Zulu–Natal region. Ongoing political violence and escalating crime associated with economic inequality and inflated expectations of liberation reinforced the principle of collaboration between the security forces enshrined in the Constitution. Although political violence has somewhat abated outside Kwa Zulu–Natal, the struggle between Inkatha and the ANC for dominance in Natal continued to demand an average monthly deployment of some 4,000 soldiers two years after the 1994 elections.[29] Yet criminal violence has largely displaced political violence as a major social problem to the point where it is seen as a threat to public order and national security. "Serious crime," the military noted, "has become a regular feature in the Republic," which "if unchecked can seriously jeopardize order and undermine the faith of the public in the government's ability, the SAPS and the SANDF more generally."[30]

The military–civil police link has consequently intensified and will continue as long as illegal trafficking in arms and drugs, car-jackings, taxi violence, and other deviant behavior define civil society. This is reflected in the National Crime Prevention Strategy, which implies national coordination between government departments, including the NDF, whose internal deployment now takes place within this framework. An undesirable situation has arisen: Much of the operational energy and conventional capability of the armed forces is now invested in cooperative work with the SAPS in conducting police operations both on and within the Republic's borders.[31] In 1997 some fifty-four Army companies (roughly 6,000–8,000 soldiers) were being maintained on a routine basis to provide support to the SAPS,[32] with approximately 60 percent in area protection, involving joint operations between the SAPS and rear-area NDF territorials to protect farming communities, and the remainder on the borders, where operations are directed at the interdiction of drugs, light weapons, and masses of illegal immigrants seeking employment and wealth in the new South Africa.[33] Most border operations take place along Mozambique and Zimbabwe, although the NDF is also used extensively at Lesotho, where stock theft by heavily armed groups is seen to "blatantly violate [South Africa's] territorial integrity."[34] During 1996, the NDF carried out 20,414 internal operations, including some 10,000 foot and vehicle patrols and 3,192 "farm visits" in rural areas. Some 4,600 operations were undertaken by Eastern Transvaal Command, 3,387 by Free State Command, and 2,741 by Witwatersrand Command in the Gauteng area. An average of seventeen companies are permanently deployed in urban and densely populated rural areas to carry out roadblocks, vehicle control, and cordon-and-search operations.

Several major operations to combat criminal activity (Jamba I–III) have been carried out jointly between the NDF and the SAPS, either to prevent crime nationwide or to eliminate crime in certain regions. Given the large scale of these activities, the NDF's rapid-deployment and rapid-reaction forces—including its elite Special Forces—have been sucked into a semi-permanent internal deployment vaguely reminiscent of total strategy but without its political framework. Internal responsibilities have also reached beyond the Army to embrace the special capabilities and assets of the other arms of service. The SAAF, as the Defence Review noted, has "air space surveillance and control capability which can . . . assist in the protection of the Republic's air space against smuggling and illegal entry." During 1996, the SAAF provided the SAPS with thousands of flying hours involving command and control, troop transport, and visual reconnaissance, mainly in the Gauteng and Kwa-Zulu–Natal areas. Since crimes such as smuggling and illegal entry have a maritime dimension, the Navy is unavoidably involved in collaboration with the SAPS (as well as Environmental Affairs, Home Affairs, and the Revenue Services) in coastal patrols. Ultimately, SAMS provides medical support to the NDF and the SAPS during crime-control operations.[35]

The effectiveness of these operations in the ongoing war against what are, in many respects, the results of past SADF operations to destabilize the region—arms smuggling, drug trafficking, and the like—is a matter of interpretation. NDF claims that it interdicted 1,922 illegal handguns and homemade weapons during 1996[36] seems paltry when measured against the massive proliferation of sophisticated light weapons estimated to be moving into the country. The 36,370 illegal immigrants apprehended by the NDF over the same period also appears disproportionately small when seen against the backdrop of the millions of illegals now presumed resident in the Republic. Yet evidence suggests that a military presence in an area reduces crime.[37]

The desirability of this intensive internal deployment of South Africa's armed forces so soon after democratization is also at issue. Public opinion, particularly among the growing numbers of crime victims, generally supports these developments when SAPS is incapable of exercising its own primary function. Weakness and contradiction in the entire criminal justice system, some of it related to the uncertainty of transition, reinforce this attitude among taxpayers (black and white) who demand that the armed forces be cost-effective and fully utilized given no discernable external threat. Public hysteria over crime has also infected interest groups within government and the wider defense community, who argue that internal deployment be elevated to a primary rather than collateral function if the armed forces are to legitimate continued claims on the national budget.

These views are not shared by military leaders or the defense establishment. They see the work of the military in the area of law and order as restoration rather than maintenance, question the training and skills of the armed forces for police support, and ultimately ascribe to the traditional notion of the military as a shield against external enemies. Opinion in these circles is concerned with the potential political spillover of internal deployment on the current process of reprofessionalism, and most officers have no desire to relive the deep social involvements and disunifying experiences of the past. Military leaders, it must be strongly emphasized, are not insensitive to the tradition of interoperability between security forces bred by apartheid (although cooperation of this type has not left a legacy of interinstitutional harmony); neither is the NDF High Command immune to social pressure in the fight against crime, especially as a threat to national security. Yet feelings against direct use of the military in this arena have been sufficient for the NDF to formulate its own crime-prevention philosophy within the context of the NCPS. The new DOD has also established liaison mechanisms to facilitate (or, some would argue, manage and even control) communication between the NDF and the SAPS. As we have noted, the support lent to democratization by the armed forces has been premised on disengagement and civilianization; in these circumstances there is, to be fair, limited enthusiasm in the higher reaches of the military for blurring the crucial distinction between civil and military affairs. This is all the more so since recent history makes clear that operations of this type tend to undermine the preparedness, capabilities, and public image of the NDF. As professional soldiers, military leaders do *not* regard the NDF as an appropriate institution for combating crime, which the generals see quite correctly as firmly within the preserve of the police force under normal circumstances. The primary task on the agenda of the armed forces is to establish legitimacy as part of the consolidation process, and hence there is anxiety that NDF participation in crime control and other internal activities will encourage repoliticization of the soldiers, undermine their credibility in the eyes of the general population, and remilitarize the community.[38] Despite the recent past, military leaders are, as pointed out by the Defence Review, "unwilling to apply military solutions to political problems except in extreme conditions where government regulates a state of emergency." Given the international experiences of democratic consolidation, which reflect the danger to civil society of using armed forces internally, this is the correct position.

The operational costs of internal deployment place stress on the defense budget and indirectly strains the economy insofar as large numbers of part-time soldiers are called up for service. During 1996, for example, the 5,000 flying hours provided by the SAAF cost R6.3 million,[39] and SAN's Operation Harder involved eighty sorties and over 564 hours for a further R744 million. Some of these costs are recoverable, yet internal deployment is antithetical to the objective of the NDF to project itself as highly professional, cost-effective, and ultimately apolitical. Military and political leaders concur that the long-term solution to escalating crime and violence is socioeconomic development to alleviate inequalities inherited from apartheid, as well as the restructuring of the SAPS on a firm financial, administrative, and community foundation. This would create the ideal situation from the perspective of the armed forces, where the SAPS could assume full responsibility for policing, allowing the military to downgrade force levels for internal operations and then exit to the barracks (barring national emergency, of course).

Given South Africa's crime and political problems, as well as the availability internal capabilities, the situation is unlikely to change. The NDF recognizes "definite responsibilities and obligations towards crime prevention and the maintenance of law and order,"[40] and so the NDF is willing, if not enthusiastic, to maintain current levels of internal deployment both for area defense and border protection as ordained in Section 227 of the Constitution. This is, however, subject to clearly specified criteria that, to military planners, limit the overall damage to institutional and corporate interests. The NDF, for example, is far more comfortable with border protection than, for example, cordon-and-search support. Illegal weapons proliferation has even been described by the NDF as "the most significant contributory factor to crime in the country."[41] Border patrol has also freed up the SAPS to combat crime. As a matter of policy, the military has insisted that distinctions be drawn between the respective roles and that the NDF abjure such routine police functions such as investigation, interrogation, and courtroom support. Although maintaining a collaborative stance, the NDF insists that it maintain independence of command and control over its troops at the national level. A liaison committee established by the DOD is intended to be a communications mechanism and will delineate the roles, methods, and duties between the police and the military.

Reflecting their reluctance, the armed forces have laid down specific directives for transitional collaboration with the SAPS (as well as local and regional authorities). As of mid-1997, these included the elaboration of a code of conduct and appropriate rules of engagement, explicit agreements on the duration of NDF deployments, ongoing reviews, and time frames for extracting the military from policing. In addition, the NDF has conditioned its participation in the NCPS on combating only those crimes that threaten the constitutional dispensation of the state, those where international practice demands military involvement, and "serious crimes" of one sort or another "where the SANDF has played a significant role in the past."[42] Although this rather ambiguous, the NDF is committed to distancing itself from criminal activity insofar as is tactically and politically possible. Still, the postmodern concept of national security embraces most anything with implications for the well being of the state: violation of national airspace, extended political unrest leading to civil disobedience, attacks on farms and stock theft, illegal immigration, and weapons smuggling.

The JPSCD has been advised that NDF involvement in the fight against crime is subject to "continuous review,"[43] and the Defence Review stated unambiguously that the long-term aim of the DOD and the Department of Safety and Security is to create conditions for total withdrawal of the NDF from a policing role. It was projected that the NCPS would bear fruit after the 1999 elections—this remains to be seen—and it is estimated that the primary rational for the military will be peace operations. This ongoing review will also conceivably include the role of the military in border protection. Until this is attained, however, SAPS-NDF cooperation, the Defence Review added, will continue under strictly regulated conditions, legislation, presidential authorization, the Bill of Rights, and parliamentary safeguards designed to inhibit military reentry into the civil arena. Insofar as it is obligated to participate in the war against crime, the NDF prefers that it be done properly and in a spirit military leaders feel comfortable with (read: strict strategic management). Hence, in 1997 the national Joint Security Staff structure, linked to security committees at provincial and local levels as well as the nine regional military commands, was established to coordinate all joint operations between the security forces along lines vaguely reminiscent of total strategy. In dealing with crime as a facet of maintaining national order, plans have also been laid to incorporate all stakeholders in the National Crime Prevention Strategy into the Joint Security Staff. The NDF would indeed welcome the replacement of the NCP Secretariat with some sort of statutory body "to ensure that all plans with regard to crime prevention and combatting thereof are coordinated and executed."[44]

The issue of the military providing collateral utility, like much else in South Africa today, is in a state of flux. This reflects the shrinking defense budget, the intensity of social demands, and finite limits in skills and institutional capacity in the military as well as other public- and private-sector organizations. The armed forces, as we have repeatedly noted, sees nonmilitary involvement as economically inefficient and politically unwise, and this colors not only reactions to the RDP but also its full range of secondary functions. The NDF would prefer to see the Service Corps transferred to some other state department and in the Defence Review clearly indicates that the armed forces will not as a matter of principle undertake secondary functions except at the specific request of other government departments, with the consent of communities, and subject to civilian control and clearly specified time frames. Force design, the military has insisted, is also "largely structured to meet the primary objectives [of the NDF] as stated in the Constitution,"[45] and collateral utility, it emphasized, is not a "force designer." This does not necessarily reflect a lack of civic responsibility on the part of the armed forces but rather the fact that collateral utility is expensive, an added administrative burden when the military is engaged in its own internal restructuring, and a strain on manpower. The system of financing collateral services through other state departments is ambiguous, and in many instances the armed forces themselves are burdened with the costs despite their own diminishing resources.

The enormous costs of integration have also forced the military to become more introspective, and for the foreseeable future the social and development services provided by the NDF will have to be balanced against its internal demands and requirements. SAMS resources, for example, have frequently been strained or outpaced by the accelerated integration of former NSF personnel who bring with them not only unique demands and claims on medical services but also a network of dependents. In the mental-health field, integration has obliged SAMS to reevaluate assessment techniques and initiate new programs to assist integrees with psychological empowerment. As rationalization takes hold, the interest and capability of the SAMS is likely to decline as its becomes preoccupied with the mental health of its primary constituency—the soldiers.[46] The collateral utility of such organizations as the Air Force and Navy also resides in equipment that is fast becoming obsolete and will have to be renewed if the armed forces are to fulfill their primary and secondary functions. As South Africa is drawn into regional and continental conflicts, it can also be anticipated that the capacity of the military to service local and international constituencies will become competitive and inconsistent.

Ultimately, the military may be unable to continue providing much in the way of collateral utility. A transformed military is all very well, but society must be prepared to carry the costs of that transformation. For the armed forces to extend their already invaluable contribution to the democratic project, the state needs to consider and then legislate social assets that meet the financial, technical, and human needs of the military. Only then will the NDF be able to maximize its input to assist the realization of the ideals contained in the Constitution, the Defence Review, and the White Paper.

External Deployment: The Dilemmas of Peacekeeping

In the meantime, the military's contribution to social development is likely to involve what the armed forces know best, that is, providing South Africa with a security framework. Within that, accelerated social reconstruction under RDP, GEAR, or any other program can conceivably function. Within this context, the Army is tasked, as always, with the mission to hold land and, if necessary, to seize territory and engage in hot-pursuit operations to defeat or deter aggression in accord with principles of international law. This, however, represents yet another departure from the past, when neighboring territory was ravaged in cavalier fashion by the SADF's permanent force of professionals serviced by a huge white conscript army. Postdemocratic strategic discourse and planning has in fact opted for a defensive posture for a mixture of political and financial reasons. The Defence Review, in addition, underwrites an affordable military, and this has come down to the core force design in which a relatively small body of high-tech professional soldiers carry out the defense mandate. As in countries where the experience of the Gulf War reemphasized the critical importance of air superiority, the Air Force is assigned the normal responsibilities of maintaining a deterrent capability to ensure local dominance in the air, performing surveillance missions along the borders, and guarding sea margins in territorial waters and the adjoining economic zones. Given South Africa's dependence on international trade and its vast yet poorly policed coastline, the force structure and design of the Navy is geared to a variety of maritime functions to secure the sea surface and submarine areas. These include defense of the sea-lanes and primary ports like Durban, Cape Town and Richards Bay, antimining activities, interdiction against piracy and smuggling, action in times of environmental crisis, and missions to show the flag in support of foreign policy in times of peace and war.

With increased global and regional interdependence, it is generally accepted in the mainstream of the post-transitional defense debate that the NDF will also have to perform several tasks along or even across the borders of states that it once attempted to destabilize as part of the total strategy to erect a curtain around the Republic and its neighbors during the 1970s and 1980s. Southern Africa, for example, contains an enormous concentration of weapons left over from the Cold War that support banditry, racketeering, political conflict, and general crime throughout the region. The availability of small arms and lack of controls over distribution are, in the words of one analyst, "a much greater threat to the Southern African region than the proliferation of weapons of mass destruction, be they nuclear, chemical or biological."[47] Since South Africa has thousands of kilometers of porous borders touching no less than six countries, many arms spill into the Republic, whose military will remain enmeshed in all sorts of missions arising out of the underdevelopment of its neighbors. As previous Deputy Defence Minister Kasrils has pointed out, these can be readily accommodated in a development-type postapartheid conception of national security, because most regional problems impact directly or indirectly on the RDP given South Africa's position as the economic powerhouse of the subcontinent.[48]

South Africa's battle-tested Army already spends a great deal of time and energy countering a rag-tag invasion of illegal immigrants who cross over from Zimbabwe, Mozambique, and Swaziland (conservatively estimated at 2,000 per month), then gravitate to the economic heartland of Gauteng where, according to some reports, they contribute to crime and community conflict over jobs and access to social services.[49] Since humanitarian activities are important mechanisms for accumulating political influence and building positive interstate relations, the military's long tradition of collateral utility will also require extension to the wider region in times of natural and human-made disasters.

Beyond this skeletal framework, there is no consensus as to the exact nature and components of national security and, by extension, the social role of the military as guardian. This partially reflects the failure of South Africa to determine a foreign policy (largely because of bureaucratic struggles within the Department of Foreign Affairs as elements of the old and new order jockey for position). The failure of the first post-transition foreign minister, Alfred Nzo, to impose a unifying framework incorporating the values of specialist personnel inherited from apartheid and upwardly mobile political and career appointees from the ANC, has meant that foreign policy, the natural handmaiden of defense, has remained erratic, incoherent, and vague. Given the Republic's unique moral status on the global stage at the moment, such uncertainty over national interest and security is ironic.

Two largely polar positions—with ethical and practical components—have emerged. On the one hand, there are many South Africans who do not regard global and regional security initiatives as a *vital* national interest, least of all when democracy remains fragile locally and domestic problems deprive the majority of citizens of economic and spiritual well-being. Although recognizing the poverty, starvation, and displacement in neighboring countries, this inward (some would argue xenophobic) vision of foreign policy is not sympathetic to the view held in other circles: South Africa carries a moral burden for the area as a result of its advantaged position as well as the havoc wrought by its security forces during the period of regional destabilization. It is at this point that developmentalists and military leaders form a curious alliance. South Africa, both would argue, should indeed disseminate its democratic experience, but it needs to avoid overexpenditure of scarce domestic resources; neither does it need to involve itself in the affairs of others, whether unilaterally or multilaterally, notwithstanding commitments to international treaties and conventions. Security is, in the strictest sense, national and essentially military.

Others take a broader view whereby security encompasses economic, cultural, and even environmental factors, keeping with the trend for interdependency in the international system. Within ruling ANC circles, for example, their is a powerful belief that the party is ethically indebted to the outside world for its survival during the years of struggle and that South Africa's consequent national interests are inextricably linked to the democratic movement worldwide. Within the continent of Africa, Deputy Foreign Minister Aziz Pahad has pointed out, South Africa has extensive reserves of "moral authority derived from its own process of national reconciliation and democratization" that can be brought to bear on other countries, particularly in the surrounding region, where few states practice democratic principles.[50] Sub-Saharan Africa, the moral lobby would add, has seen approximately three dozen conflicts with 10 million deaths since the end of World War II, and newly liberated South Africa has the duty and the opportunity to play a constructive role in stabilization and the alleviation of human suffering. The moral stature of Mandela must inevitably diminish with his departure from the political stage, and South Africa must now grasp the nettle by exploiting the possibilities for international influence through its adherence to the UN Charter and membership in the Organization of African Unity (OAU). Less sentimentally, trade with East Africa and southern Africa has risen sharply since transition, and the positive balance of payments is strong inducement for local businesses to favor an inclusive and participatory vision of foreign policy, particularly on the subcontinent.

The private sector in particular sees an outward foreign policy—ideally in tandem with other powerful international actors—as essential in accessing the commodities, markets, and foreign investment that support the South African economy.[51] For its part, the military is supportive of international engagement at least partially because the armed forces see modernization through international contacts as part of the payback for participation in the democratic process.[52]

Democracy has opened up South Africa. The result is a flood of international representatives to Pretoria as well as a distinct trend in public and government opinion away from cultural isolationism. Beyond the ANC's feelings of historic debt to those who supported the liberation struggle, at a more practical level South Africa is the heartland of power relationships (economic, military, political) in the subcontinent. Ex-Foreign Minister Nzo has consequentially labeled isolation from the region as "unrealistic and hazardous," and President Thabo Mbeki has reinforced a regional agenda that designates southern African countries and the Southern African Development Community (SADC) as priorities in international relations, particularly in terms of South Africa's newfound commitment to the concept of an African Renaissance.[53]

Despite this shift toward international participation, however, it remains debatable which international commitments are vital interest category. Any interest can become vital if it is worth defending militarily. Complex issues of international relations are, however, outside the scope of this book. Suffice it to say that the broader perspective on security and foreign policy increases the likelihood of military intervention in Africa by a historically insulated South Africa with "special knowledge." Despite (or possible because of) South Africa's unhealthy tradition of regional intervention, former Deputy Minister of Defence Kasrils has tentatively added his voice to the regionalists who emphasize the potential of South Africa to play a role in continent-building by extending its democratic experiences into Africa, southern Africa in particular.[54] South Africa, he has argued, has an obligation to make Africa "safe for democracy"—and, one might add, safe for South Africa as well.

It is unrealistic to expect South Africa to avoid any future military commitment, at least in the adjacent region, where it enjoys economic, military, and political hegemony. The nature of such a commitment could, however, take various forms and conceivably include a reversion to policies of regional intervention in which the military has some element of accumulated experience. Despite the Republic's newly democratic character and disavowal of militarism, one cannot entirely exclude the dangerous possibility of South Africa becoming an imperial power (consciously or not) through its natural regional hegemony or acting energetically, as would any state, to counter outright future threats by hostile governments, organizations, states, or individuals. Chapter 4.8 of the draft White Paper, one suspects, is perhaps a little too enthusiastic (or naive) in its understanding of national interests in its assertion that South Africa "does not now and will not in the future have aggressive intentions towards any other state." Protecting friendly neighbors could, for example, induce intervention in a structurally unstable environment characterized by insufficient development, chronic unemployment, and excessive population growth. South Africa's impatience with the inability of Mozambique to interdict the movement of guns, narcotics, and hijacked cars across their common eastern border has already led to an agreement that allows hot-pursuit operations by South African forces seeking to combat smugglers in areas where police forces on both sides lack access.[55] Regional involvement (as opposed to outright aggression) implies South African development aid to assist basic infrastructure and social reforms, cooperative action between states of the subcontinent, and traditional peacekeeping, peace enforcement, and humanitarian and law-and-order missions.

Economic interdependence between southern African countries with the Republic at the center has existed (and been exploited by the South Africans) for many years, and today South Africa is the only regional actor with the capacity to partially fill the financial and material gap that continues to hinder collective peacekeeping in the region. Since transition, the Republic has moved rapidly (perhaps too rapidly) to participate in organizations to enhance cooperative behavior and responsibility for regional security. A newly democratic South Africa became a member of the Southern African Development Community in 1994 and is now prominent in many of its councils and sectoral committees. This includes the key new institution for regional defense and security, the Organ for Politics, Defence, and Security (OPDS), whose role encompasses summit-level, accelerated, joint, and flexible responses in the interests of peacekeeping.[56] Its objectives also include, inter alia, a common foreign policy and a joint international lobby, a Mutual Defence Pact, training for peacekeeping, and mechanisms to address extraregional conflicts that impact peace and security in southern Africa.[57]

The interoperability of military training and equipment is an item on the agenda of the Inter-State Defence and Security Committee (ISDSC), to which South Africa adhered in 1994 and which is designated as the security organ of SADC. The end of the Cold War and the termination of the struggle against apartheid have also energized the OAU to consider permanent structures for resolving interstate conflict. Since the end of apartheid, South Africa has become actively involved in the OAU; in June 1993 the Republic became a founding member of the transitional Central Mechanism for Conflict Prevention, Management,, and Resolution and South Africa is now a member of the peacekeeping arm of the continent, the Organ for Politics, Defence, and Security. In his capacity as deputy president, Mbeki previously held persistent talks with the OAU on issues of collective security where South African participation would doubtlessly raise its own esteem, both continentally and within the United Nations, where the Republic is now in the process of seeking Security Council membership.

From the strictly military perspective, international involvement could well assist integration in the NDF as soldiers from different racial and political backgrounds become engaged in operations in neutral areas outside the country. Peace-related operations would also test the mettle of new recruits and create career incentives for recruits and officers from the former NSFs. This conceivably could take the edge off white anxiety about artificial affirmative-action promotions, and many soldiers would welcome the opportunity to use their professional skills for promotion purposes rather than wait until a tangible threat confronts South Africa. It is still, however, far from clear that South Africa "has . . . firmly place its armed forces in the regional context" and whether peacekeeping within the region will emerge as a primary mission of the NDF in the immediate future.[58]

Notwithstanding the fact that a dedicated regional peacekeeping force is still relatively far in the offing, Minister Modise has made the point that other countries are "desperate" for South African regional involvement (particularly in protecting undefended coastlines).[59] In June 1995, Namibia entered a comprehensive agreement with South Africa on crossborder policing to combat drug, arms, and vehicle smuggling through joint patrols and the sharing of specialist technology. A border liaison committee has been established between Mozambique and South Africa to deal with illegal crossborder movement of goods and people, which might lead to a cooperative defense agreement. Illegal movement on a large scale also takes place across the northern border with Zimbabwe; comparable agreements are likely to be more difficult in this case given Zimbabwe's frustration in being displaced as the regional powerhouse.[60]

The rhetoric of regional cooperation is diffusive; a good beginning, there is little substance in most of the multilateral institutions set in place. In the OPDS, for example, there is a keen sense of the power disparity between the Republic and its neighbors. Despite its responsibility for regional defense and security, OPDS is conceived of as an "informal" organization whose chairmanship is annually rotatable "in order to avoid suspicion in this highly sensitive area."[61] This is not unrelated to the power struggles between small actors with an inflated sense of prestige despite South African hegemony. Most of the SADC's dozen members appear to recognize the need for Africans to take responsibility (especially in light of growing Africa fatigue worldwide) or, as some would put it more diplomatically, "primary ownership of their own problems."[62] This must inevitably involve South Africa. At the same time, all are sensitive to the fact that their ability to make independent choices is seriously constricted by South Africa's dominance of the regional agenda.

As evidenced by such gatherings like the SADC Secretariat meeting in Lilongwe in February 1995, or the attempt to establish an Association of Southern African States as the security arm of SADC in Johannesburg a few months later, ideas exported from South Africa are viewed with considerable trepidation. South Africa, in turn, is inclined to ride roughshod over initiatives originating from other sources. Among these sources, including some of the world's poorest states, there is a distinct fear that behind the benign language of nation-building and peaceful engagement lies a well-developed tradition of South African economic coercion and military interference. Although it was the work of the apartheid government, the track record does not inspire confidence. The NDF has echoed its deputy minister's concern with democratic continent-building by defining help to "emerging democracies in building civil-military relations consistent with democracy" through educational programs and practical support.[63] In a suspicious environment, however, innocent gestures contain a subtext of interference and intervention, since most countries in the region are not stable, democratic, or embodiments of civil-military systems as in South Africa.

The case of Mozambique, whose internal problems are unremittingly consequential for the Republic, is particularly instructive of the harsh power framework within which polite dialogue over regional peace is conducted. South Africa is impatient with its neighbor's inability to help secure the common border against smuggling and the turmoil sown by struggle between Renamo and Frelimo (the two movements that fought the civil war in Mozambique until the national elections of 1994). The situation is complicated by South Africa's growing vested interest in the planned Maputo Corridor (a major development corridor running from the industrial heartland through the Mpumalanga region and eventually to the port of Maputo), and the massive Cahora Bassa hydroelectric scheme. This will ultimately allow the Electricity Supply Commission to dominate the power networks of sub-Saharan Africa.[64] These are, by any definition, vital interests for South Africa, where peace is likely to become more fragile should Mozambique's demobilization deteriorate into renewed civil violence. In that eventuality, Mozambique's military has not entirely discounted South African intervention to secure the Cahora transmission lines and the narrow territory on both sides of the corridor should security circumstances warrant.

There is a possibility that the ISDSC will become a major player in preventative diplomacy and the mechanism for multilateral military, police, and intelligence coordination. Yet the ISDSC is not without problems. Like the OPDS, ISDSC has an agenda embracing everything from the prevention of coups d'état to exchange of information on drug trafficking and measures to combat "religious extremism."[65] As an instrument for military cooperation and collaboration in the interests of regional peace, ISDSC is also an important step forward by virtue of its Defense Sub-Committee, with its various substructures concerned with operations, intelligence, maritime, and aviation affairs. Yet ISDSC remains an informal institution without a permanent secretariat. Competitive struggles over leadership have plagued initial attempts to set the ISDSC in place, and a rotatable chairmanship has similarly come to be seen as a way out of the impasse. South Africans have nevertheless played a preponderant role from the outset, with Modise as chair and NDF personnel in key positions throughout the committee system. At one point, General Meiring was head of the Defense Sub-Committee, Vice Admiral R.C. Simpson-Anderson was chair of the Standing Maritime Committee, and the SAAF was strategically placed in the Aviation Committee. This may well reflect regional power realities, but to some southern Africans, particularly military leaders sensitive to their marginal status, such arrangements institutionalize South African dominance.

NDF offers to assist the development of professionalism, though well-intentioned, are regarded as particularly galling and paternalistic. Although reluctant to comment on the internal affairs of other officer corps, some senior personnel in the regional armies privately express reservations about the NDF's own integration program, which they regard as an unfortunate prototype for interstate military relations. The structural facilitation and coordination currently on offer from South Africa and essential for regional initiatives is given due credit by most regional leaders, military and political. Much less welcome, however, is South African enthusiasm for pooling defense resources inherent in what Modise has termed "joint defensive concept and capability."[66] Some of the sensibilities are not lost on South Africans. Deputy Minister Kasrils has previously indicated that it is undesirable for South Africa to become a continental "big brother,"[67] while in the NDF there is some caution about flexing military muscle and encouraging perceptions of auxiliary status among other continental countries at this point. A regional nonaggression pact to encourage a sense of participation among all actors will probably be concluded in the near future, but a more fundamental mutual defense treaty (of the order proposed at the Windhoek conference of July 1994) is most unlikely despite the fact that the Republic has opted for a nonthreatening force design and defensive posture.

South Africa will have to tread cautiously in the framework for common security in southern Africa.[68] Regional security initiatives will have to surmount structural constraints that mirror the abject conditions of most African countries. The OAU, despite indications of arousal from Cold War inertia, is composed of profoundly underdeveloped nations, most of whom are far from contributing in any meaningful way to collective security. This is reflected at the regional level, where there is limited institutional capacity for any sort of security operation. As made clear at the Council of Ministers meeting held in Johannesburg in January 1996, SADC is no exception to the rule: It lacks funds, logistical support structures, managerial expertise, and the staff to drive integrative visions. Here, the failure of the Secretariat to consult ministries (especially Defence and Police) in drafting recommendations is indicative of serious shortfalls in organizational capacity for liaison and communication among component militaries.

The Department of Foreign Affairs and the military largely concur in the belief that regional initiatives require considerable sensitivity to the structural weaknesses of neighboring states and should be paced according to their very limited developmental capacity. Behind such polite conceptions, both institutions are keenly aware that South Africa runs the risk of bearing the brunt of regional security, a situation that is likely to worsen rather than improve. Regional involvement, particularly in peacekeeping, will also require much closer cooperation between these two actors, which continue a tradition of separate policymaking. Under militarization, defense considerations tended to have a first-order impact over foreign policy decisions for the subcontinent, and as recent peacekeeping operations in Lesotho indicate, the legacy of institutional struggles is still a factor in MOD–Foreign Affairs relations, irrespective of the changes taking place in both organizations. The different pace of change, however, is also a problem given the tendency of some senior policymakers in Foreign Affairs to regard it as far more representative and psychologically attuned to the progressive nature of the new South Africa and southern Africa.

Even were the NDF to develop a consultative and mutually reciprocal policymaking relationship with the Foreign Affairs, inclusion of peacekeeping in its mission would have implications for the organization, size, and structure of the military. The universal experience indicates peacekeeping demands a special configuration of personnel and equipment that emphasizes enhanced air- and sea-lift capacity, light infantry, organic intelligence collection, the development of specialist observer-monitoring battalions, dedicated communications surveillance equipment, special nonlethal weaponry, special training programs for civic actions in support of operations short of war, and appropriate command structures.[69] Some of these elements can be factored into the NDF's current force design as it moves toward light, deployable, and maintenance capabilities appropriate to the rapid-reaction forces now being developed in the United States and NATO.[70] Yet several powerful doctrinaire interests, particularly in the conservative ranks of the Army, have a mixture of professional and institutional stakes in maintaining the NDF as a heavy force. They are not especially open to strategic reorientation as an additional item on an agenda that includes financial shortfalls, integration, and changes in organizational culture. Irrespective of strategic orientation, virtually all senior officers are cautious about peacekeeping being able to create effective government and promote national reconciliation in war-torn foreign countries. Training for peacekeeping, it should be added, normally presupposes the existence of a conventional capacity on the part of soldiers. This means that until such a time as these capabilities are developed among new members of the armed forces from MK and APLA, peace work is likely to be the preserve of members of the former SADF component. "Units sent on peace-keeping operations at this stage," it has been noted, "would still reflect the old order."[71]

This problem of representivity in advanced training has in turn led some commentators to conclude that the armed forces lack the special military and political dynamics appropriate to peacekeeping . This is especially pertinent to the weaker service arms fighting for their very existence. Some moves to counter the backlog have, however, been initiated by organizations such as the Institute for Security Studies working in collaboration with the Norwegian government and the British Army Staff College to educate Southern African militaries in conflict containment and stabilization work outside the framework of normal missions and training. The NDF agreed to collaborate with ISS in a three-month series of orientation exercises designed to introduce the doctrine, planning, command, and control of peace-support operations at strategic, tactical, and operational levels. In September 1996, for example, Exercise Morning Star (involving officers from the NDF, SADC, the ISDSC and Ghana) began with a series of seminars at the Army College at Voortrekkerhoogte and culminated in tactical exercises geared to peacekeeping and peace enforcement at Lohatla battlefield in the following November.[72] This, however, is a rare collaborative program between civil society and a military largely accustomed to an apartheid heritage of maximum unilateralism and autonomy in the management of its own affairs.

There is in principle and practice a vast difference between soldiers attending lectures on humanitarian law, conflict resolution, and the nature of UN peacekeeping, on the one hand, and the actual commitment of resources on the other. Civil society organizations such as ISS, IDASA, and the University of the Witwatersrand's Public and Development Management Program play a valuable role in suggesting agendas for regional cooperation to government officials and the NDF, but they are very much on the margins of NDF policymaking. There are also limits to the pressure that can be exerted by international military institutions on the decisionmaking of the NDF. Despite past pressure from the U.S. military, for example, the NDF has studiously avoided making any substantial commitments to intervention in Central Africa. The armed forces in the process of defining their future are understandably reluctant to risk the possibility of inextricable involvement in the Byzantine world of African social conflicts even while professing that they have that special knowledge of the area, particularly the immediate region.

Regional involvement is also not especially attractive to a public that is tantalized by new prospects to raise the prestige of South Africa abroad yet continues to see domestic priorities as the key to public policymaking. From a developmental perspective, it is far from clear how occasional military forays into Africa can contribute to meaningful change given the deep structural nature of conflict in most African countries—certainly not to the degree necessary to justify allocations of scarce resources from local programs of reconstruction and development. Supporters of the RDP tend to concur with the isolationist vision of foreign policy that precludes diversions for peacekeeping, on much the same grounds as arguments for cutting the defense budget. The loss of South African lives in the international interest is an emerging issue in the defense debate following the deaths of half a dozen NDF soldiers in the 1998 Lesotho incursion—and this is more likely to dampen rather than encourage enthusiasm for future peace operations. The dedicated and rapid reaction capability supplementary to mainstream military work of the type now being discussed in U.S. defense circles is clearly ruled out in such circumstances where South Africa is still "not apparently crowding to buy into the notion of an African peace-keeping body."[73] Even more limited regional involvement continues to remain on the margins of national security. Still, peacekeeping operations could route new members from the former NSFs with limited capabilities for conventional operations.

Other pressures, domestic and international, also lever peacekeeping into the operational universe of the South African military. As the draft White Paper indicated, South Africa is committed (subject to reasonable conditions) to international peacekeeping as a member of the global community. Although the military is not about to be steamrolled into casual force deployments, low-risk and brief missions with clear objectives are not anathema, particularly if they have no impact on the already strapped defense budget.

With a eye to many expensive yet abortive UN peacekeeping missions in places such as Somalia, Liberia, and Angola, the major players in the Security Council are also keen that Africa, particularly the OAU, take on more responsibility for its own peace, especially at the regional level. This includes the British, who have convened various bilateral and multilateral workshops on African peacekeeping in such diverse places as Cairo, Harare, and Gaberone over the last few years, and the French, who proposed a Rapid African Intervention Force working at the subcontinental level during the 1994 Biarritz Summit. Against a backdrop of ongoing war in Angola and ethnic violence in the Great Lakes area and the Congo, the United States in particular would like to maneuver South Africa into its own OAU-endorsed African Crisis Response Force to create safe areas where civilians can receive humanitarian assistance in cases of insurrection, civil war, or genocide. Former U.S. Secretary of State Warren Christopher sought to exploit this avenue with an offer to organize, train, equip, and finance such a initiative with $25 million during his visit to the Republic in October 1996. Whether such a surrogate initiative is sustainable, however, depends on energizing South African support in military and foreign policy circles. With the exception of the odd African country such as Mali and Ethiopia, there is little support for this Americentric initiative in OAU circles with its emphasis on African solutions to continental problems. France, with its own African interests, is also not especially responsive, which is important in shaping the attitudes of the European Union, whose financial contribution is necessary to make the project viable.[74]

In a post–Cold War world, where bipolar confrontation has given way to peace interventions, regional and international expectations of South African being savior to Africa are also likely to intensify, particularly if countries like Tanzania and Zimbabwe continue to participate in collective security operations involving forces other than those of the permanent members of the UN Security Council.[75] Africa's supposed decade of democracy is drowning in blood, and subregional conflict resolution is very much on the agenda as the United Nations runs into capacity problems related to global overcommitment. Even though certain leaders, such as President Robert Mugabe of Zimbabwe, temper their enthusiasm for South African participation with a eye to personal and national prestige in the post-Mandela era, South Africa will in all probability have to participate in multilateral peacekeeping, relief, or enforcement operations—particularly in circumstances with moral appeal, along the lines of Rwanda. This does not necessarily mean the Republic becomes a full-fledged member of the core group of "middle nations" regularly contributing to peacekeeping forces through the United Nations Stand-By Arrangement, at least not in the intermediate future.[76]

Apart from any other consideration, military leaders are sensitive to the actual and hidden costs of commitments of this type at a time when the NDF and the UN face financial austerity. Still, should South Africa send its troops across territorial boundaries in support of peace in the near future, it will probably prefer to do so on a multilateral basis, or under the authorization of SADC (as was recently the case in Lesotho), than under OAU or UN auspices. Such would reduce the security burden and risks and counteract suspicions of the Republic's intentions. This has been clearly reflected in the debate following South Africa's undemocratic incursion into Lesotho as well as in discussions between Mandela and the United States over the latter's proposed African crisis force. Lukewarm enthusiasm on the part of the OAU has clearly been influential in shaping South African opinion. Mandela has in turn indicated that such a force must originate within the continent rather than represent an extension of American interests to disengage from costly operations in Africa that figure low among U.S. global priorities in any case.[77] UN endorsement of the project would enhance its marketability to the military and foreign policy establishment, as would additional consultation with sub-Saharan countries and more detail on issues of membership, funding, duration, and control. Even then, NDF leaders are likely to remain skeptical of the primary responsibility envisioned by the Americans for South Africa.

Several items are on the agenda that reflect the cautious but distinct interest of the military to give practical content to the injunctions of the White Paper (i.e., that the NDF take on regional and continental responsibilities). The military and operations subcommittees of the ISDSC have endorsed common planning between member states, standardization of staff, tactics, and equipment, and coordination of intelligence and counterintelligence activities.[78] Inasmuch as these are followed up by annual joint training exercises along the lines of Morning Star, this could contribute to the development of subcontinental esprit de corps among regional armies. Whether this will also help export democratic models of civil-military relations remains an open question.[79] The MOD is also keen to justify maintaining as much of the huge Lohatla battlefield as possible in the face of land-reform pressure emanating from communities, local developmental interests, and the Department of Land Affairs. This augers well for combined military exercises with other countries on the subcontinent and farther afield (if not the local communities with claims to military-owned land at Lohatla and elsewhere). Regional cooperation at this level will doubtlessly include the exchange of military intelligence and cooperation in the use of medical services with states such as Mozambique.

Effective peacekeeping implies the loss of South African lives, and it behooves the NDF (and other regional militaries) to emulate their U.S. and European counterparts in developing contingent capabilities consisting of people and units "trained and equipped to bring non-lethal power, appropriate rules of engagement, and a good deal of patience to bear on situations ranging from the merely disordered to the seriously chaotic, only some of which resemble the kinds of missions to which the military is accustomed and for which it has traditionally been trained."[80] Several staff colleges in African countries such as Ghana, Nigeria, Zambia, and Zimbabwe already offer peacekeeping courses as component features of advanced military training, and South Africa is now adapting to this trend with its emphasis on doctrine, logistics, and the development of early-warning systems.

Since its first involvement (along with Zimbabwe and Botswana) in Lesotho in 1994, South Africa has facilitated peace negotiations and undertaken preventative diplomacy in places such as Angola or Swaziland; this is likely to continue to figure on the agenda of organizations such as ISDSC as a cost-effective means to preempt fighting missions. Suggestions have been made for joint weapons acquisition programs and the creation of hotlines between regional leaders and senior officials.[81] The implications of the former are probably too complex and contentious, but more effective means of communication at the leadership level could well blossom into a regional version of the continental early-warning network envisioned by the Central Organ of the OAU.

Humanitarian assistance is also likely to increase as the South African military struggles between desire for international involvement and anxiety at overinvesting scarce resources.[82] Humanitarian assistance was provided by the NDF to Rwanda in 1994, which is likely to be stepped up along with logistical support, observer missions, cease-fire, and elections monitoring as an extension of collateral utility on the domestic front. Peace-support operations, such as South Africa's air support to the Angolan and Mozambique national elections of 1992 and 1994 respectively, can also be expected to be replicated elsewhere. Collateral utility derived from peacekeeping in the region has been explicitly recognized by senior officers,[83] although many still have difficulty in calculating the costs and benefits so soon after South Africa's preoccupation with forward defense in depth to destabilize the surrounding environment.[84] Lesotho notwithstanding, it appears that a major intervention of South African troops is unlikely until the new domestic order is more fully consolidated and the military is fully disengaged from local law enforcement.

An emerging network of bilateral security arrangements has, however, appeared with early democratization: The national government has signed agreements with various states covering matters from drug smuggling to disaster relief; even provincial governments are in on the act (to the point where the Department of Foreign Affairs was concerned with overlap and discrepancies in foreign policy between the center and the periphery).[85] Mpumalanga, for example, concluded an agreement with the neighboring Mozambican provinces of Gaza and Maputo regarding security, tourist promotion, wildlife protection, and water resources.[86] Such joint ventures will, no doubt, create the infrastructure for more profound multilateral defense and security. Yet South Africa is most likely to lean toward peacekeeping activities (Chapter 6 the UN Charter) rather than peace-enforcement operations (Chapter 7).

The NDF has issued various policy statements that incorporate the above missions, as well as several others, that together indicate its newfound mission in development beyond national boundaries. These include engineering operations, particularly mine-clearing in Mozambique and Angola, assistance with demobilization in both these war-ravaged countries, and the disarmament of paramilitary and irregular forces in the process of peace-support operations.[87] At the ISDSC session held in Cape Town in September 1995, Minister Modise then reiterated the commitment of the NDF to stem crossborder crime and the illegal flow of armaments; to undertake joint intelligence exercises and training; and to assist with confidence- and security-building exercises (such as invitations to SADC countries to observe exercises at Lohatla).[88] A number of measures designed to give operational content to these goals of conflict prevention are already in place. They include the mutual secondment of soldiers, assistance in land-mine clearance, and multilateral structures to coordinate doctrine and logistics. On the downside, official references to peacekeeping, least of all actual deployment of personnel, remain curiously circumscribed.

Bloc Obsolescence and Rearmament

Whether the military can effectively carry out any external function is an intriguing question. Defense funding, it has been noted, "has always been chronic."[89] After World War I, for example, the Union Defence Force came perilously close to disbanding on several occasions with personnel retrenchments, equipment cutbacks, and the disestablishment of units in the face of Depression, all reminiscent of the situation today.[90] Between 1945 and 1960, reduction and decay was common, and virtually no new equipment was procured (apart from a few British Centurion tanks in 1952 and two squadrons of Sabre aircraft three years later).[91] Fortunes fluctuated with an increasingly hostile international environment and domestic mass mobilization, and as late as 1983 military spokesmen were still warning that the apartheid state would have to rely on antiquated weapons systems were the monies devoted to armaments not raised a further percentage point of GNP to compensate for the eroding value of the rand.[92] Even in the years of total strategy, the SADF never entirely escaped the threat of rising domestic inflation combined with the falling purchasing power of the local currency in the underground international arms market.

Yet the "affordable" defense force now proposed clearly impinges the ability of the military to defend current national interests (however defined) and to buy against future contingencies by investing in the defense sector. Even the ongoing transformation of the military from a vast conscript army to a small professional core force is beset by strategic problems related to funding that preclude operational content and clarity. Generally speaking, such base forces should be at once defensive, deterrent, flexible, adaptive, affordable, and cost-efficient. The core-force capability should, in the words of one commentator, consist of such elements as "a balanced and sustainable nucleus with the ability to handle a range of contingencies," the capability "to expand the defence force timeously," sufficient resources to ensure the "upgrading or replacement of equipment and weaponry," and an "an efficient intelligence capability."[93]

This, however, requires funding that in the last analysis is impervious to alternative claims like peace operations. Operational readiness is also a factor in the strategic equation given the fact that the more ready a force the more expensive it becomes—, which itself opens up complex planning issues in the relationships between core, active, and reserve forces. Ultimately, defense planners will have to come to detailed technical decisions regarding the natural level of spending given the overall posture, missions, capabilities, and resources of the armed forces in relation to the industrial base and domestic and international contexts.

Various theorists have argued that "all militaries tend to adhere to more demanding standards of national security than do civilians. . . . Given the soldier's defense responsibilities it is better to err on the side of additional safety by spending more on men and weapons."[94] Be that as it may, some defense analysts and South African military leaders would argue that the budget should be in the region of 3 percent of GNP in order to allow the armed forces to maintain their edge. Any lower is "unnaturally" low and portends the loss of combat capability with appropriate and sustained logistical support.[95] Without available finance, many training programs have already been curtailed, and since 1990 staff levels in command, training, and administrative structures have fallen precipitously (an estimated 11.4 percent).[96] Budget cuts have carried over into the industrial base to negatively affect reconstitution capacity, and the defense industries face a major crisis, with half its workers being laid off. Cutbacks have also had a major effect on morale as officers concur with the CSANDF that the military is fast approaching a dysfunctional state. Esprit de corps has also been deeply affected by the uncertainties generated by impending rationalization, expected to lead to job losses for thousands of people.

All this stands in sharp contrast to the apartheid past, when procurement policies were shaped by political circumstance and opportunity rather than criteria for balanced force design. The result today is weapons systems that face obsolescence, which has important implications for the security framework and, hence, economic development and consolidation.

Budgetary pressures have compounded the problem, forcing the NDF to defer replacement and expansion programs even in the Army, which currently absorbs almost 50 percent of the total defense budget. Despite its role as the main instrument for taking and holding ground in any military, the Army now urgently requires replacement of its internationally acclaimed G5 artillery piece, its Ratel armored cars, and its main battle tanks, such as the Oliphant and its successors.[97] Its armor capacity has been drastically reduced, with both the Buffel and Eland armored cars about to be scrapped. Upgrading is necessary for the Rooikat tank destroyer, and antiaircraft capabilities function at dangerously low levels. The high-tech Air Force, the recipient of 31.9 percent of the 1994–1995 budget, has also been hit by cutbacks, the falling value of the rand, and the rapid obsolescence of tactical aircraft. Bases have been closed following democratization, training programs have been curbed, and some of the SAAF's most famous squadrons have been disestablished with a resultant loss of highly specialist personnel. Long-range patrol capabilities in support of the Navy effectively ended with the demobilization of South Africa's long-serving Shackleton aircraft at the end of the 1980s, and the number of aircraft in the SAAF (791 in 1989) is expected to decline to 390. This implies ten fighter squadrons being reduced to one single supersonic Cheetah squadron if further equipment cannot be procured.[98]

Some procurement needs have already been satisfied with the local production of the Impala Mk2 jet trainer (a new name for the Italian Aeromacchi MB-326M) since 1966 and the delivery of several dozen Pilatus Astra PC-7 MKII trainers to replace Harvards that have been in service for fifty years.[99] Yet the poor quality of available equipment, struggles over representivity between old and new personnel from the former NSFs, low morale, and the lure of the private sector have encouraged the flow of personnel from the SAAF, particularly those strapped to aircraft, that is, combat instructors (each of whom costs an estimated R83 million to train; seven out of twenty have now resigned) and pilots (whose training costs a mere R3 million).[100] The Air Force had in fact lost about 130 pilots between 1995 and 1997 and is now roughly two-thirds undercomplement (bearing in mind the simultaneous resignation of flight engineers, ground crew, air-traffic controllers, and support personnel). The state has lost an estimated R515 million due to resignations between 1993 and 1995, which caused the Chief of the SAAF, General James Kriel (now retired) to break the armed forces' implicit code of silence to endorse the sentiments of former CSANDF General Meiring that the armed forces are fast losing their collateral utility in the provision of emergency services, technological infrastructure, and operational capability.[101] Although this has prompted plans to upgrade the fleet of existing French Mirage fighters (currently known as Cheetahs) in cooperation with the Israeli Defence Force at a cost of R2.6 billion, the SAAF now actually consists of the Cheetahs (some with Russian engines), thirty-year-old Impalas of questionable airworthiness, older Dakotas used in coastal patrols, upgraded C-130 transports, Oryx helicopters, and an assortment of other minor support aircraft.[102]

Obsolescence and limited force levels in major weapons systems confronts the Navy, which has traditionally suffered from the obsession among South African defense planners with landward invasion.[103] Traditionally the guardian of the Cape sea route during the Cold War, the South African Navy, much like its American counterpart, has lost its principle adversary and force-building foil with the collapse of the Soviet Union. The Navy continues to have multiple tasking appropriate to a largely island nation that includes coastal rescue and environmental protection, deep-sea patrolling, monitoring of foreign fishing fleets (in South Africa's 64,000 square kilometers of territorial sea and in its massive Economic Exclusion Zone, more than 1 million square kilometers), the protection of sea-lanes out to two hundred nautical miles, and guarding major ports such as Cape Town and Durban that service trade to the major growth points in the country, including Gauteng.[104]

Its ability to conduct both green- and blue-water operations of both a political-military and maritime nature has, however, been seriously compromised over the years by the inability of the Navy claim a reasonable proportion of the national budget. Today, the Navy still has some capability in surface warfare, mining countermeasures, combat support, and hydrographic services, but, as with the Air Force, it is questionable whether it possesses even a core capability in the form of good all-weather craft with effective sea-keeping qualities.[105] The Navy currently receives a mere 7.4 percent of the defense budget, and in these strained circumstances, naval officers readily admit, many missions are impossible. That includes antisubmarine activities that effectively came to an end with the withdrawal from service of the last Rothesay-class ships and their accompanying Wasp helicopters during the 1980s and the protection of secondary ports such as Mossel Bay, Port Elizabeth, and East London.[106]

In the years following 1984, the personnel component of the Navy dropped from 15,000 to 9,200, and the number of ships has declined from thirty-seven to twenty-four. As in the Army and Air Force, obsolescence has set in, and between 1997 and 2005 it is expected that the Navy will decommission most of its remaining combat vessels.[107] Admiral Simpson Anderson, former Chief of the Navy, has added his voice to that of his Air Force counterpart (former General Kriel) in speaking out sharply—perhaps too sharply as far as the Army is concerned—against budgetary imbalances that sap the ability of the smaller service arms to effectively meet generic defense contingencies. With the exception of two combat support vessels, all naval ships are either too small or too light to cope with the rough seas around the Cape. Unless problems are addressed in the near future, Simpson-Anderson has emphasized, the nation's mediocre Navy can be expected to disappear entirely from the South African armed forces shortly after the turn of the century.[108]

Yet that is unlikely given the survival instincts of bureaucratic institutions. Despite (or because of) its disadvantage, the Navy has begun to take decisive steps to ensure that it does not disappear. As the navy is traditionally the most liberal of the three major service arms, some 55 percent of its personnel our now nonwhite (12 percent African, 12 percent Indian, 30 percent colored); in a time emphasizing equal opportunities and affirmative action, this racial makeup is increasingly used to the advantage of the Navy in accessing the budget.[109]

In a radically new environment absent of definable foes, and in a manner vaguely reminiscent of its U.S. counterpart in the post–Cold War setting, the Navy has also turned to marketing joint operations based on regional and continental contingencies as part of its claims to the public purse. For example, it played a key role in the establishment of the Strategic Maritime Committee to promote peace and regional cooperation under the auspices of the ISDSC following a regional maritime conference held in Cape Town in October 1994 attended by representatives from all Southern African states south of the Equator. Naval personnel repeatedly emphasize that the very real problems of port protection and prevention of mining to disrupt trade routes are replicated several times over in neighboring countries, which also depend on trade but lack maritime forces. Simpson-Anderson frequently alluded to the fact that South Africa is the only state apart from Gabon and Kenya with a meaningful naval capability. This means Namibia, Mozambique, and even Tanzania are unable to protect themselves from giant trawler fleets denuding their rich fishing grounds. The Republic, other naval advocates add, sits aside while vital world sea routes and many countries, both African and non-African, benefit for its provision of various maritime services.

A regional security regime must become, in the words of one maritime defense analyst, "an unnegotiable referent point for any South African naval restructuring."[110] Restructuring, the Navy believes, should also provide for a defensive zone incorporating the Cape Town–Saldanha Bay and Durban–Richards Bay complexes. Ideally, this would be interchangeable with Mossel Bay, Port Elizabeth, and East London. In addition, the Navy would like a maritime warfare capacity, attack strike craft, support vessels, a deterrent submarine capacity, and a heavier platform for deep-sea operations in the economic maritime zone. This was the backdrop to the Navy's efforts during transition to acquire four light corvette-type patrol vessels at a cost of R1.7 billion to upgrade regional capability in blue-water operations. Although a relatively modest request, it was still the largest procurement request and sparked one of the major debates within the defense-development nexus since the initiation of democracy.

The technicalities and movement of this debate have been adequately explored in other studies and follow familiar lines.[111] Thus, proponents of the procurement have projected South Africa as an island economy within which the corvettes are crucial for national and regional maritime defense. In support of the corvette acquisition, local defense analyst Helmut Heitman has, for example, noted that South Africa dominates both the 11,500-kilometer sub-Saharan coastline stretching from Gabon to Kenya and the greater proportion of the EEZ in the area.[112] Other supporters have indicated the fact (often ignored by developmentalists) that the SAN is constitutionally obliged to protect South Africa both above and below water and that it is internationally responsible for hydrographic and search-and-rescue operations in the region by virtue of its membership in the International Maritime Organisation and the International Hydrographic Organisation.[113] Critics have nevertheless predictably questioned the need for corvettes that would be five times bigger than any combat ship in service at a time of financial austerity, reconstruction, and development. What is critical, however, is that years after the initiation of a debate that has come to typify the struggle between military and civil society for scarce social resources, there was every likelihood that the state will soon accede to Navy demands despite intense pressure from various peace and developmental lobbies.[114]

A similar drift toward reinvigorated militarism applies to other service arms, such as the Air Force, where the question is less whether it will acquire the advanced fighting equipment it desperately desires but from whom and at what cost.[115] An armed version of the standard Puma helicopter, in service with the SAAF for several years, was on the agenda, with sixty-one operational and training helicopters planned for delivery at a cost of R1.35 billion within ten years.[116] The Air Force has already decided to purchase six of the locally manufactured, state-of-the-art Rooivalk attack helicopters; according to the dubiously named Project Impose, seven more are expected to follow.[117] The acquisition of this leading-edge technology will help develop pilot skills in antitank warfare; it is also intended as an act of faith in the domestic arms industry with an eye to the international market. Plans are also afoot to provide the SAAF with much needed advanced light jet trainers with the capacity to double up as combat fighters. Several European defense contractors have displayed interest in this project. These include the French, who have enjoyed a long relationship with the South African armed forces, particularly the Air Force, extending from the apartheid years and the Swedes, whose Grippen fighters have attracted high praise from the SAAF. The frontrunner for the tender, however, appears to be British Aerospace, whose Hawk 100 has already been tested by the SAAF over the Cape.[118] Favored for its functionality and international track record, some five dozen are expected to be designated for the Air Force.[119] The Army will also be a recipient of unexpected largesse. By 2009, the Olifant battle tank is projected to be replaced by ninety-four main battle tanks at a cost of R3.38 billion, and by 2011 some 3,100 general-purpose mine-protected infantry vehicles will follow at a cost of R764 million. And 242 locally produced Rooikats are envisioned by the MOD.[120]

The development-peace complex is, needless to say, aghast at these proposals. Although a technical case can be made for the corvettes, it is difficult to justify advanced and expensive technology such as the Hawk (its sophistication precludes use for training purposes even in the Royal Air Force). The Rooivalk is also a target for criticism insofar as its acquisition by the armed forces provides a spur to the defense industries. The MOD has nevertheless forged ahead with its intentions to replace most fixed-wing aircraft, helicopters, ships, submarines, main battlefield tanks, and heavy armor over ten to twenty years, in what Joe Modise describes as the largest reequipping in local military history.[121] Most of the projected equipment in this exercise is expected to come from Britain, the United States, other NATO countries, as well as the local defense industry, with the corvettes and trainers-fighters in the forefront. Thereafter, new aircraft are projected to replace the Cheetah upgrades and SAAF helicopters. To the delight of the Navy, current plans include new submarines to replace the three aged French platforms currently in use as well as the corvettes originally requested.

It is not yet clear how massive refurbishment, involving some 145 projects, will be financed; this has led some commentators to believe that the MOD is simply grandstanding to appease its constituency among the soldiers. South Africa nevertheless signed a historic defense-equipment agreement with Britain in March 1996 in developing closer defense relations with its old mentor; years into democracy, there are clear signs of departure from the spirit of the April 1994 transition, when rhetoric focused on demilitarization and the development of the disadvantaged. Less than eighteen months later, Minister Modise was waxing lyrical on the access of the armed forces to international military markets from which it was excluded under apartheid, and there are now clear signs that the defense establishment is in the process of flexing much of its traditional muscle on matters of defense policy—at least regarding weapons procurement.[122]

The inexplicable major rearmament of Botswana is sometimes cited as one of the factors that changed defense policy dynamics.[123] Some commentators even anticipate that this could set off a regional arms race that would derail current peace and integration initiatives. Botswana is no doubt advantageous to the South African military in its struggles with local developmentalists by virtue of its ability to provide the phantom threat that justifies more defense expenditure. More fundamentally, however, is the changing profile and marketability of the RDP within South Africa, where two years after formal initiation as a policy platform of the ANC it ran into problems of institutional incapacity. These have led to the dismantling of special RDP structures in favor of the traditional line departments of government, as well as a reconsideration, if not full-blown reassessment, of the relationship between defense and development within the context of the new GEAR program. This has, needless to say, not been discouraged by the military establishment, particularly defense industries in the doldrums after apartheid. Minister Modise and, to a lesser extent, his successor as defense minister, Patrick Lekota, have long been strong advocates of a strongly armed state, and it is ironic, as Modise noted to the satisfaction of local arms producers, that apartheid assisted the creation of an armaments industry that can be turned to positive RDP purposes like boosting local exports and creating jobs. The public's ability to absorb these militaristic notions behind the polite face of development is assisted by high levels of crime and violence linked to rising expectations and delivery problems in the transitional environment.

Although this does not directly translate into an enhanced defense budget, which is likely to remain at current levels for some time to come, the convergence of many South Africans of divergent racial backgrounds around security as a common priority is, from the perspective of the military establishment, clearly advantageous. Given the growing propensity of a growing majority of threatened people to resort to quick-fix solutions involving arms for themselves and security organizations in both the private and public sectors, the peace and development interests are faced with an increasingly uphill battle. Many of these grassroots sentiments are shared in the highest of official circles, including the MOD, where Modise and his previous deputy, Ronnie Kasrils, once archenemies of the SADF, have become converts to the view that capital investment in defense is a prerequisite to development. Although Parliament differs from the U.S. Congress in many respects, including the absence of articulate and organized defense and reservist lobbies, many ANC members, reared in the virtual xenophobia emerging a few years after democratization, are sympathetic to the prestigious notion of South Africa as the most advanced fighting force on the continent. Others, looking to their own past, are sensitive to the difficulties of waging warfare without effective resources. As the transition years pass, the defense establishment, both the armorers and the soldiers, have moved with increasing aggression to exploit this mixture of nationalism and historic sentiment for their own institutional purposes.

None of this is incompatible with a working democracy, and it does not augur a return to civil-military patterns of the past in which soldiers dominated the budget process. The emergence of interventionist motives as a consequence of the inability to extract resources from society Latin American–style is also not in the cards. What this does signal, however, is that the military, like many other interest groups following the first shock of democracy, has come to realize the importance of proactivity to cultivate strategic constituencies in the public and private sectors in order to avoid becoming empty vessels or mere targets in the policymaking process.[124] This is entirely legitimate, even desirable, given that democracy is enriched by interest-group competition in the marketplace of public opinion. Throughout the democratic universe today, the armed services (and the defense establishment more generally) rarely hesitate to make a case for their own well-being when given the opportunity to do so; this is perfectly acceptable provided they remain loyal to higher authority.[125]

There is considerable truth in the view that the Navy failed in its original motivations for corvettes (now granted) because of its initial inability to understand the needs and agendas of many stakeholders in what emerged as a consultative public policy process. Magnetized by the requirement to procure weapons platforms capable of operating two hundred nautical miles out to sea in the rough conditions of the Cape and unaccustomed to political intrigue and bargaining, the "silent service" simply barged ahead "in the correct military manner" under the misplaced assumption that by simply presenting its technical case it would swing the political leaders behind its defense interests.[126]

In the wake of the subsequent debacle, however, the Navy (and the other services) have absorbed the lesson that defense policy procedures require a higher level of political maturity in demands and negotiation. In the learning curve that followed, the armed forces came to understand that civilian compliance with defense appropriations can no longer be taken as automatic and that institutional interests require military leaders to lobby at all levels in aligning policy with their perceptions of national interests, military missions, and capabilities. Their ability to do so is, perhaps ironically, assisted by the democratic framework, which requires the military to be accountable and more transparent in a way that runs counter to the culture of secrecy under total strategy. On the contrary, democracy means greater accessibility of the military to a network of power interests, some of whom are undoubtedly hostile to the military establishment; but others can be used, maneuvered, and manipulated behind the scenes.

At this point in time the NDF has no official parliamentary lobby in Cape Town. Much like its counterparts in other areas of the world, including the United States, where the armed forces are legally prohibited from lobbying, the NDF now actively "liaises" with various strategic institutions in both the public and private sectors. In doing so, moreover, its advocates have come to realize that emergent civil society is not particularly well equipped to manage the technicalities of defense policy over and beyond some threshold when general vigilance and criticism on the part of those who defend the public realm become quite useless.

The armed forces, to their own surprise, have come to recognize, for example, that the end of the culture of secrecy is not necessarily disadvantageous and can actually be bent to the manufacture of corporate capital. Armed with a virtual monopoly of knowledge over the esoterica of military matters, the leaders of the NDF are finding to their astonishment that they can effectively leverage the conception and implementation of defense policy with little informed resistance. In the legislature, for example, the technically powerful JPSCD performs important oversight functions but is grossly underequipped to counter the complex ideograms and data brought by senior officers. This imbalance in specialist power, favorable to the inculcation of military views, is not uncharacteristic of organizations linked to defense policymaking—including the Defence Secretariat, the major instrument for civilianization—where sheer experience and accumulated information frequently allow soldiers to carry the day. The corvette procurement, according to one anonymous official commentator in 1996, is assured because of "the large amount of educational work which has over the last few months been undertaken by the Navy and other sectors of the SANDF."[127]

The armed forces are fighting hard to protect their turf, and a document for procurement plans until 2015, incorporating the corvettes and much else in earlier announcements governing major reequipment by Joe Modise, has been lodged with the JPSCD.[128] The fact that this rearmament initiative has now succeeded in obtaining legislative support is testimony to the growing comparative advantage of the military in the rough-and-tumble world of public policy.

Organizations prefer to keep control of the process of change, particularly militaries that have to blend particular interests with the broader requirements of national security. The worst-case scenario for any military comes when change is not only controlled but imposed by external forces. This is no less true of the NDF, seeking to keep ahead of demands for change in the now completed Defence Review. The nature of the situation has tended to encourage the military to become much more streetwise in adapting to the competitive nature of interest-group politics, and should it succeed in its goal to divest massive public funds away from development objectives, it will be clearly indicative of ground lost to the defense establishment by the antimilitarists, peace lobbies, and the developmentalists. Many individuals and organizations in these networks have already tailored their initial agenda to disestablish the defense establishment along with democratization and are now pressing for a more minimalist goal—a "socio-economic based national security outlook," as one analyst put it.[129] Whether this more limited objective is even realizable in this policymaking environment (with signs of cynicism, corruption, and self-service as the ideal of liberation come up against reality) is another unanswered question.

The development of a veteran's lobby, including past members of the SADF and MK, will also increase military leverage over defense policy-making, although it is unlikely that such a lobby will wield the enormous influence of its American counterparts.[130] The political weight of the military in protecting its institutional essence can also be expected to increase if South Africa moves after 2000 to the coupling of military and local defense interests tending to emerge in the United States and in European societies with parliamentary systems of representation. Centralist tendencies in the political system could work equally well to the advantage of the military, provided its leaders maintain the key personal and organizational means of access to exploit the policymaking environment. In many Pacific Rim countries, such as Taiwan and South Korea, advanced defense industries have also become an overall component of economic development, with interactive benefits of civilian and military production contributing to technological progress. Some aspects of this process are likely to be replicated in South Africa, where there continues to be close relations between government, the defense industries, and the armed forces given that the initial claims of development on defense have lost much of their policy impact.

It is extremely unlikely that South Africa will see a reversion to the past, where the armed forces made massive claims on national budgets. For the foreseeable future, most analysts predict, defense expenditures are unlikely to rise substantially. Nevertheless, as the state's new neoliberal and market-driven GEAR policy has displaced the RDP, some space has been created within which the armed forces are far better placed to maneuver for public funds to support various initiatives, from rearmament to peace-support operations on the African continent. The genuinely transformed and representative military projected for the first years of the next century, part of wider initiatives to accelerate the institutionalization of the postapartheid state, will doubtlessly enhance the capacity of the armed forces to project their financial and political interests at the national policy level. Much, of course, depends on the future character of the state and civil-military relations. It is to these matters that we now turn.

Notes

1. See, for example, Lucian Pye, "Armies and the Process of Political Modernisation," in *The Role of the Military in Underdeveloped Countries*, ed. J. Johnson (Princeton: Princeton University Press, 1964); Morris Janowitz, *The Military in the*

Political Development of New Nations: An Essay in Comparative Analysis (Chicago: University of Chicago Press, 1964).

2. See Anita Isaacs, *Military Rule and Transition in Ecuador, 1972–1992* (Basingstoke: Macmillan, 1993).

3. Relatively early intimations of the negative impact of militaries on development appear in such works as Henry Bienen ed., *The Military and Modernisation* (Chicago: Aldine Atherton, 1971); Ellen Kay Trimberger, *Revolution From Above: Military Bureaucrats and Development in Japan, Turkey, Egypt, and Peru* (Brunswick,N.J.: Transaction Books, 1978); and Abraham Lowenthal, *The Peruvian Experiment: Continuity and Change Under Military Rule* (Princeton: Princeton University Press).

4. See Claude Welch, "The Roots and Implications of Military Intervention," in *Soldier and State in Africa: A Comparative Analysis of Military Intervention and Political Change*, ed. Claude Welch (Evanston: Northwestern University Press, 1970).

5. Philip Frankel, *Pretoria's Praetorians: Civil-Military Relations in South Africa* (Cambridge: Cambridge University Press, 1984), p. 73.

6. Ibid., p. 74.

7. *Mail and Guardian* (Johannesburg), April 22, 1994.

8. Rocklyn Williams, "Overview and Backdrop to the Defence Review," presentation to the Defence Review Workshop, Jan Smuts House, University of the Witwatersrand, Johannesburg, July 29, 1996.

9. *The Star* (Johannesburg), August 4, 1994.

10. Nan Cross at Defence Review Workshop, ibid; see Philip Frankel, "Report on Proceedings: Defence Review Workshop, presented to Defence Secretariat, July 1996.

11. *Mail and Guardian* (Johannesburg), April 19, 1996.

12. *The Star* (Johannesburg), August 15, 1995.

13. *The Star* (Johannesburg), August 4, 1995.

14. *Mail and Guardian* (Johannesburg), May 20, 1994.

15. Frankel, *Pretoria's Praetorians*, p. 76.

16. *Mail and Guardian* (Johannesburg), April 19, 1996.

17. For regional statistics on defense expenditures, see *Africa At A Glance: Facts and Figures, 1996/97* (Pretoria: African Institute of South Africa).

18. *The Star* (Johannesburg), July 18, 1996.

19. *The Star* (Johannesburg), June 22, 1995.

20. Ibid.

21. See Barry Blechman, "U.S Interests and Military Power," in Blechman et al., *The American Military in the Twenty-first Century* (New York: St Martin's Press, 1993), p. 84.

22. Samuel Huntington, *The Soldier and the State: The Theory and Practice of Civil-Military Relations* (Cambridge: Harvard University Press, 1968; rev. ed., 1995).

23. South African National Defence Force (SANDF), Defence in Transition, Annual Report 1994/95 (Pretoria: SANDF), p. 57

24. Ibid.

25. Ibid.

26. *Sunday Times* (Johannesburg), November 29, 1995.

27. The Dunnottar Centre is at one of the air bases being closed as a result of the constraints of the defense budget. Should the Corps fail or move, both or which appear likely, this facility is likely to be converted into an alternative international airport for Johannesburg.

28. See Lieutenant General Reg Otto, presentation to the conference Preparing the South African Army for the 21st Century, Council for Scientific and Industrial Research (CSIR), Pretoria, October 15, 1995.

29. Department of Defence (DOD), New Era Defence, Annual Report 1995/96, p. 41.

30. Andre Bestbier, Briefing to Joint Parliamentary Standing Committee on Defence, June 1997.

31. Ibid.

32. Ibid.

33. SANDF TR3/96 DCC

34. Bestbier, Briefing to JPSCD.

35. DOD, New Era Defence, p. 128.

36. SANDF, TR 5/96 DCC

37. Bestbier, Briefing to JPSCD.

38. Ibid.

39. SANDF, TR8/96 DCC

40. Bestbier, Briefing to JPSCD.

41. Ibid.

42. Ibid.

43. Ibid.

44. Ibid.

45. Ibid.

46. DOD, New Era Defence, p. 122.

47. Jakkie Cilliers, "Towards Collaborative and Cooperative Security in Southern Africa: The OAU and SADC," in *About Turn: The Transformation of the South African Military and Intelligence*, ed. Jakkie Cilliers and Markus Reichardt (Midrand: Institute for Defence Policy, 1996), pp. 194–223.

48. *The Star* (Johannesburg), November 3, 1995.

49. *The Star* (Johannesburg), July 3, 1995.

50. Aziz Pahad, "South Africa and Preventative Diplomacy," paper presented at the Conference on South Africa and Peacekeeping in Africa, Johannesburg, July 13–14, 1995, p. 6.

51. *Sunday Times* (Johannesburg), June 4, 1995.

52. See, e.g., Paul Preston, *The Politics of Revenge: Facism and the Military in Twentieth-Century Spain* (Unwin Hyman, 1990.)

53. *Sunday Independent* (Johannesburg), September 17, 1995.

54. *The Star* (Johannesburg), November 3, 1995.

55. *The Star* (Johannesburg), February 7th 1996.

56. J. Cilliers, "The Evolving Security Architecture in Southern Africa," *African Security Review* 4(5) (1995).

57. Summit of Heads of State or Government of the Southern African Development Community, Communiqué, Gaberon, June 28, 1996. See also Kgomotso

Monnakgotla, "From Ambivalence and Adversity to Stability in Southern Africa," in *New Partners in Peace: Towards a Southern African Peacekeeping Capacity*, ed. Mark Malan (Midrand: Institute for Defence Policy, Monograph Series No. 5, July 1996), p.22.

58. *The Star* (Johannesburg), January 8, 1996.

59. *The Star* (Johannesburg), November 3, 1995.

60. *Mail and Guardian* (Johannesburg), August 25, 1995.

61. Monnakgotla, "From Ambivalence and Adversity," p.20

62. See W. Nhara, "The OAU and the Potential Role of Regional and Subregional Organisations," in *Peacekeeping in Africa*, vol. 2, ed. J. Cilliers and G. Mills (Midrand: Institute for Defence Policy and South African Institute for International Affairs, 1995), p. 100.

63. South African Defence Force, *Communication Bulletin* 92(95), September 12, 1995.

64. The massive Cahora (or Cabora) Bassa hydroelectric scheme was constructed by the Portuguese prior to their decolonization of Mozambique. It was subsequently rendered inactive during the civil war that followed. Attempts to reactivate this enormous initiative since 1994 have been delayed by many factors, including the existence of massive minefields along the power lines running toward South Africa. These have to a large extent been cleared within a narrow corridor.

65. See R.S. Shikhapwashya, "Presentation of the Aim, Roles, Functions and Organisation of the Standing Aviation Committee of the Inter-State Defence and Security Committee for the Southern African Region," paper presented at the Sir Pierre van Ryneveld Air Power Conference, Pretoria, October 3, 1995. See also Cilliers, "Towards Collaborative and Cooperative Security," p. 212.

66. *The Star* (Johannesburg), January 8, 1996.

67. *The Star* (Johannesburg), November 9, 1995.

68. *The Star* (Johannesburg), September 26, 1996.

69. John Henshaw, "Forces for Peacekeeping, Peace Enforcement, and Humanitarian Missions," in Blechman et al., *The American Military*, pp 397431.

70. W.G. Lombard, "Armour in the SADF: A Strategic and Practical Perspective," in *Mailed Fist: Developments in Modern Armour*, ed. J. Cilliers and B. Sass (Midrand: Institute for Defence Policy, Monograph Series No 2, March 1996), p. 11.

71. Cilliers, "Towards Collaborative and Cooperative Security," p. 204.

72. *The Star* (Johannesburg), September 10, 1996.

73. Henshaw, "Forces for Peacekeeping"; *The Star* (Johannesburg), July 7, 1995.

74. *Sunday Independent* (Johannesburg), October 6, 1996.

75. Henshaw, "Forces for Peacekeeping," p. 404.

76. These include, inter alia, Austria, Australia, Canada, Finland, Ireland, the Nordic countries, and Poland.

77. *The Star* (Johannesburg), October 11, 1996.

78. *Pretoria News*, March 13, 1996; see also D. Hamman, "The Inter-State Defence and Security Committee: Defence Sub-Committee," paper presented at the seminar on South African and Global Peace Support Initiatives, Cape Town, May 17, 1995, p. 5.

79. See Samuel Huntington, *The Soldier and the State: The Theory and Practice of Civil-Military Relations* (Cambridge: Harvard University Press, 1968; rev. ed., 1995).

80. Henshaw, "Forces for Peacekeeping," p. 397.

81. *The Star* (Johannesburg), September 13, 1995.

82. Pahad, "South Africa and Preventative Diplomacy," p. 8.

83. Lombard, "Armour in the SADF."

84. Bill Sass, "The Union and South African Defence Force, 1912–1994" in *About Turn: The Transformation of the South African Military and Intelligence*, ed. Jakkie Cilliers and Markus Reichardt (Midrand: Institute for Defence Policy, 1996), pp. 118–140.

85. *The Citizen* (Johannesburg), June 13, 1995.

86. Ibid.

87. See, e.g., South African Policy on Global Support Efforts, quoted in Cilliers, "Towards Collaborative and Cooperative Security," p. 201.

88. SANDF, Communication Bulletin 92(95), September 12, 1995.

89. Philip Frankel, *Pretoria's Praetorians: Civil-Military Relations in South Africa* (Cambridge: Cambridge University Press, 1984), p. 75.

90. Ashley Lillie, "The Origins and Development of the South African Army," *Militaria* 12(2) (1982): 12.

91. DOD, *White Paper on Defence and Armaments Production, 1969* (Pretoria: DOD, 1969), p. 1.

92. DOD, *White Paper on Defence and Armaments Supply, 1982* (Pretoria: DOD, 1982.

93. Mohlolo Siko, "Regional Defence Restructuring: A Southern African Maritime Perspective," paper presented at Southern African Regional Workshop on Defence and Restructuring of the Armed Forces, Helderfontein, Johannesburg, March 1–4, 1996.

94. Eric Nordlinger, *Soldiers in Politics: Military Coups and Governments* (Englewood Cliffs, N.J.: Prentice-Hall, 1977), p 68.

95. *The Star* (Johannesburg), August 4, 1994, and May 1, 1996.

96. *The Star* (Johannesburg), July 18th 1996.

97. *The Star* (Johannesburg), March 18, 1996; September 29, 1995.

98. *The Star* (Johannesburg), August 9, 1994, and June 22, 1995.

99. *Mail and Guardian* (Johannesburg), May 20, 1994; *The Star* (Johannesburg), September 13, 1995, and September 19, 1995.

100. *The Star* (Johannesburg), April 10, 1996, and May 1, 1996; *Sunday Times* (Johannesburg), March 24, 1996.

101. *The Star* (Johannesburg), September 13, 1995, and May 1, 1996.

102. *The Star* (Johannesburg), September 29, 1995, and April 30, 1996.

103. *The Star* (Johannesburg), November 3, 1995.

104. *The Star* (Johannesburg), October 27, 1995, and April 10, 1996; see also T.J.N. Beukes, *Naval and State Activities in the Exclusive Economic Zone: A Comparative Perspective* (Pretoria: Institute for Maritime Technology, 1995).

105. Helmut-Roemer Heitman, "Southern African Maritime Security Agency," paper presented at the National Maritime Strategic Conference: Navies in Peace and War, Simonstown, October 26, 1995.

106. *The Star* (Johannesburg), October 27, 1995, and April 10, 1996.

107. *The Star* (Johannesburg), June 22, 1995.

108. *The Star* (Johannesburg), April 10, 1996.

109. Ibid.

110. Siko, "Regional Defence Restructuring."

111. Martin Edmonds and Gregg Mills, *Uncharted Waters: A Review of South Africa's Naval Options* (South African Institute for International Affairs, Johannesburg; and the Centre for Defence and International Security Studies, Lancaster University; Lancaster 1996).

112. Heitman, "Southern African Maritime Security Agency."

113. Siko, "Regional Defence Restructuring."

114. *The Star* (Johannesburg), April 30, 1996. The SAN's demands for corvettes and a submarine form part of the R30 billion remarmament package approved in 1999.

115. Ibid.

116. *Sunday Times* (Johannesburg), September 22, 1996.

117. Ibid.

118. *The Star* (Johannesburg), April 30, 1996.

119. *The Star* (Johannesburg), September 29, 1995. The Hawks, along with the Grippen fighters, are part of the R30 billion remarmament package approved in 1999.

120. *Sunday Times* (Johannesburg), September 22, 1996.

121. *The Star* (Johannesburg), March 25, 1996.

122. Ibid.

123. *New Nation* (Johannesburg), February 23, 1996.

124. *Mail and Guardian* (Johannesburg), April 19, 1996.

125. See, e.g.,, Gordon Adams, *The Politics of Defense Contracting: The Iron Triangle* (New Brunswick, N. J.: Transaction Books, 1982), and Kenneth R. Mayer, *The Political Economy of Defense Contracting* (New Haven: Yale University Press, 1991).

126. Edmonds and Mills, *Uncharted Waters; The Star* (Johannesburg), November 3, 1995. See, e.g., "Position Paper on the Management of Military Veterans Affairs," presented by the Military Veterans Association to the Defence Review Workshop, July 1996.

127. *The Star* (Johannesburg), April 30, 1996.

128. *Sunday Times* (Johannesburg), September 22, 1996.

129. *Siko*, "Regional Defence Restructuring."

130. See, e.g., Military Veterans Association, "Position Paper on the Management of Military Veterans Affairs."

Epilogue: Beyond the Millennium

An armed disciplined body is, in essence, dangerous to liberty. Undisciplined, it is ruinous to society.

—***Edmund Burke, Speech on the Army Estimates (1770).***

The principal armed services of its country—in its professional attitudes, its equipment, its officer corps—is an extension, a reflection, of the country's whole society.

—***Corelli Barnett, The Swordbearers (1963).***

There are no universal formulas for measuring the success of democratic transitions, partially because of conceptual problems in pinpointing performance, partially because the medium- to long-term outcomes of the so-called third wave of transitions (starting in the late twentieth century and continuing today) are still uncertain.[1] When asked to comment on the consequences of the French Revolution for world history almost two hundred years later, the great Chinese statesman Chou En-lai is reputed to have replied that it was too soon to tell. Much the same applies to more recent, if less dramatic, social experiments that have converted authoritarian states to democracy. Transitology, that curious science fueled by the worldwide breakdown of closed regimes in recent years, generally favors the contextual factors promoting democratization as opposed to their consequences; this deflected into the more specialized literature on the variables shaping the political behavior of militaries in postauthoritarian situations.[2] Here, despite several studies on armed forces in the democratizing societies of Eastern Europe and Latin America, we still do not know with any exactitude how, for example, the legacies of an authoritarian past, the distinctive features of transitions, and political activity following founding elections come together into one compound that either simulates or suffocates the new political system. Neither are we certain that pacted transitions of the South African type, once considered most propitious to democracy, now ensure sustainable democratic governance with an appropriate supportive system of civil-military relations.[3]

South Africa, it appears, is no exception to the general rule that judgments on structural change require considerable historic distance, particularly in cases where the decomposition of the state during transition, is, as in this case, neither evident nor unambiguous. In addition, unlike most Latin American countries with deep traditions of civil-military conflict, the Republic of South Africa lacks historic precedents from which we can infer scenarios for ongoing relations between its postauthoritarian government and its soldiers. The guardian or arbitrator character of previous local militarization—somewhere between full-blown praetorianism and legally constituted civilian control—adds further difficulty to making predictions. What we have in the end is a surprising negotiated transition out of which, despite the continued cultural and institutional residues of apartheid, there appear to be real, if tentative, prospects for an enduring and stable democratic order.

The civilianization of the military—a prerequisite for such a political system—has not been deeply disturbed by, for example, the activities of the Truth and Reconciliation Commission, established in the wake of transition to investigate human rights abuses committed by the security forces under apartheid. The resilience of the state during transition, the negotiated character of the shift from authoritarian apartheid to democracy, the ability of the armed forces (if not the police) to close ranks around allegations of human rights violations, and the nature of the Truth and Reconciliation Commission itself have ensured that the old leaders of the SADF and MK, for better or worse, have escaped being brought to justice for their behavior during the pretransition years.[4] Still, critical issues remain to be resolved before a clearly articulated system of civil-military relations can be emplaced, including the rationalization of the armed forces, probably the most consequential of all the issues. It is an irritant to other organizational conflicts within the military and has the potential to spill over into civil society and jeopardize the early stages of democratic consolidation.

During the initial JMCC discussions in 1993, some of this was already suspected while planning the integration of the armed formations. One consequence would inevitably be a massively overinflated military in relation to strategic requirements. Participants from all sides in these early talks recognized that for integration to succeed in the longer term it would require that the armed forces also downsize (or "rightsize") before too long. This was consequently projected into the first-draft Interim Constitution, which provided that all adherents to the CPR automatically become members of the NDF but then goes on to refer to the necessity of managing "personnel exceeding needs."[5] In subsequent years, as the principle of pruning the bloated state bureaucracy inherited from apartheid has taken root in policy circles, the notion of a comparably inflated military has become increasingly untenable, particularly with strategic changes in the philosophy governing national security architecture. The threat from the North—the cardinal concept shaping national security policy under apartheid—has evaporated, and there is no justification—at least in civil society—for bloated armed forces when South Africa faces no conventional threat across its borders. This is at least partially recognized by strategic planners within the armed forces, who have opted for a small but highly professional core as the appropriate force design for discharging military missions within the Republic, at its borders, and in the surrounding subcontinent. Rationalization is also consistent with transition, moving into a climate of social reconstruction and development where public finances to sustain armed forces have diminished significantly.

The huge, newly integrated NDF, with its projected 135,000 members, simply contradicts the principle enshrined in the Defence Review of an "appropriate and affordable" defense force. Given security requirements and financial imperatives, the size of such a force has been pared down in transformative negotiations and military estimations and is now some 70,000 personnel maximum.[6] This represents, in effect, cutting the armed forces almost in half if one discounts natural attrition, which poses more than the normal stresses inherent in rationalization taking place in most post–Cold War militaries because of the structural characteristics of the South African military.

Transition-integration in the NDF has involved the extraordinary contradiction of revolving people into and out of the military, which has aggravated the political fault lines that appear in military institutions under the pressure of disengagement and democratization. Logic dictates that rationalization or demobilization should have preceded integration, but due to the political circumstances surrounding civil-military relations in transitional South Africa, the converse has occurred. As an uncertain white minority negotiated the sharing of power in the early 1990s, it was considered desirable that the antiapartheid armies be located with speed under the watchful wing of the statutory SADF, and this view was endorsed by the military leaders who saw the armed might of MK and APLA as a dangerous, unpredictable factor. ANC leaders confronted by a mass of repatriated fighters and new recruits in the first years of the 1990s were equally keen to quickly concentrate and institutionalize their fighters, whose hunger for the fruits of liberation posed an imminent threat to stable transition. Many of the newer MK recruits, the self-styled

Self-Defence Units in the vortex of township violence, were—even to their leaders—an unknown. With elections looming in 1994, retrenchment, with its image of armed men on the streets in an uncertain political climate, was utterly unacceptable to all parties, both civil and military.

The consequence, six years down the line, is an imperfectly cohesive military whose internal fractures still largely conform to racial cleavages and that is of a size unprecedented in South African history. Integration has been completed at massive organizational cost, and now, with rationalization in gear, the esprit de corps in the NDF has also sunk to unprecedented low levels.

Ambiguous combat performance always induces depression in the ranks, and the uncertain track record of the SADF in apartheid's wars on the subcontinent was a powerful stimulus to progressive military managers to press vigorously for political restructuring since the late 1980s as a prerequisite to reprofessionalization, the enhancement of organizational capability, and the restoration of morale. The prospect of rationalization, however, also impacts negatively on the driving spirit of bureaucratic institutions, and the NDF officer corps, subsequently shaken by the traumas of democratization, is no exception to the universal principle. Integration has, for example, exacted a serious toll on the cadre of still largely white professional officers, most of whom are of the old school and have seen career-development programs and other initiatives essential to upward mobility either proscribed or reshaped to meet the requirements of a process that appears to be dictated, despite all evidence, by MK, APLA, and their allies in the political classes.

Integration in a climate of financial austerity has meant a much higher workload for leadership elements and, as amalgamating the various armed forces has become an institutional obsession (presumably driven once again by the ubiquitous politicians), many white former SADF officers have watched aghast and angry as standards of training and discipline have fallen to subterranean levels. The Military Police, for example, has found itself in a pernicious situation between enforcing discipline and igniting flames of racial conflict. Without prior experience or enthusiasm for their new roles, white NCOs are an especially frustrated group, particularly when confronted with new, complex, and sometimes incomprehensible demands from raw troops without adequate administrative backup in experimental situations. Bridging training in all arms of service has shifted the emphasis away from what many former SADF members see as real soldiering and has reinforced reconsideration of the military as a future career path.

The diminishing defense budget, obsolescence of equipment, and the in-built demographics of the armed forces fuel this crisis of raison d'être, particularly among conservative white officers who, having backed a political settlement as a matter of corporate interest, now face the consequence of being placed under black command. Many of the more senior officers, including at least half the current complement of white generals whose careers have run their course at the edge of an uncertain future, are saddened but not especially anxious at the prospect of leaving a bedeviled African military with generous retirement packages offered by the state to create space for black leadership in the upper echelons of the state bureaucracy. Middle-level officers with management, administrative, or technical experience in the functional divisions of the NDF are also potential resettlers in civil society with similarly mixed feelings about rationalization. Still, the situation is turbulent and demoralizing for more commissioned or noncommissioned officers who lack the seniority, confidence, or skills to disengage into civil society after years of sheltered employment.

Cleavage and mutual distrust in the officer corps became fairly pervasive in the 1990s in the wake of rationalization. Retrenchment sows conflict and personal competition, and many white officers saw themselves as pawns in a political chess match. This feeling has become pervasive in the Army since the appointment of General Nyanda as chief of the NDF and the infiltration of his MK colleagues into the most senior service positions. In the middle and lower reaches of the chains of command in all four service branches, there is widespread opinion that senior leadership (black or white) has been lacking, even disingenuous, in explaining the practical implications of organizational transformation in the armed forces and, more generally, democratization. Many in this constituency fall within the most dislocated category, where life inside the barracks is increasingly uncomfortable and life outside virtually impossible (unless padded by generous severance provisions).

The forced and accelerated exodus of predominantly Afrikaner officers predicted at the point of transition has largely not materialized.[7] As in other areas of the state bureaucracy, however, much of this has less to do with professional or corporate commitments than with administrative delays in the finalization of severance packages and, ultimately, the so-called sunset clauses built into the Constitution during the course of transitional negotiations that effectively prohibit the state from laying off existing members of the public service until after the 1999 elections. These resulted in a strengthened ANC majority, thereby creating more space for restructuring the public service, including the military. In the armed forces, there are also administrative provisions that enable the hierarchy to block exit on numerous grounds, which has certainly worked to halt what might have been a veritable flood of displaced and disoriented personnel. Still, by 1993, a year before democratic elections, already some 7,000 members of the Permanent Force, including 18 percent of its professional officers, had already accepted voluntary severance packages.[8] Since then, some 10,000 white personnel, including seasoned professionals, have trickled out of the military with the tide of democracy. These conservative estimates will doubtless escalate now that the new government is no longer constitutionally required to safeguard the careers of state bureaucrats who might impede progress.

The landscape beyond the wire is today increasingly dotted with former SADF personnel who have gravitated toward allied work in the defense industries. With crime burgeoning, military personnel have drifted into the highly lucrative private security industry. Many development projects forming part of the postapartheid reconstruction program—the flagship Katorus Presidential Project, for example—are reliant on former senior SADF officers for security. Other professional warriors have moved into the shady and equally lucrative world of transnational mercenary activity as members of such controversial organizations as Executive Outcomes.[9] In light of the universally recognized fact that training is no substitute for experience, however, this situation has potentially enormous implications for the skills base of South African armed forces, particularly at strategic middle and upper leadership levels. There is no shortage of people for military service: In 1995, for example, almost 40,000 volunteers (mainly black) came forward to fill a shrinking number (3,500) of designated posts.[10] While one anticipates that a new equilibrium will emerge as the cadre of black officers acquires the skills for effective military management, it is reasonable to expect that the intervening period is likely to be dysfunctional. Over this period, as aggrieved officers on the verge of resignation are quick to point out, combat capability is sacrificed on the altar of representation. These older officers are, for better or worse, the major reservoir of institutional excellence, although their departure will eliminate a significant source of internal resistance to transformation.

The recent Lesotho debacle (in which the SANDF "rescued" the small mountain kingdom at great expense in the face of minimal resistance), appears to fulfill some of the worst predictions of brutality, ill discipline, and poor leadership. Much of the old guard remains at the helm, and few are uncontaminated by deep anxiety and an ambiguous sense of mission eighteen months after South Africa's first attempt at peacekeeping. Yet many senior leaders welcome the opportunity to leave the service, though some still fear the implications of that for career prospects. Although there have been two previous rationalizations in the armed forces since 1985, both have been essentially belt-tightening exercises. Neither has been on the scale of the current undertaking[11] or taken place on the heels of a process consciously concerned with expanding the military and, in the process, exacerbating the management problems of organizational overload. Preliminary research indicates that at least half the total complement suffers extreme apprehension over the alternative prospects of retrenchment.[12] This pervasive sense of being at risk is concretized by the fact that all NDF members (the CSANDF excepted) are now temporary staff as the vanguard of the rationalization process moves into full acceleration.[13] Informal rationalization has already been initiated, and already by late 1995 seventy-five part-time and thirty-four full-time units, many with decades-long histories, had already been disestablished; at the time, a further thirty-nine were earmarked for obsolescence in what is fast becoming a seriously depressed corporate environment.[14] Suggestions by former President Mandela and other senior ANC politicians that many remaining units be renamed after the heroes of the liberation struggle adds grist to the mill of the white personnel who see themselves as locked into a decomposing situation.[15]

This apparently includes a large proportion who, in the words of one commentator, are "simply biding their time in the unenthusiastic fulfillment of their duties while calculating the benefits that will accrue to them when they receive the much hoped for 'package.'" This is, he added, "the financial crutch that would enable them to make some sort of transition to civilian life."[16] This will no doubt challenge institutional cohesion and promote internal competitive struggles. Despite the efforts of NDF chiefs to target excess administrative personnel and the fairly bloated civilian component of the military services, retrenchment will inevitably carry over into the teeth of the NDF to reduce combat capacity unless the new core force envisioned is equipped with supportive technology and new weapons systems to compensate for losses in manpower. Even then, this is likely to be a long-lead process, during which the professional capability of the military to either defend the new democratic state or advance its interests will suffer. The Lesotho intervention stands in testimony.

Perhaps most important, the dynamics of rationalization are far different and potentially more explosive in the case of newly integrated personnel from MK, APLA, and other NSFs. Esprit de corps among these sectors is still highly tentative because of the adverse experiences of former guerrilla fighters being converted to fight in a conventional military. This is particularly true outside the new black officer corps among low-level recruits, many of whom see incorporation into the NDF as relatively forced, unfair, and conducted within a power framework dominated by the very people whom they were once recruited to fight. This also produces demoralization, albeit of a different order than that encountered among the white soldiers. Many former freedom fighters have joined the armed forces (as legions of Afrikaners did under apartheid) because they provide employment in a competitive job market. Given high unemployment in the postapartheid economy and the few convertible civilian skills among former MK-APLA cadres, this group has even bigger stakes in the rationalization process. Given the heterogeneity and class differences among integrated black personnel, the situation necessarily varies. The black officer class, for example, has every incentive to remain on the professional career track and is probably least at risk given its political leverage. Having adapted to the hierarchy with zeal, many in this group, particularly those with professional training prior to integration, are now equally zealous in their claims to accelerated promotion. This excludes the small clutch of former TBVC officers, many of whom identify with the whites' suspicion that the new NDF will inevitably demand political correctness and who, like white officers, are eagerly awaiting severance packages. Outside this limited circle, however, rationalization issues are fast becoming a site of struggle with dangerous racial connotations.

The frustration among black recruits from MK and APLA is illustrated by the Tempe incident in 1999, in which a black officer opened fire upon and killed white colleagues at the vast military complex outside Bloemfontein. Although the NDF has tried to write off the incident as an isolated incident by a disturbed individual, it represents the thin edge of simmering tension.

To some extent the edge has been taken off by the failure of almost half the persons on the CPR to report for duty. This assisted integration and will facilitate rationalization by reducing the numbers to be managed. Approximately 6,000 former cadres have also taken the option of voluntary demobilization or chosen to transfer to the Service Corps, where they remain auxiliaries under NDF authority while receiving some minimal conversion training. This has included 1,500 veterans and vulnerables who were not considered suitable for integration at the outset, as well as MK and APLA personnel who did not take to the military life. For the rest of the former NSFs, however, rationalization is problematic. Rationalization, for example, spurs people to complete their bridging training, since those who have completed the obligatory course are eligible for higher packages. Given that logistic and administrative roadblocks have occurred in bridging training, considerable resentment is evident among the mass of lower-grade black troops who cannot complete their training as quickly as planned yet are the primary targets for rationalization.

NDF leaders repeatedly emphasized that rationalization will be implemented on a justiciable basis independent of political or racial considerations. This will, according to official statements, involve a formula based on "principles of operational readiness, fair labour practice, transparency, productivity, representivity and the maintenance of expertise with all the members and employees of all constituent forces being equally eligible."[17] Yet this is not especially reassuring to blacks in the military hierarchy (the middle and lower ranks, operationally the least ready), where there is a widespread perception that key internal decisions are still made by the old regime behind the back of General Nyanda. This tends to fuel mutual suspicion throughout the chain of command from the middle upward. Indicative of the suspicion surrounding rationalization, some cadres believe that the slow pace and failures in bridging training are parts of a conspiracy by NDF leadership to primarily target former MK and APLA personnel for retrenchment. Notwithstanding official statements to the contrary, there is a widespread belief that the guiding principle of rationalization will be last hired, first fired.[18]

The unfortunate tendency of military spokespersons to draw a distinction between rationalization (which applies to career soldiers from the former SADF) and demobilization (all others) fuels suspicions and reinforces racial tensions to the point where white management has even been accused of doctoring personnel files in order to present new integrees in the worst possible light. Since the great majority of the others, that is, the new integrees, are also enlisted on STSCs that are now renewable every two years, former MK and APLA personnel feel especially vulnerable to any policy that keeps only those "with appropriate performance and/or potential according to the new demands of the SANDF."[19] Reading between the lines, less experienced (i.e., black) personnel will eventually be excluded from the core force. Ultimately, there are disagreements over the potential size of severance packages between former statutory and NSF personnel. While the former are expected to walk away with generous benefits, former cadres, many with decades of service in the liberation armies, can expect a once-off payment ranging from R12,000 to R42,000—barely sufficient, as one commentator has put it, "to buy a house in a location."[20]

Equal-opportunity and affirmative-action programs compound the equation, and it is far from certain that the armed forces are psychologically or organizationally ready to handle rationalization with a minimum of internal disturbance. Although the position of historically disadvantaged groups surfaced in the first negotiations between the SADF and MK, the practical implementation of these policies has been delayed in the face of old-guard resistance. As in all public and private sectors in early transitional South Africa, the mere mention of affirmative action strikes fear into the ranks of the privileged, let alone military personnel quick to label anything designed to correct historical discrimination in power relations as reverse racism. Hence, affirmative action has been slow in the armed forces despite the early rush to appoint senior NSF personnel. At the time of the 1994 elections, contacts were initiated with the U.S. Defense Equal Opportunities Management Institute with a view to transplanting some facets of the American experience, yet little concrete policy emerged over the next three years because most senior former SADF leaders saw this experience as a triple threat—to combat capacity, skills, and their own power base. Among this group there is very little of the intuitive sympathy for equal opportunities that played an important a part in energizing their counterparts in the U.S. officer corps. On the contrary, many white officers believe that "MK veterans were inducted with grossly inflated ranks and that certain of the TBVC states' soldiers were inducted with highly inflated salaries."[21]

Others see affirmative action as another nasty element of the organizational restructurings that account for deteriorating standards. The controversial decision to allow bridging trainees two chances to pass courses was widely labeled discriminatory during 1995–1996, even though some MK officers saw it as condescending and dangerous to the long-term maintenance of professional standards. Blacks have moved upward in the organizational hierarchy, but there are still discrepancies in power relations between the old and new orders, particularly in the specialist services, where it is difficult, if not dangerous, to adjust standards.[22] As in other sectors of the state bureaucracy, new appointments to address disadvantages have been studiously camouflaged, if only to halt the outflow of specialist white personnel. In these circumstances, affirmative action in the military remained largely a paper exercise until recently.

Former SADF members nevertheless remain convinced that they will be disadvantaged should affirmative action become practice.[23] Indeed, this is likely, in tandem with rationalization now that the honeymoon period of the democratic transition is over. With the end of Nationalist participation in the Government of National Unity and the expiration of civil-servant tenure provisions, massive cutbacks are currently contemplated for the public sector. Throughout the state bureaucracy, the dialectic between standards and representivity is likely to echo as a policy variable for years to come. But in the case of the military, there is particular pressure to move assertively forward to set the example. The NDF is, to an extent, hoist on its own petard since it continues to present itself as one of the most (if not *the* most) successful state sector in dealing with transformation. Former Deputy Minister Kasrils consistently urged its leaders to step up the pace of affirmative action,[24] as did his then-superior, the far more cautious Joe Modise. In the electoral run-up following the appointment of General Nyanda, Modise displayed unprecedented activism on equal opportunity. Since late 1996 Modise also displayed considerably less compliance with the agenda of the white generals. This resulted in March 1997, for example, in several significant appointments (but not necessarily promotions) that should go some way toward empowering senior black officers at operational and tactical levels once "final decisions are taken as a result of the re-engineering [i.e., rationalization] process."[25] The successors to Kasrils and Modise, Defence Minister Lekota in particular, are bound to advance the case for affirmative action and equal opportunity as the ANC tries to deliver on its promise during the 1999–2004 interelection period.

The Air Force is also being pressured to dilute its rigid insistence on standards that tend to act as mechanisms of exclusion and has agreed to revisit its procedures.[26] In the Army, the predominant arm of service, the debate over affirmative action has tended to be sidetracked by issues such as whether it applies only to black personnel or to women as well. Nevertheless, even in this most conservative organization, democratization took its toll with the appointment of General Andrew Masondo as chief director for equal opportunities, tasked "to establish in conjunction with the Defence Secretariat and then maintain within the SANDF, the DOD's policy with regard to equal opportunity and affirmative action." This implies a broad mission to prevent any "unfair discrimination [while] ensuring cohesion and morale among SANDF members." Provision is made not only for black personnel but also women and "other previously disadvantaged personnel," including those who might require basic adult education.[27] One can generally anticipate greater energy on the part of the new Directorate to research discriminatory practices in the armed forces, investigate complaints, develop programs to ensure affirmative action for each arm of service down to unit level, and ensure general linkage between future training and the concept of the military as an equal-opportunity employer.

All of this would be disturbing for any conservative military hierarchy. Concentrated within the short time frame of transition, the impact is potentially traumatic for the military and civil society. The relocation of former NSF guerrillas is likely to be especially problematic, as very few have convertible skills for civilian use. Many latter-day MK personnel (i.e., those joining after its legalization in 1991) have come directly from the volatile SDUs, which, along with Inkatha's SPUs, were a major source of political-criminal violence in the run-up to elections. Since the primary criteria for rationalization include skill levels and disciplinary record,[28] this group (with generally low skills and a history of disrupting the integration process), is a prime but explosive target for forced retrenchment. It is also the least absorbable into civil society, along with thousands of other black SDU-SPU former paramilitary personnel who continue to roam the streets. Yet the track record of the Service Corps is dubious and its programs increasingly redundant. Today, there are few successful graduates from its low-caliber courses, and unless substantially greater resources are pumped in by the NDF, the state bureaucracy, and civil society, it faces complete disappearance in the near future.

Retrenchment of former NSFs recently recruited into the armed forces is fraught both political and practical dangers. Except for a thin layer of highly professional officers maintained as the vanguard of the new black officer corps, all newly integrated former MK and APLA members who are underqualified are at risk. Since most MK and APLA personnel are members of the generation of 1976 (young people with incomplete educations forced into exile and then military service in the wake of the Soweto rebellion), effective downsizing will be difficult and dangerous. Rationalized or demobilized women (particularly black women) present a particular problem given the gender barriers that have to be surmounted in their reintegration to civil society. Other African states have experienced considerable instability as a result of inadequate support being extended to soldiers cast out of the barracks to join the ranks of the poor and unemployed once their severance packages have been exhausted, and former SANDF General Meiring has said as much with regard to South Africa's tentative democracy in his assertion that "to leave these individuals in the streets is . . . to invite trouble."[29] Subsequently, the Personnel Rationalization Work Group (PRWG) was designated to be as consultative, fair, and transparent as possible in working to blunt the personal and social impacts of rationalization. A subgroup to examine social and psychological support for those unfortunate enough to be laid off has been established, while BMATT has been co-opted into the process with a special oversight (but not adjudicative) responsibility for former NSF personnel. With an eye to the latter, NDF leaders have emphasized that bridging training "is meant to give everyone a fair chance to remain in service."[30] Assurances have been given that severance payments will also be made on a "humane" basis with respect to background, talent, qualifications, and past performance—but with due regard to representivity.[31] According to some plans, at least some personnel whose services are no longer required could find themselves deployed to allied state departments (such as the SAPS), retrained, remustered, or even reemployed as consultants under special contract.

It is notoriously difficult to manage or predict the consequences of rationalization for civil-military relations or society more generally; much depends on the sociodemographic profile of those affected (age, military experience, life skills, and readjustment capability) as well as the type of conversion mechanisms emplaced at the borders with civil society. South Africa is fortunate in that its armed forces are proactively planning the process that now takes precedence over integration, and civil society is sufficiently differentiated, all things being equal, to meet the challenge of thousands of soldiers disgorged from the military ranks. Yet the fledgling democracy still has to contend with coinciding class and race cleavages in conditions of gross inequality, burgeoning criminal violence, a society awash with weapons, and massive structural joblessness. Rootless unemployed soldiers drawn from lower-grade personnel in former guerrilla armies constitute an aggravating factor. There is, for example, evidence to suggest that armed gangs of former freedom fighters who have scorned integration—so-called Mkaplas—operate at the borders of crime and politics in the interminable violence in Kwa-Zulu–Natal. During late 1997, the rural areas of the Free State region were rocked by a spate of killings of white farmers. Attributed to renegade former APLA personnel working across the Lesotho border, such violence remains an important lever for political mobilization by the Afrikaner right, still with strong roots in conservative rural areas. In urban areas, spectacular heists conducted along military lines by large armed gangs (allegedly former MK personnel) also fueled fears at the highest levels about a resurgent third force with an agenda to destabilize the nascent democratic system.[32]

Civil society has not risen to the challenge. Despite virtual paranoia about crime and its impact on foreign investment, the private sector and the armed forces remain distinct worlds. With the exception of the loosely formed National Defence Liaison Council, whose purpose is to assist the recruitment of part-time forces around the professional core, there is little collaboration between business and the military on rationalization. Despite examples of conversion programs from other parts of Africa and Latin America, business remains largely unconcerned with the social impact of movements to downsize the military. South Africa's powerful union movement (which goes by the acronym COSATU) is also a nonactor because of its primary involvement in issues concerning the privatization of the economy and the neoliberal GEAR initiative. ANC involvement in rationalization-demobilization is conducted largely with the feeling that MK's problems are now those of the NDF. Given mass unemployment, there is in fact strong support for the view that former soldiers not be treated on a favored basis. As for the armed forces, six years into democratization, there is still built-in resistance to civilian involvement in what is seen to be an internal matter. This tends to inhibit possible developments to upgrade the Service Corps or some successor organization as the transition point between the military and civil society thus avoiding a situation where, as in many Eastern European economies, hopelessly uncompetitive former soldiers become the victims of unconstrained market forces.

It has been suggested that the armed forces could fragment, with disastrous political consequences in the face of half-baked integration followed by conflicts over rationalization.[33] This is unlikely, although the immediate future will probably see a variety of conflicts as the NDF seeks to attain equilibrium and representivity through structural changes that progressively erode the current situation of white predominance. Rationalization will inevitably impact these struggles, particularly inside the high-tech ranks of the Air Force and Navy, where it is reasonable to assume white control will continue for some time regardless of rationalization.[34] In the Army, the early years of the twenty-first century are likely to see an institution fundamentally transformed by natural attrition, rationalization, and affirmative action. This means an increasingly black officer corps in the medium term alongside young men of all backgrounds united by a common commitment to professional soldiering. Already at the Army Gymnasium, there is a healthy esprit de corps among intakes.[35] Given the continued inability of the new military to magnetize white South Africans, however, the lower ranks of the core force will almost inevitably be staffed by blacks, some of whom will be the more highly trained survivors of rationalization, others of whom will be new recruits attracted to a military career. The part-time forces and Rear Area Protection Units will also in all likelihood become more national, provided it is possible to quickly develop a military service ethic among black South Africans, the majority of whom still carry distasteful memories.

All of this depends on how successfully rationalization is creatively managed by state ministries (e.g., Housing, Labour, Education), which have yet to develop a meaningful policy dialogue on rationalization. These numerous options remain to be explored and have even proved relatively successful in diminishing the impact of letting loose trained soldiers on civil society in other contexts. These include counseling and outplacement services (used in the Netherlands), preferential hiring practices negotiated with the business community (the United States), and the recruitment of former soldiers into other areas of the civil service—even as the public sector is the process of downscaling. Rationalization, however, is only one factor in future civil-military relations, and the determining element for successful democratization is the creation of strong civil institutions to catch the fallouts from the transforming military.

At this level, there are infinite variables. South Africa's transition and the civil-military system reflect the enormous charismatic and moral influence of Nelson Mandela. The former president is widely attributed a major personal role in directly, if quietly, facilitating some of the most severe interpersonal and interinstitutional tensions arising out of integration,[36] and his official departure from the political scene following the 1999 elections constituted the end of an important, if idiosyncratic, hedge against conflicts between soldier and soldier as well as soldier and civilian. While President Thabo Mbeki has eased into Mandela's footsteps, albeit with a different and less personalized style of governance, struggles over future successions among the ruling ANC cannot be ruled out. This has important implications for relations between warrior and managerial elements in the armed forces. Transformation is now the stuff and measure of political identity in all institutions, not excluding the NDF, and as various elements in the armed forces contest its speed and content, struggles of this type will inevitably interconnect with civil society following the end of the transition honeymoon.

Retrograde, resurgent militarism is unlikely given the constraints of a resurrected local society, the international decline of militarism, and intensifying global interdependence. Yet the establishment of electoral democracy is only one step toward the culmination of a full-blown democratic system, and six years into the transition many of the ingredients for stable and effective governance remain to be emplaced. Authoritarian traditions and practices are notoriously residual, and South Africa's new constitutional leadership may experience difficulty in independently managing the cascade of events that accompany transition in its second stage. The mission of the armed forces has significantly shifted from the offensive to the defensive, from maintaining national security—the watchword of total strategy—to defending the nation. Yet the nation remains to be built in conditions of coinciding race and class division that do not augur well for a newly civilianized military that is not without its own internal tensions. Power relations within South Africa ultimately involve a highly tentative and intricate arrangement of elite bargains and trade-offs remarkably similar to the consociational ideas discredited during the years of the tricameral parliament. The stabilizing black middle class dismissively referred to during those years has emerged with a vengeance in the form of what some grassroots critics vociferously condemn as a venal black bourgeoisie in alliance with white elites and divorced from its populist base. History is, after all, replete with examples where the military has moved to protect complex mixtures of corporate and class interests, either unilaterally or, just as dangerously, by invitation.

Now that the initial gloss on the transition has begun to dull, a growing number of writings and statements, both in South Africa and abroad, are beginning to reluctantly conclude that the democratic experiment has run into a degree of trouble as new mechanisms for social control and cohesion are inadequate to maintaining economic growth and sociopolitical stability. As South Africa continues to wrestle with unemployment, inequalities, and imploding systems of law enforcement, several bleak scenarios undermine the optimism accompanying the birth of the rainbow nation. Presumptions concerning the deterioration of civil-military relations are implicit in these visions of decay, not excluding the outside possibility of eventual military intervention. South Africa, fortunately, cannot compete with many of its continental counterparts at the level of coup pedigree. Still, social history is such that one can never entirely exclude military intention in some form or another, particularly if the transition falters.

Whether the state will succeed in delivering on its development promises, inherent in the original RDP and inflated during 1994 for political purposes, remains a moot point as the economy moves into a market-driven, neoliberal mode for growth and reconstruction. Ultimately, civil disturbances stemming from the unremittingly unsatisfied aspirations of the great majority of South Africans could provide the trigger for characteristic military action to save the constitution. Variations on this tragic theme include a breakdown in the unity of the ruling ANC, political meddling with the promotional system of the military hierarchy as various political stakeholders jockey for influence, growing distance between the elite and the volatile masses, coup coalitions, economic decline in the face of inability to magnetize foreign capital inputs, added structural unemployment, civil violence that only the soldiers can contain—indeed, the full combination of depressing factors that have together fueled the coup as a frequent political event in Africa and elsewhere.

None of this is meant to imply that South Africa is firmly on the road to civil-military conflict. Much of the earlier literature on the military under apartheid tended to overinfer: What was true for Nigeria or Argentina was wrongly translated to South Africa, despite vast differences in structural conditions. The necessary motive, means, and disposition of the military to act against legally constituted civil authority also requires, as eminent military sociologist and author Samuel Finer noted some years ago, much more than the simple existence of political conflict intrinsic to a civil society, like South Africa, struggling to forge a democratic identity. Much the same circumspection needs to be applied to the consequences for the various horizontal and vertical tensions within the armed forces, linked to such issues as black aspirations to upward mobility, interservice rivalries over weapons acquisitions, and tensions between soldiers and civilians over national budget allocations. These may not augur well for the democratic experiment, or perhaps they are signs of normal and healthy political competition in a society emerging from authoritarianism.

Still, the chapters herein are subtexted by the view that there are many combustible points within the military that carry danger for the democratic order. Rationalization may or may not prove to be the thin edge of the wedge that transforms invisible tensions into conflict in or with the civic realm. This reflects the deeper truth that the military pact built into transition has not produced what many persons of power, in the barracks and without, consider an appropriate restructuring of the armed forces.

Neither has it produced a coherent bureaucratic formation based on transcending professional identities resistant to the claims of power-hungry politicians seeking to exploit the coincidence of organizational and racial cleavages. Despite public disclaimers by senior officers that the armed forces are beginning to fall behind other institutions, race relations in many regional commands remain volatile, in a climate of undiscipline.[37]

In many respects, the armed forces have indeed been at the forefront. Yet many officers continue to fear contamination should civil values become more intrusive. The academic notion that militaries who share values with civilians are less prone to intervention and repression[38] remains to be more effectively marketed in the officer corps, guided by a mixture of discipline, combat capacity, and social distance. At this point in time, the principles of subjective control in the NDF are still insufficiently intense to entirely guarantee that some factions within the armed forces will not respond positively to overtures from rogue elements in society, populists, or reactionaries, the former Generals Holomisa or Viljoen, or lesser public figures still emerging onto the political landscape who see the military as a fertile arena for accumulating political capital. The mutually reinforcing objective controls for peacefully subordinating the armed forces are also still germinal in their role of what one theorist has termed "politically sterilising" the armed forces.[39]

Relations between South Africa's constitutionally democratic government and its postauthoritarian military have tended to lean heavily on idiosyncratic factors and personal relations, with the charismatic Mandela at the center. These include ties forged between some of the senior NDF generals and Mandela once he was released from prison and then undemonized to the military in the process of becoming South Africa's first democratic president. Although these relations have been correct rather than close, there has been a delicate symbiosis of interests between the executive branch and military leaders that may or may not be maintained by succeeding generations of leaders. More formal regulation of the military is also fairly tentative, even in the powerful JPSCD, where the first generation of antimilitarists is now giving way to a milder and less militant (if better informed) group of legislators.

The elections of June 1999 confirmed the ruling ANC's grip on state power; in their wake, we also saw the resignation of South Africa's first postapartheid defense minister, Joe Modise. His successor, Patrick "Terror" Lekota, is still a largely unknown quantity, at least in the defense arena. Clearly, a new and stronger defense minister directly linked to the increasingly powerful executive (which President Mbeki seems intent on fashioning with Mandela now in retirement) does not in itself ensure firmer civil control over the military. This ultimately depends on civil society being armed with effective organizational mechanisms for the management of the armed forces. Here there is still some cause for concern.

While it is certainly an exaggeration that "government attempts to establish civilian control over the defense force are foundering,"[40] it is nonetheless true that the newly reinvigorated MOD remains to prove its mettle as a lever for civilianization. South Africa's disastrous peacekeeping operation in Lesotho in late 1998 not only displays poor planning and uncertain cohesion within the SANDF as a military institution but also castes into bold relief the capability of the MOD to shape interbureaucratic power relations and policy decisions within the state when the chips are down. Current proposals to elicit South African participation in peacekeeping initiatives to halt the ongoing political decay in the Democratic Republic of the Congo and the Great Lakes region of central Africa are also likely to test the MOD. Certainly, the MOD likely will require considerably more human resources, institutional experience, and administrative skills if it is to effectively shape public policy, least of all take on the military establishment.

The Defence Secretariat, an important step forward, is equally circumscribed in its oversight capacity by its continued reliance on the goodwill of the armed forces and their sense of compliance. Personality and political differences in the triad formed by the NDF, the MOD, and its Secretariat continue to be an important facet of interinstitutional relations, but the new acting defence secretary, Mamatho Netsianda, is an even more unknown quantity than Modise was. In the past, Modise's tendency to avoid conflict where possible tended to act to the advantage of the generals. This could conceivably continue unless the new minister and his secretary constitute a more forceful instrument for dealing with the more conservative of senior and midlevel white officers who speak the rhetoric of transformation but stymie its implementation.

As previous Defence Secretary Pierre Steyn himself pointed out to Parliament in August 1997, there is a definite gap between budget and policy commitments within the nascent MOD that clearly requires much more in the way of human resources, institutional experience, and administrative skills if it is to effectively take on the NDF.[41] Despite the fact that military finances have technically been transferred to the Secretariat, its actual oversight and control capability is severely circumscribed by its reliance on the goodwill of military personnel in the day-to-day running of organizational matters. This means heavy dependency on the cooperation of many old-fashioned bureaucrats, schooled under total strategy, who have yet to fully internalize the spirit and logic of compliance with civil society as an elementary facet of defense management in democracy.

It will take many more years to effectively inculcate this policy culture into the mainstream military psychologies, not only in the diminishing ranks of the former SADF complement but also their counterpart MK populists. In the absence of these new mind-sets, one can anticipate a series of running battles for institutional influence at the ministerial level for the foreseeable future. Within this time frame, the established bureaucracy of the NDF is likely to enjoy the upper hand, partly because of the current financially induced moratorium on the hiring of new staff (including civilian staff in the Secretariat), partly because progressive officers in the NDF remain unattracted to service in the Secretariat, where under existing regulations they lose a variety of service benefits. Overall, as Secretary Steyn lamented publicly prior to his departure, "the rate of change is too slow."[42]

Public opinion as a constraint on reinvigorated militarism is also problematic because arbitrary behavior by political and military leadership was casually accepted as a matter of national interest. Notwithstanding efforts to democratize defense through such instruments as the Defence Review, defense matters are still generally regarded as highly specialist and secretive in nature—best left to central decisionmakers. This natural deference, a legacy of authoritarianism, is expressed in multiple ways, including little sophisticated debate on defense control and a general lack of analytical skills and interests in the academic sector. The inability of antimilitarist groups, such as Gun-Free South Africa or the Cease-fire Campaign, to effectively extend their activities beyond specialist microdisarmament activities indicates the wider, serious, and continuing problems of effectively regulating civil-military relations in a partially reconstituted civil society largely devoid of vigilant and critical opinion on defense issues.

None of this is to suggest that the NDF still sets the terms of the dialogue between the military and civil society as in the recent past; it does not suggest that the military would like to do so—except on such specific institutional issues that concern all militaries, such as weapons procurement, defense budgets, the internal autonomy of the armed forces, and their tasks and mission. Appropriate participation that allows social institutions to maintain their maximum goals is crucial to a working democracy,[43] and it is important that militaries make available their specialist expertise to government, subject to the proviso that they do so as a state sector and not as a political actor.

Civil society, for its part, also has responsibilities to its soldiers, and the way it behaves, particularly in the transitional strategies of government, is critical to new democracies.[44] The Latin American experience, for example, shows that the institutional autonomy of the armed forces must be honored. Policies that seek to neuter the military by fostering interservice competition over resources and power have a nasty tendency to backfire, to draw civil society into the military, and perhaps embroil the military in civil society. Military behavior in the post-transitional phase is also sharply conditioned by the status accorded the armed forces, partly expressed through the material means of the defense budget, partly through symbolic actions that encourage the self-perception that the military is a valued, credible, and contributory institution. While the new NDF does not enjoy the historic centrality possessed by many of its counterparts in Latin America, considerations of institutional dignity are vitally important in promoting military loyalty to the new political order. Although it may not be possible, as in South Africa, for civil society to secure its military with lavish rewards at a time of social reconstruction and competing demands by other interest groups with possibly more valid claims on the public purse, it is important that the armed forces be given some compensation that feeds its raison d'être, its sense of purpose, morale, and, ultimately, its collaboration and compliance with civil society. It is probably with this in mind that the development-versus-defense debate swung decisively in favor of the militarists in the late 1990s. Despite the controversy over reequipping the armed forces, the state committed some R30 billion for weapons acquisitions.

The line between subordination and alienation in civil-military relations is always dangerously thin, especially at the point where vested authoritarianism gives way to democratization. Thus, it was unavoidable that the armed forces would bear the brunt of responsibility for past injustices even as those in the National Party escaped the same. Budget cuts, new systems of civilian control, Lesotho, Tempe, and technical obsolescence—all have sapped the institutional confidence and status of the armed forces. A career in the military, relative to other public service, has already ceased to be seen as a promising path for the socially mobile, the seekers of technological skills, and those who quite simply seek to serve their country. Certainly the new system of voluntary military service remains to capture the public imagination. Civil control and budget cuts are all very well, but more emphasis needs to be placed on professional restructuring if one is not to demoralize those who are its targets. Human rights trials serve an important ethical and consolidative purpose in the wake of extended authoritarianism, but when they turn into a generalized condemnation of the military, they cement the conviction of the soldiers that democracy is hostile.[45] In South Africa, it is inconceivable that every member of the entire military, or even the Army, is implicated in human rights violations.

Civil society is under no obligation to pander to its soldiers even in the shaky circumstances of democratization. Yet governments need to educate their militaries as to what is acceptable and what is undesirable in the uncertain conditions of transition. More important, government has a responsibility to define and support the mission of the armed forces on the basis of the understanding that missionless militaries become political militaries. This means that in aligning militarism with tentative democracy in South Africa the military needs to receive appropriate respect and positive reinforcement, due recognition, and, above all, a clear set of professional responsibilities that accords with their proven capacity as members of a fighting institution.

The pacted context of South Africa's transition has insulated the military from popular discreditation, their inability to come to terms with the new political order, and the subsequent insurrections.[46] South African civil-military relations during the 1990s have evolved in a far more favorable political context, with many of the preconditions for the depoliticization and organizational evolution of the armed forces already emplaced.[47] The South African military has followed the path of extricating itself from power politics before choices have been snatched from its control; in doing so it has succeeded in emerging from the militarism of the last days of apartheid with a fair degree of social credibility. Many of the objectives for legitimacy first articulated in transitional negotiations have been realized, while the Defence Review process has opened unprecedented possibilities for public participation in defense matters. Inasmuch as demilitarization involves the transfer of power and resources to civil society, a considerable amount has been achieved in a remarkably short period. Much, however, remains to be done to reverse the culture of militarism engendered by apartheid. Although democratic transition represents a fundamental move forward in race relations within the Republic, both oppressor and oppressed have been so ethically desensitized by the sheer destructiveness of apartheid that it will take generations for people to break free of the reinforcing virulence of militarism, nationalism, class exclusion, and the pervasive belief that violence is an acceptable means to manage conflict. Certainly the military, as elsewhere, remains locked to the view that war is normal social activity.[48]

South Africa remains a society without the economic foundations for sustaining democracy. Following two rounds of democratic elections, there are still gross inequalities between blacks and whites, and there can be little consensus on defense issues. The debate over how the military fits into the new democracy, and its claim on national resources, will be debated for years. Many questions surrounding demilitarization remain unanswered, including the role of the local arms industry in the economy, the moral and economic dimensions of arms exports, and the value-based policy frameworks for national security. Within the narrower confines of the NDF itself, the objective of a unified and representative military also remains elusive. Overall, civil-military relations appear to fall short of the mark when compared to the world's stable and enduring democracies. Transformation is clearly in motion, but one suspects it is far from concluded.

The process of organizational redesign, disengagement, and civilianization of the armed forces will continue well into the twenty-first century and will no doubt be punctuated by struggles that reflect the wider problems of democratic consolidation. This is a political system seeking to find its feet in a socioeconomic environment that lacks many of the prerequisites for stable and sustainable government performance in its first generation. The challenge facing the military is to perform its professional mission, whatever it might be, within these shifting contours. In so doing, some of the wider social struggles could well deflect back into the armed forces. Others could originate within the military and spread across the boundaries from the barracks into broader society. Apartheid has broken down, but democracy has yet to deal with the excruciating and incomplete business of fully breaking through. Should it succeed in doing so—and one hopes it will—it will justify the enormous investment of lives and resources in the restoration of human dignity in a society once so very deeply divided by its disparate peoples.

Notes

1. See Samuel Huntington, *The Third Wave: Democratization in the Late Twentieth Century* (Norman: University of Oklahoma Press, 1991).

2. See, e.g., Deborah Norden, *Military Rebellion in Argentina: Between Coups and Consolidation* (Lincoln: University of Nebraska Press, 1996), p. 99.

3. On pacted transitions and transitional outcomes, see Terry Lyn Karl and Philippe Schmitter, "Modes of Transition in Latin America, South and Eastern Europe," *International Social Science Journal* 128 (May 1991): 264–284.

4. For a detailed analysis of relations between the armed forces and the TRC since the latter's inception until its Final Report, see Philip Frankel, "Recivilianisation and Reconciliation: South Africa's Armed Forces and Democratic Transition," paper presented to the International Political Science Association, Research Group into Armed Forces and Society Conference, University of the Negev, Israel, Sede Boker, July 1999.

5. See Interim Constitution, 236(8), 237(1b), sec. 189.

6. Major General P.J. Venter, "Restructuring, Integration, and Rationalization: An Overview of the Future Size and Shape of the National Defence Force," unpubl., n.d.

7. Greg Mills, "Armed Forces in Post-Apartheid South Africa," *Survival* 35(3) (Autumn 1993).

8. Recent Statements by the Minister and Deputy Minister of Defence,South African National Defence Force (SANDF), Internal Communications Bulletin 15(95), March 1, 1995.

9. *The Star* (Johannesburg), April 3, 1997.

10. SANDF, The National Defence Force in Transition, Annual Report 1994/95.

11. Colonel L.B. van Stade, "Rationalization in the South African National Defence Force: The Next Challenge," paper presented at the conference on the South African National Defence Force and Transformation, University of South Africa, Pretoria, October 15, 1996.

12. Charl Schutte, "People's Army, People's Choice: The Results of a Human Sciences Research Council/Institute for Defence Policy Public Opinion Survey," paper presented at the conference on Preparing the South African Army for the 21st Century, Council for Scientific and Industrial Research (CSIR), October 19, 1995.

13. Recent Statements by the Minister and Deputy Minister of Defence.

14. *Salut* (February 1995).

15. Suggestions have, for example, been made that units be named after various MK heroes, such as the late Chris Hani. This would effectively dispose of many regiments, including the Transvaal Scottish, for example, which maintained British nomenclature even during the apartheid years.

16. Mark Malan, "Yesterday's Heroes," *Natal Witness* (Durban), February 22, 1996. A situation of this type is highly undesirable as noted in recent reports of the Directorate for Intelligence: Current conditions, it notes, negatively affect discipline, effective administration, training and logistics, leadership capacity, corporate self-perceptions and loyalty, internal communication within structures, and the motivations of members of the NDF to carry out their professional tasks—in sum, all the attributes of what we indefinably term "morale." As far as rationalization is concerned, however, demoralization is at least part positive in principle in that it encourages voluntary retrenchment and natural attrition. Unfortunately, it does not do so to the point where forced retrenchment can be obviated as a policy option. Despite the reservations governing their position in the armed forces, most white personnel have not taken the decisive step of crossing the dangerous borders into civil society. Hence, as of the beginning of 1998, the NDF announced that it would have to compulsorily lay off a conservative 20,000 members (the figure is, privately, far higher) due to the failure of natural attrition to reduce numbers during the previous four years. It is currently estimated that rationalization requires downsizing the NDF complement by 25,000–30,000 personnel over the next two to three years.

17. van Stade, "Rationalisation in the South African National Defence Force."

18. Parliamentary Integration Oversight Committee (PIOC), Report on Visits to South African National Defence Force Units and Headquarters, June 14, 1997.

19. van Stade, "Rationalisation in the South African National Defence Force."

20. Malan, "Yesterday's Heroes."

21. Malan, "Yesterday's Heroes."

22. In the Air Force, for example, looming affirmative action rubs raw internal relations in an organization frequently labeled racist by NSF recruits and where, until 1997, only a tiny handful of former MK personnel was allowed to fly unaccompanied by white instructors. *The Star* (Johannesburg), October 6, 1995.

23. PIOC, Report on Visits to SANDF Units.

24. *The Star* (Johannesburg), May 15, 1996.

25. SANDF, "Transformation in the Ministry of Defence: Second Level Appointments," *Internal Communications Bulletin*, March 11, 1997, FOD No. 55520.

26. *The Star* (Johannesburg), July 5, 1996.

27. SANDF, Management Directive: Chief DirectorEqual Opportunities, Personnel Division, CSP/DPD/501/7, July 4, 1996.

28. Criteria of this type will somehow have to be aligned with issues of representivity if the goal of achieving a legitimate military is to be at all realized.

29. General Georg Meiring, "Keynote Address," presented at the conference on Taking the South African Army into the Future, University of South Africa, Pretoria, November 15, 1993.

30. *The Star* (Johannesburg), August 11, 1995.

31. Major General Deon Mortimer, "Integration, Rationalization, and Demobilisation."

32. Increasing reference is made in the local media, for example, to large-scale robberies of cash-in-transit by gangs acting with military precision.

33. Malan, "Yesterday's Heroes."

34. *The Star* (Johannesburg), October 6, 1995.

35. *Sunday Independent* (Johannesburg), February 11, 1996.

36. *Sunday Independent* (Johannesburg), March 15, 1998.

37. *Mail and Guardian* (Johannesburg), January 10, 1997.

38. See Samuel Huntington, *The Soldier and the State: The Theory and Practice of Civil-Military Relations* (Cambridge: Harvard University Press, 1957), p. 83.

39. Ibid.

40. *Mail and Guardian* (Johannesburg), August 15, 1997.

41. Ibid.

42. Ibid.

43. See, e.g., Ted Gurr and Harry Eckstein, *Patterns of Authority: A Structural Basis for Political Inquiry* (London: John Wiley and Sons, 1975), p. 485.

44. Norden, *Military Rebellion in Argentina.*

45. Ibid, p. 105.

46. Ibid.

47. On these preconditions, see, e.g., Samuel Finer, *The Man on Horseback: The Role of the Military in Politics* (New York: Frederick Praeger, 1962).

48. See, e.g., M. Mann, "The Roots and Contradictions of Modern Militarism," *New Left Review* 62 (1987): 71.

Select Bibliography

Books

Abrahamson, Bengt. *Military Professionalism and Political Power*. Beverly Hills, Calif.: Sage Publications, 1972.

Adams, Gordon. *The Politics of Defense Contracting: The Iron Triangle*. New Brunswick, N.J.: Transaction Books, 1982.

Beaufre, Andre. "*Introduction de la Strategie.*" In *Strategie de l'Action*. Paris: Armand Collin, 1966.

Beukes, T.J.N. *Naval and State Activities in the Exclusive Economic Zone: A Comparative Perspective*. Pretoria: Institute for Maritine Technology, 1995.

Blechman, Barry, et al. *The American Military in the Twenty-first Century*. New York: St. Martin's Press, 1993.

Boraine, Alex, Janet Levy, and Ronel Scheffer, eds. *Dealing with the Past: Truth and Reconciliation in South Africa*. Cape Town: Institute for Democracy in South Africa, 1994.

Cawthra, Gavin. *Brutal Force: The Apartheid War Machine*. London: International Defence and Aid Fund, 1986.

______. *Policing South Africa: The South African Police and the Transition from Apartheid*. Cape Town: David Philip, 1994.

Charnay, J-P. *Essai General de La Strategie*. Paris: Editions Libre, 1973.

Cilliers, Jakkie. *Counter-Insurgency in Rhodesia*. London: Croom Helm, 1985.

Cilliers, Jakkie, ed. *Dismissed: The Demobilisation and Reintegration of Former Combatants in Africa*. Midrand: Institute for Defence Policy, 1995.

Cilliers, Jakkie, and G. Mills, eds. *Peacekeeping in Africa*. Midrand: Institute for Defence Policy and South African Institute for International Affairs, 1995.

Cilliers, Jakkie, and Markus Reinhardt, eds. *About Turn: The Transformation of the South African Military and Intelligence*. Midrand: Institute for Defence Policy, 1996.

Cock, Jacklyn, and Nathan Laurie. *War and Society: The Militarisation of South Africa*. Cape Town: David Philip, 1989.

Dabat, Alejandro, and Luis Lorezano. *Argentina: The Malvinas and the End of Military Rule*. London: Verso, 1984.

Danopoulos, Constantine, ed. *From Military to Civilian Rule*. London: Routledge, 1992.

Diamond, Larry, Juan Linz, and Seymour Martin Lipset, eds. *Democracy in Developing Countries*. 4 Vols. Boulder: Lynne Reiner Publishers, 1988.

______. *Politics in Developing Countries: Comparing Experiences with Democracy*. Boulder: Lynne Rienner, 1990.

di Palma, Guiseppe. *To Craft Democracies: An Essay on Democratic Transition*. Berkeley: University of California Press, 1990.

Edmonds, Martin, and Gregg Mills. *Uncharted Waters: A Review of South Africa's Naval Options*. Johannesburg: South African Institute for International Affairs; and Lancaster, U.K.: Centre for Defence and International Security Studies, Lancaster University, 1996.

Enloe, Cynthia. *Ethnic Soldiers: State Security in a Divided Society*. Harmondsworth: Penguin, 1980.

Finer, Samuel. *The Man on Horseback: The Role of the Military in Politics*. New York: Frederick Praeger, 1962.

Fontana, Andres. *Fuerzas Armadas, Partidos Politicos y Transicion a La Democracia en Argentina*. Buenos Aires, Argentina: CEDES, 1984.

______. *La Politica Militar en un Contexto de Transicion Argentina, 1983–1989*. Buenos Aires, Argentina: CEDES, 1990.

Frankel, Philip. *Pretoria's Praetorians: Civil-Military Relations in South Africa*. Cambridge: Cambridge University Press, 1984.

______. *Marching to the Millennium: The Birth, Development, and Transformation of the South African National Defence Force*. Pretoria: South African National Defence Force, Directorate of Corporate Communications, 1998.

Frankel, Philip, Noam Pines, and Mark Swilling, eds. *State, Resistance, and Change in South Africa*. London: Croom Helm, 1988.

Friedman, Steven, and Doreen Atkinson, eds. *The Small Miracle*. Johannesburg: Ravan Press, 1994.

Geldenhuys, Jannie. *A General's Story: From an Era of War to Peace*. Johannesburg: Jonathan Ball, 1995.

Goodman, Louis, Johanna Mendelson, and Juan Rial, eds. *The Military and Democracy: The Future of Civil-Military Relations in Latin America*. Lexington, Virg.: Lexington Books, 1990.

Grundy, Kenneth. *Soldiers Without Politics: Blacks in the South African Armed Forces*. Berkeley: University of California Press, 1983.

______. *The Militarisation of South African Politics*. London. I.B. Tauris, 1986.

Gurr, Ted, and Harry Eckstein. *Patterns of Authority: A Structural Basis for Political Inquiry*. London: John Wiley and Sons, 1975.

Hanlon, Joe. *Begger Your Neighbour: Apartheid Power in Southern Africa*. London: Catholic Institute for International Relations, 1986.

Hansson, D.S. *Policing and the Law*. Cape Town: Juta, 1989.

Heitmann, H-R. *South African War Machine*. Johannesburg: Central News Agency, 1985.

Herz, John. *From Dictatorship to Democracy*. Westport, Conn.: Greenwood Press, 1982.

Huntinton, Samuel. *The Third Wave: Democratisation in the Late Twentieth Century*. Norman: University of Oklahoma Press, 1991.

______. *The Soldiers and the State: The Theory and Practice of Civil-Military Relations*. Cambridge: Harvard University Press, 1968 (rev. ed., 1995).

International Defence and Aid Fund. *Namibia: The Facts.* London: International Defence and Aid Fund, 1989.

Isaacs, Anita. *Military Rule and Transition in Ecuador, 1972–1992.* Basingstoke, Hamphire: Macmillan, 1993.

Janowitz, Morris. *The Military in the Political Development of New Nations: An Essay in Comparative Analysis.* Chicago: University of Chicago Press, 1964.

Janowitz, Morris, and Jacques van Doorn, eds. *On Military Ideology.* Rotterdam, Netherlands: Rotterdam University Press, 1971.

Jaster, Robert. *South Africa in Namibia: The Botha Strategy.* Lanham, Md.: University Press of America, 1985.

Kemp, Arthur. *Victory or Violence: The Story of the AWB.* Pretoria: Forma Publishers, 1990.

Linz, Juan. *The Breakdown of Democratic Regimes: Crisis, Breakdown, and Re-Equilibrium.* Baltimore: Johns Hopkins University Press, 1978.

Mainwaring, Scott, Gullermo O'Donnell, and J. Samuel Valenzuela, eds. *Issues in Democratic Consolidation.* South Bend, Ind.: University of Notre Dame Press, 1992.

Maniruzzaman, Takuldar. *Military Withdrawal from Politics: A Comparative Study.* Cambridge: Bollinger, 1987.

Matthews, Anthony. *Freedom, State Security, and the Rule of Law: Dilemmas of Apartheid Society.* Cape Town: Juta, 1986.

Mayer, R. *The Political Economy of Defence Contracting.* New Haven: Yale University Press, 1991.

McCuen, J.J. *The Art of Counter-Revolutionary Warfare.* London: Faber and Faber, 1966.

McSherry, J. Patrice. *Incomplete Transition: Military Power and Democracy in Argentina.* Basingstoke, Hamphire: Macmillan Press Ltd, 1997.

Minnaar, Anthony, Ian Liebenberg, and Charl Schutte, eds. *The Hidden Hand: Covert Operations in South Africa.* Pretoria: Human Sciences Research Council, 1994.

Nathan, Laurie. *The Changing of the Guard: Armed Forces and Defence Policy in a Democratic South Africa.* Pretoria: Human Sciences Research Council Publishers, 1994.

Norden, Deborah. *Military Rebellion in Argentina: Between Coups and Consolidation.* Lincoln: University of Nebraska Press, 1996.

Nordlinger, Eric. *Soldiers and Politics: Military Coups and Government.* Englewood Cliffs, N.J.: Prentice-Hall, 1977.

Nunn, Frederick. *The Time of the Generals: Latin American Professional Militarism in World Perspective.* Lincoln: Universisty of Nebraska Press, 1992.

O'Donnell, Guillermo, et al. *Transitions from Authoritarian Rule: Latin America.* Baltimore: Johns Hopkins University Press, 1986.

O'Meara, Daniel. *Forty Lost Years: The Apartheid State and the Politics of the National Party, 1948–1994.* Athens: Ohio University Press, 1996.

Pauw, Jacques. *In the Heart of the Whore.* Johannesburg: Southern Book Publishers, 1991.

Peralta Ramos, Monica, and Carlos Waisman, eds. *From Military Rule to Liberal Democracy in Argentina.* Boulder: Westview Press, 1987.

Potash, Robert. *The Army and Politics in Argentina, 1928–1945* and *1945–1962*. 2 Vols. Stanford: Stanford University Press, 1969 and 1980.

Pottinger, Brian. *The Imperial Presidency: P.W. Bothe—the First Ten Years*. Johannesburg: Southern Book Publishers, 1988.

Preston, Paul. *The Politics of Revenge: Facism and the Military in Twentieth-Century Spain*. London: Unwin Hyman, 1990.

Preston, R. *Demobilising and Reintegrating Fighters After War: The Namibian Experience*. Warwick, U.K.: International Centre for Education in Development, University of Warwick, 1994.

Rees, M., and C. Day. *Muldergate: The Story of the Info Scandal*. Johannesburg: Macmillan, 1980.

Ruiz Moreno, Isidoro. *Comandos en Accion: El Ejercito en Malvinas*. Buenos Aires, Argentina: Emec, 1986.

Sarkesian, Sam, John Allen Williams, and Fred B. Bryant. *Soldiers, Society, and National Security*. Boulder: Lynne Rienner, 1995.

Seegers, Annette. *The Military and the Making of Modern South Africa*. London: Tauris Academic Studies, 1996.

Shaw, Mark, and Jakkie Cilliers, eds. *Peacekeeping in Africa*. Vol. 1. Midrand, South Africa: Institute for Defence Policy, 1995.

Simons, H.J., and R.E. Simons. *Class and Colour in South Africa, 1850–1950*. London: Defence and Aid Fund, 1983.

Steenkamp, Willem. *South Africa's Border War, 1966–1989*. Gibraltar: Ashanti Publishing, 1989.

Stepan, Alfred. *Rethinking Military Politics: Brazil and the Southern Cone*. Princeton: Princeton University Press, 1988.

Totemeyer, Gerhard, Vezer Kandetu, and Wolfgang Werner, eds. *Namibia in Perspective*. Windhoek, Namibia: Council of Churches in Namibia, 1987.

Varas, Augusto, ed. *Democracy Under Siege: New Military Power in Latin America*. Stamford, Conn.: Greenwood Press, 1989.

Welch, Claude. *Civilian Control of the Military*. Albany: SUNY Press, 1976.

______. *No Farewell to Arms: Military Disenagagement from Politics in Africa and Latin America*. Boulder: Westview Press, 1987.

Zagorski, Paul. *Democracy versus National Security: Civil-Military Relations in Latin America*. Boulder: Lynne Rienner, 1992.

Articles, Monographs, Reports, and Public Presentations

Acuna, Carlos, and Catalina Smulovitz. "Ni Olvido ni Perdon? Derechos Humanos y Tensiones Civicos-Militares en Las Transicion Aregentina." Paper prepared for Latin American Studies Association Congress, 1991.

Aguero, Felipe. "The Military and Limits to Democratisation in South America." In *Issues in Democratic Consolidation*, edited by Scott Mainwaring, Guillermo O'Donnell, and J. Samuel Valenzuela. South Bend, Ind.: University of Notre Dame Press, 1992.

______. "Autonomy of the Military in Chile: From Democracy to Authoritarianism." In *Democracy Under Siege: New Military Power in Latin America*, edited by Augusto Varas. Stamford, Conn: Greenwood Press, 1989.

Amnesty International. "Statement to the United Nations Ad Hoc Working Group of Experts on Southern Africa." London: Amnesty International, 1991.

Andersen, Martin Edwin. "The Military Obstacle to Latin Democracy." *Foreign Policy* 73 (Winter 1988–1989).

Anglin, J. "The Life and Death of South Africa's National Peace-Keeping Force." *Journal of Modern African Studies* 33(1) (1995): 21–52.

Bestbier, Andre. "Briefing to Parliamentary Joint Standing Committee on Defence." June 1997.

Boraine, Andrew. "The Militarisation of Local Control: The Security Management System in Mamelodi, 1986–1988." In *War and Society: The Militarisation of South Africa*, edited by Jacklyn Cock and Laurire Nathan. Cape Town: David Philip, 1989.

Borzutsky, Silvia. "The Hidden Hand of the Military: The Impact of Human Rights Abuses on the New Democracies." Paper presented to the Eighteenth International Congress of the Latin American Studies Association, Atlanta, Georgia, March 10–12, 1994.

Buchanan, Paul. "The Varied Faces of Domination: State Terror, Economic Policy, and Social Rupture During the Argentine 'Processo,' 1976–1981." *American Political Science Review* 31(2) (February 1987).

Cilliers, Jakkie. "A Factual Overview of the Armed Forces of the TBVC Countries." *South African Defence Review* 13 (November 1993).

______. "Towards Collaborative and Cooperative Security in Southern Africa: The OAU and the SADC." In *About Turn: The Transformation of the South African Military and Intelligence*, edited by Cilliers and Markus Reichardt. Midrand: Institute for Defence Policy, 1995.

______. "The Evolving Security Architecture in Southern Africa." *African Security Review* 4(5) (1995).

Cock, Jacklyn. "The Link Between Security and Development: The Problem of Light Weapons Proliferation in Southern Africa." *African Security Review* 5(5) (1996).

Danopoulos, Constantine. "Military Dictatorships in Retreat: Problems and Prospects." In *The Decline of Military Regimes: The Civilian Influence*, edited by Danopoulos. Boulder: Westview Press, 1988.

______. "Intervention and Withdrawal: Notes and Perspectives." In *From Military to Civilian Rule*, edited by Danopoulos. London: Routledge, 1992.

de Klerk, W.J. "Behind Closed Doors." *Leadership South Africa* 6(6) (1987).

______. "Word Die Afrikaners Nou Liberaliste?" *Die Suid-Afrikaan* 18 (December/January 1988–1989).

Dix, Robert H. "Military Coups and Military Rule in Latin America." *Armed Forces and Society*. 20(3) (Spring 1994).

Dorning, W.A. "A Concise History of the South African Defence Force, 1912–1987." *Militaria* 17(2) (1987).

Dosman, E. "Understanding the Cuban Role in Angola, 1975–1990." Paper presented to the Workshop on Angola, Canadian Research Consortium on Southern Africa, Queens University, Kingston, October 2, 1993.

de Kock, Chris, and Charl Schutte. "The Public's Perception of the National Peace-Keeping Force at Deployment at Katorus." Midrand: Institute for Defence Policy, NPKF Research Project, May 1994.

du Pisani, Andre. "Beyond the Barracks: Reflections on the Role of the SADF in the Region." Johannesburg: South African Institute of International Affairs, 1988.

du Toit, A. "Editorial." *Die Suid-Afrikaan* (August/September 1990).

Fitch, Samuel. "Military Professionalism, National Security, and Democracy: Lessons from the Latin American Experience." Paper presented at the Latin American Studies Association Conference, Miami, Florida, September 1989.

______. "Democracy, Human Rights, and the Armed Forces in Latin America." In *The United States and Latin American in the 1990s*, edited by Jonathan Hartlin, Lars Schoultz, and Augusto Varas. Chapel Hill: University of North Carolina Press, 1992.

Foster, Don, and Dianne Sandler. "The Black Man's Burden: Policing the Police in South Africa." *South African Journal of Human Rights* 2(2) (November 1986).

Fourie, Deon. "Control of the Armed Forces in South Africa: Constitutional Formulae." *South African Defence Review* 5 (1992).

Frankel, Philip. "South Africa: The Politics of Police Control." *Comparative Politics* 12(14) (July 1980).

______. "Race and Counter-Revolution: South Africa's 'Total Strategy.'" *Journal of Commonwealth and Comparative Politics* 18(3) (November 1980).

______. "Pretoria's Praetorians: The Military in South African Politics." Paper presented to the South African Political Science Association conference, Pretoria, June 1985.

______. "The Military and Political Transition in South Africa." Paper to the Military in Africa conference, Joint Analysis Centre, European Command, Alconbury, U.K., May 1993.

______. "From Soldiers to Democrats? South Africa's Military in Political Transition." Paper presented to the International Political Science Association World Congress, Berlin, August 1994.

______. "Report on Proceedings: Defence Review Workshop." Jan Smuts House, University Of the Witwatersrand, Johannesburg, July 1996. Presented to Defence Secretariat in July 1996.

______. "Democratisation and Integration in the South African Armed Forces." Paper presented to the International Political Science Association World Congress, Seoul, August 1997.

______. "Rationalisation and Transformation: The South African Armed Forces on the Brink Of the Millenium." Paper to the Thirty-fourth World Congress of the International Institute of Sociology, Tel Aviv, July 1999.

______. "Recivilianisation and Reconciliation: The South African Armed Forces and Democratic Transition." Paper presented to the International Political Science Association, Research Group on Armed Forces and Society, University of the Negev, Israel, Sede Boker, July 1999.

Garro, Alejandro M. "Nine Years of Transition to Democracy in Argentina: Partial Failure or Qualified Success?" *Columbia Journal of Transnational Law* 31(1) (1993).

Garro, Alejandro M., and Henry Dahl. "Legal Accountability for Human Rights Violations in Argentina: One Step Forward and Two Steps Backward." *Human Rights Journal* 8(2–4) (1987).

Geldenhuys, Deon, and Hennie Kotze. "P.W. Botha as Decisionmaker: A Preliminary Study of Personality and Politics." *Politikon* 12(1) (June 1985).

Giliomee, H. "Oktober Verkiesing: Nuew Gesig vir die Nasionale Partie." *Die Suid Afrikaan* (October 17, 1988).

Grundy, Kenneth. "The Rise of the South African Security Establishment: An Essay on the Changing Locus of State Power." Johannesburg: South African Institute for International Affairs, 1983.

Hamman, D. "The Inter-State Defence and Security Committee: Defence Sub-Committee." Paper Presented at seminar entitled "South Africa and Global Peace Support Initiatives," Cape Town May 17, 1995.

Haysom, Nicholas. "Mabangalala: The Rise of Right-Wing Vigilantes in South Africa." Johannesburg: Centre for Applied Legal Studies, University of the Witwatersrand, 1986.

Heinecken, Lynley. "The Effect of Industrial Democracy and Unionisation on the South African Security Forces." Paper presented at the Conference of the South African Political Science Association, Bloemfontein, October 20–23, 1993.

Heitman, H-R. "Southern African Maritine Security Agency." Paper presented at the National Maritime Strategic Conference, Navies in Peace and War, Simonstown,South Africa, October 26, 1996.

Human Rights Commission. "Briefing on Political Assassination in the 1990s." Human Rights Commission, March 21, 1992.

Karl, Terry Lynn, and Philippe Schmitter. "Modes of Transition in Latin America, Southern, and Eastern Europe." *International Social Science Journal* 128 (May 1991).

Kentridge, Matthew. "The Unofficial War in Natal: Pietermaritzburg Under the Knife." Paper presented to the Department of Applied Psychology/Project for the Study of Violence, University of the Witwatersrand, Johannesburg, 1990.

Liebenberg, I., and Rocklyn Williams. "The Impact of the Truth and Reconciliation Commission on the SANDF." Midrand: Institute for Defence Policy, Occassional Papers No. 13, November 1996.

Lilley, Ashley. "The Origins and Development of the South African Army." *Militaria* 12(2) (1982).

Lodge, Tom. "The Post-Apartheid Army: Political Considerations." Paper presented to conference entitled "Taking the South African Army into the Future," University of South Africa, Pretoria, November 15, 1993.

Lombard, W.G. "Armour in the SADF: A Strategic and Practical Perspective." In Jakkie Cilliers and Bill Sass, eds. *Mailed Fist: Developments in Modern Armour.* Midrand: Institute for Defence Policy, Monograph Series No. 2, March 1996.

Louw, C. "Die SAP en die Pyning van Oorgang." *Die Suid-Afrikaan* 24 (December 1989).

Loveman, Brian. "Protected Democracies and Military Guardianship: Political Transitions in Latin America, 1978–1993." *Journal of Interamerican Studies and World Affairs* 36(2) (Summer 1994).

______. "Mision Cumplida? Civil-Military Relations and the Chilean Political Transition." *Journal of Interamerican Studies and World Affairs* 33(3) (1991).

McSherry, J. Patrice. "Military Political Power and Guardian Structures in Latin America." *Journal of Third World Studies* (Spring 1995).

______. "Institutional Legacies of Military Rule in Argentina." Paper presented to the Nineteenth International Congress of the Latin American Studies Association, Washington, D.C., September 1995.

Malan, M.A. de M. "Die Aanslag Teen Suid-Afrika." *ISSUP Strategic Review* (November 1980).

______. *Submission to the Truth and Reconciliation Commission.* May 7, 1997.

Malan, Mark. "Yesterday's Heroes." *Natal Witness* (Durban), February 22, 1996.

Malan, Mark, ed. *New Partners in Peace: Towards a Southern African Peacekeeping Capacity.* Midrand: Institute for Defence Policy, Monograph Series No. 5, July 1996.

Mann, M. "The Roots and Contradictions of Modern Militarism." *New Left Review* 162 (1987).

Meiring, Georg. "Keynote Address." Taking the South African Army into the Future, University of South Africa, Pretoria, November 15, 1993.

Mills, Greg. "Armed Forces in Post-Apartheid South Africa." *Survival* 35(3) (Autumn 1993).

Monnakgotla, Kgomotso. "From Ambivalence and Adversity to Stability in Southern Africa." In Mark Malan, ed. *New Partners in Peace: Towards a Southern African Peacekeeping Capacity.* Midrand: Institute for Defence Policy, Monograph Series No. 5, July 1996.

Mortimer, Deon. "Integration, Rationalisation, and Demobilisation." Paper presented to conference entitled "Preparing the South African Army for the Twenty-first Century," Council for Scientific and Industrial Research, Pretoria, October 19, 1995.

Nathan, Laurie, and Mark Philips. "Security Reforms: The Pen and the Sword." *Indicator SA* 8(4) (1991).

______. "Crosscurrents: Security Developments Under F.W. de Klerk." In Glenn Moss and Ingrid Obery, eds. *South African Review 6.* Johannesburg: Ravan Press, 1992.

______. "Beyond Arms and Armed Forces: A New Approach to Security." *South African Defence Review* 4 (1992).

Norden, Deborah. "Democratic Consolidation and Military Professionalism: Argentina in the 1980s." *Journal of Interamerican Studies and World Affairs* 32(3) (1990).

______. "Shadows of Military Rule: Legacies of Bureaucratic-Authoritarianism in Latin America." Paper presented at the Latin American Studies Association Meeting, Los Angeles, 1992.

O'Donnell, G., P. Schmitter, and L. Whitehead. "Tentative Conclusions About Uncertain Democracies." In Guillermo O'Donnell et al., eds. *Transitions from Authoritarian Rule: Prospects for Democracy.* Baltimore: Johns Hopkins University Press, 1986) Section IV.

Otto, Reg. "Preparing the Army for the Next Century." Paper presented to conference entitled "Preparing the South African Army for the Twenty-first Century," Council for Scientific and Industrial Research, Pretoria, October 19, 1995.

Pahad, Aziz. "South Africa and Preventative Diplomacy." Paper presented to conference entitled "South Africa and Peacekeeping in Africa," Johannesburg, July 13–14, 1995.

Perelli, Carina. "From Counterrevolutionary Warfare to Political Awakening: The Uruguayan and Argentine Armed Forces in the 1970s." *Armed Forces and Society* 20(1) (Fall 1993).

Pion-Berlin, David. "Military Autonomy and Emerging Democracies in Latin America." *Comparative Politics* (October 1992).

Pye, Lucian. "Armies and the Process of Political Modernisation." In J. Johnson, ed. *The Role of The Military in Underdeveloped Countries*. Princeton: Princeton University Press, 1964.

Remmer, Karen. "New Theoretical Perspectives on Democratisation." *Comparative Politics* (October 1995).

Sass, Bill. "The Union and the South African Defence Force, 1912–1994." In Jakkies Cilliers and Markus Reichardt, eds. *About Turn: The Transformation of the South African African Military and Intelligence*. Midrand: Institute for Defence Policy, 1996.

Scheepers, L. "Two Percent of GDP: Enough for a Secure Future?" *African Armed Forces Journal* (March 1996).

Scheetze, Thomas. "The Macroeconomic Impact of Defence Expenditures: Some Econometric Evidence for Argentina, Chile, Paraguay, and Peru." *Defence Economics* 2 (1991).

Schutte, Charl. "People's Army, People's Choice: The Results of a Humand Sciences Research Council/Institute for Defence Policy Opinion Survey." Paper presented to conference on Preparing the South African Army for the Twenty-first Century, Council for Scientific and Industrial Research, Pretoria, October 19, 1995.

Seegers, Annette. "From Liberation to Modernisation: Transforming Revolutionary Paramilitary Forces into Standing Professional Armies." In Bruce Arlinghaus and Pauline Baker, eds. *African Armies: Evolution and Capabilities*. Boulder: Westview Press, 1986.

______. "South Africa's National Security Management System, 1972–1990." *Journal of Modern African Studies* 29(2) (1991).

______. "The Head of Government and the Executive." In R. Schrire, ed. *Leadership and the Apartheid State: From Malan to De Klerk*. Cape Town: Oxford University Press, 1994.

Selfe, James. "The Total Onslaught and the Total Strategy: Adaptions to the Security Intelligence Decision-Making Structures Under P.W. Botha's Administration." Unpubl. thesis, University of Cape Town, 1987.

______. South Africa's National Security Management System." In Jacklyn Cock and Laurie Nathan, eds. *War and Society: The Militarisation of South Africa*. Cape Town: David Philip, 1989.

Shaw, Mark. "Negotiating Defence for a New South Africa." In Jakkie Cilliers and Markus Reinhardt, eds. *About Turn: The Transformation of the South African Military and Intelligence*. Midrand: Institute for Defence Policy, 1995.

Siko, Mohlolo. "Regional Defence Restructuring: A Southern African Maritime Perspective." Paper Presented to South African Regional Workshop on Defence and Restructuring of the Armed Forces, Helderfontein, South Africa, March 1–4, 1996.

South African Catholic Bishop's Conference. *Report on Namibia*. Presented to conference on Namibia, Johannesburg, 1982.

Stepan, Alfred. "The New Professionalism of Internal Warfare and Military Role Expansion." In Alfred Stepan, ed. *Authoritarian Brazil: Origins, Polices and Future*. New Haven: Yale University Press, 1973.

Steyn, Pierre. "The Defence Industry and the Role of the Defence Secretariat." *African Security Review* 5(6) (1996).

______. "The Defence Secretariat and the South African Army." *African Security Review* 5(1) (1996).

Sunhaussen, Ulf. "Military Withdrawal from Governmental Responsibility." *Armed Forces and Society* 104 (Summer 1984).

Swilling, Mark, and Mark Philips. "The Power of the Thunderbird: Decision-Making Structures and Policy Strategies in the South African State." In *Policy Perspectives 1989: South Africa at the End of the 1980s*. Johannesburg: Centre for Policy Studies, 1989.

Toase, Francis. "The South African Army: The Campaign in South West Africa/Namibia Since 1966." In Ian Beckett and John Pimlott, eds. *Armed Forces and Modern Counter-Insurgency*. London: Croom Helm, 1985.

van Zyl Slabbert, F. "The Causes of Transition in South Africa." Johannesburg: Institute For a Democratic Alternative in South Africa, Occasional Papers No. 32, 1990.

Venter, P.J. "Restructuring, Integration, and Rationalisation: An Overview of the Future Size and Shape of the National Defence Force." Unpubl., n.d.

van Stade, L.B. "Rationalisation in the South African National Defence Force: The Next Challenge." Paper presented to conference entitled "The South African National Defence Force and Transformation," University of South Africa, Pretoria, October 15, 1996.

Varas, Augusto. "Democratisation and Military Reform in Argentina." In Varas, ed. *Democracy Under Siege: New Military Power in Latin America*. New York: Greenwood Press, 1989.

Wandrag, A.J. "Political Unrest: A Police View." *Strategic Review*. University of Pretoria, Institute for Strategic Studies, October 1985.

Welch, Claude. "Military Disengagement from Politics: Paradigms, Processes, or Random Events." *Armed Forces and Society* 18(3) (Spring 1992).

Williams, Rocklyn. "Back to the Broker: The SADF and the Nature of Civil-Military Relations under the Botha and de Klerk Administrations." London: Institute of Commonwealth Studies, 1990.

______. "Changing the Guard." *Work in Progress* 13 (September 1992).

______. "Overview and Backdrop to the Defence Review." Presentation to the Defence Review Workshop, Jan Smuts House, University of the Witwatersrand, Johannesburg, July 29, 1996.

Zagorski, Paul. "Civil-Military Relations and Argentine Democracy: The Armed Forces Under the Menem Government." *Armed Forces and Society* 20(3) (Spring 1994).

Zaverucha, Jorge. "The Degree of Military Autonomy During the Spanish, Argentine, and Brazilian Transitions." *Journal of Latin American Studies* 25 (May 1993).

______. "Civil-Military Relations During the First Brazilian Post-Transition Government: A Tutelary Democracy." Paper presented to the Eighteenth Congress of the Latin American Studies Association, Atlanta, Georgia, March 10–12, 1994.

Official Sources

British Military Advisory and Training Team (BMATT). Situation Reports: Army, Navy, Royal Air Force, and Medical Services, June 1994–August 1997. BMATT, South African National Defence Force Headquarters (SANDF HQ), Pretoria.

______. Report on Weekly Commander's Conference: Record of Proceedings. June 1994–August 1997. BMATT, SANDF HQ, Pretoria.

______. SA/710/2, July 7, 1994. BMATT, SANDF HQ, Pretoria.

______. Report on Intelligence Corps and Chief of Staff Intelligence Board, August 17, 1994. AMS/Int/5. BMATT, South African National Defence Force, Pretoria.

______. Report on Bridging Training for the Parliamentary Integration Oversight Committee, June 12, 1995. BMATT, SANDF HQ, Pretoria.

______. Response to Questions from the Joint Parliamentary Standing Committee in Defence, September 29, 1995.

______. CDFS/R/303/3. BMATT, SANDF HQ, Pretoria.

______. Report on South African National Defence Force Transformation to the Parliamentary Integration Oversight Committee, January 1996. BM/SA/150/2, February 22, 1996. BMATT, SANDF HQ, Pretoria.

______. Report on the South African National Defence Force Transformation to the Parliamentary Integration Oversight Committee, February 26, 1996. BMATT, SANDF HQ, Pretoria.

______. Report on the South African National Defence Force Integration as at 1st April 1997 for the Parliamentary Integration Oversight Committee, April 8, 1997. BMATT, SANDF HQ, Pretoria.

______. Army Accreditation Board, January 21, 1997: Observations Sumbitted by BMATT to the 80th Meeting of the Integration Committee, May 28, 1997.

Department of Defence (DOD). *White Paper on Defence and Armaments Production, 1969*. Pretoria: DOD, 1969.

______. *White Paper on Defence and Armaments Supply, 1982*. Pretoria: DOD, 1982.

______. New Era Defence. Annual Report, Financial Year 1995/96. Pretoria: DOD, 1996.

______. Reports of the Defence Review. 3 Vols. Pretoria: DOD, 1997.

Joint Military Coordinating Council (JMCC). Register of Decisions.

______. Minutes of Sessions.

______. Proposed Terms of Reference of JMCC Legal Workgroup. MA/JMCC(1)/AEG/ALL/DOC, February 15, 1994, Appendix to Fourth Session.

______. Abridged Minutes for the Logistics Workgroup on the Control of Arms and Armaments, March 9, 1994, Appendix R to the Sixth Session.

______. Post-Electoral Control and MOD Structure, JMCC/DSM/501/6, Appendix B to the Sixth Session.

______. Aims, Roles, Goals, Objectives, and Functions of the JMCC Liaison Team, March 3, 1994, Appendix A to the Sixth Session.

______. Recommendations of the Personnel Workgroup Re: Promotions, Appointments, and Recruiting in Participating Forces, March 1994, Appendix G to the Seventh Session.

______. Defence Force Promotions Policy, March 1994, Appendix H to the Seventh Session.

______. Progress Report from the JMCC to the Sub-Council on Defence on the Assembling of the Non-Statutory Forces, Appendix M to the Seventh Session.

______. Communications Policy. Concept Strategy for the Communications Function in the South African National Defence Force, JMCC/C/S/511/1/1/1/3/B, March 30, 1994, Appendix H to the Eighth Session.

______. Plans for Taking NSF Forces on Strength and Maintaining Them until They Enter into an Agreement with the South African National Defence Force, Appendix N to the Ninth Session.

______. Report on Additional Structures and Models for the RSA's National Defence Force, HSP/DMANP/S/101/9, Report to the Ninth Session.

______. Position Re: NSF Members Outside the Borders of the RSA, Appendix O to the Ninth Session.

______. Bulletin.

Joint Parliamentary Standing Committee on Defence. (JPSCD). Report of the Joint Parliamentary Standing Committee on Defence, June 9, 1994. Parliament of South Africa, Cape Town.

______. Report of the Joint Parliamentary Standing Committee on Defence, November 9, 1994. Parliament of South Africa, Cape Town.

______. Draft Report on Bridging Course Training, November 23, 1995. Parliament of South Africa, Cape Town.

National Peace-Keeping Force. Directive of the Command Council: Concept for Operations and Training. 1994.

Parliamentary Integration Oversight Committee (PIOC). Report to the Joint Parliamentary Standing Committee on Defence, September 16, 1996. Parliament of South Africa, Cape Town.

______. Report of Visits to South African National Defence Force Units and Headquarters, September/October 1996, January 14, 1997. Parliament of South Africa, Cape Town.

______. *Defence in Democracy: White Paper on Defence for the Republic of South Africa*, May 1996.

South Africa. *White Paper on Defence and Armaments Production, 1969*. Pretoria: Government Printer, 1969.

______. *White Paper on Defence and Armaments Supply, 1982*. Pretoria: Government Printer, 1982.

______. *The White Paper on Defence and Armaments Supply, 1984*. Pretoria: Government Printer, 1984.

______. *The White Paper on Defence and Armaments Supply, 1986*. Pretoria: Government Printer, 1986.

South African Defence Force (SADF). Operational Instruction 15/85.

Communication and Liason Between the SADF and the Sub-Council on Defence of the Transitional Executive Council, Appendix A, October 4, 1993, CSADF Directive 3/6 DD.

______. Verkennende Gesprek 2 Met ANC/MK. N.d. Private collection of Brigadier C.S. Steijn (Steijn collection).

______. Verkennende Gesprek 3 Met ANC/MK. N.d. Steijn collection.

______. Working Paper in Preparation for SADF/ANC Discussions on Unrest/Conflict Before, During, and After Elections. N.d. Private collection of Major General M. Oelschig (Oelshig collection).

______. Proposals for an Exchange of Strategic Ideas, Views, and Perceptions. Directorate for Transitional Liason to Chief of South African Defence Force, HS/OPS/S/302/S. N.d.

______. Notes: Working Group on Defence. N.d. (May 1993?).

______. Details on Given Guidelines Worked Out by the Working Group of the Bilaterals Meeting Between the SADF and MK on Defence Matters. N.d. (May/June 1993?).

______. Memorandum: Chief of South African Air Force to Chief of the South African Defence Force, LMH/G/IGLM/203/2/18, March 23, 1993.

______. Letter: Chief of the South African Defence Force, CSADF/HSF/DPB/11/6, March 28, 1994. Appendix D to the Eighth Session of the JMCC.

______. Bilateral Meetings SADF/ANC(MK), April 23–24, 1993, Admiralty House, Cape Town. Unpublished Notes and Proceedings. N.d. Oelschig collection.

______. Areas of Discussion and Tentative Consensus Arrived at Simonstown in Bilateral Meeting of Week Ending April 25, 1993, and as Amended in Pretoria, May 25, 1993. Steijn collection.

______. Notes: Meeting of the Workgroup of the SADF Negotiating with Other Internal Forces at H.S. Ops 061030B, May 1993. Oelschig collection.

______. Notes: Workgroup Between the SADF and the ANC, Pretoria, May 6, 1993. Oelschig collection.

______. Negotiations Between the South African Defence Force and the ANC. May 6, 1993. Oelschig collection.

______. Confirmatory Notes: Meeting of the Workgroup of the SADF Negotiating with Other Internal Forces at Blenny, 101200B, May 1993. Oelschig collection.

______. Notes for Communication to Chief of the Army and Air Force: Chief of the Army, Conference Room 111500B, May 1993. Oelschig collection.

______. Confirmatory Notes: Communication of Chief of the South African Defence Force on Standpoints for Further Negotiations with ANC(MK), Monday, May 17, 1993. Oelschig collection.

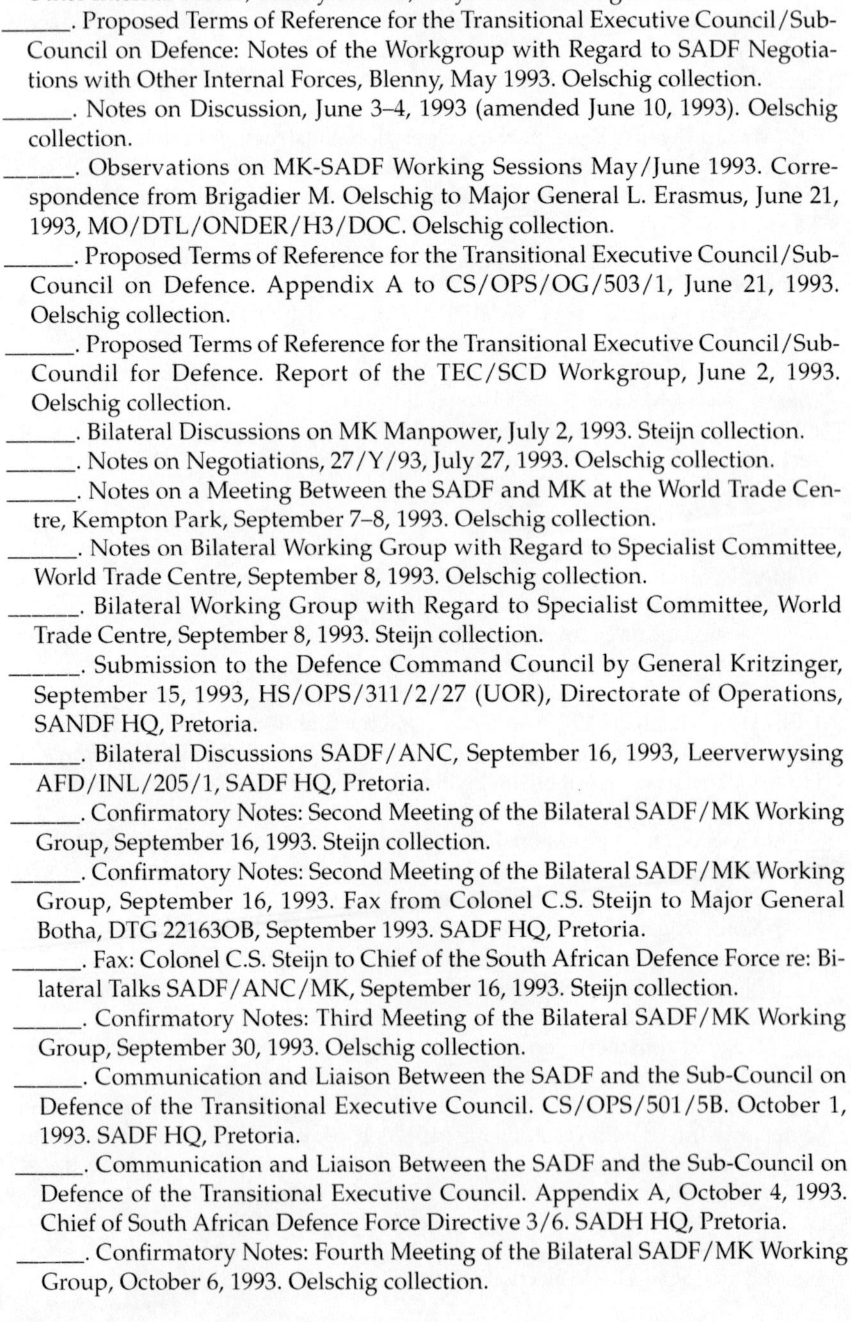

______. Notes of Workgroup on South African Defence Force Negotiations with Other Internal Forces, Blenny 10120B, May 1993. Oelschig collection.

______. Proposed Terms of Reference for the Transitional Executive Council/Sub-Council on Defence: Notes of the Workgroup with Regard to SADF Negotiations with Other Internal Forces, Blenny, May 1993. Oelschig collection.

______. Notes on Discussion, June 3–4, 1993 (amended June 10, 1993). Oelschig collection.

______. Observations on MK-SADF Working Sessions May/June 1993. Correspondence from Brigadier M. Oelschig to Major General L. Erasmus, June 21, 1993, MO/DTL/ONDER/H3/DOC. Oelschig collection.

______. Proposed Terms of Reference for the Transitional Executive Council/Sub-Council on Defence. Appendix A to CS/OPS/OG/503/1, June 21, 1993. Oelschig collection.

______. Proposed Terms of Reference for the Transitional Executive Council/Sub-Coundil for Defence. Report of the TEC/SCD Workgroup, June 2, 1993. Oelschig collection.

______. Bilateral Discussions on MK Manpower, July 2, 1993. Steijn collection.

______. Notes on Negotiations, 27/Y/93, July 27, 1993. Oelschig collection.

______. Notes on a Meeting Between the SADF and MK at the World Trade Centre, Kempton Park, September 7–8, 1993. Oelschig collection.

______. Notes on Bilateral Working Group with Regard to Specialist Committee, World Trade Centre, September 8, 1993. Oelschig collection.

______. Bilateral Working Group with Regard to Specialist Committee, World Trade Centre, September 8, 1993. Steijn collection.

______. Submission to the Defence Command Council by General Kritzinger, September 15, 1993, HS/OPS/311/2/27 (UOR), Directorate of Operations, SANDF HQ, Pretoria.

______. Bilateral Discussions SADF/ANC, September 16, 1993, Leerverwysing AFD/INL/205/1, SADF HQ, Pretoria.

______. Confirmatory Notes: Second Meeting of the Bilateral SADF/MK Working Group, September 16, 1993. Steijn collection.

______. Confirmatory Notes: Second Meeting of the Bilateral SADF/MK Working Group, September 16, 1993. Fax from Colonel C.S. Steijn to Major General Botha, DTG 22163OB, September 1993. SADF HQ, Pretoria.

______. Fax: Colonel C.S. Steijn to Chief of the South African Defence Force re: Bilateral Talks SADF/ANC/MK, September 16, 1993. Steijn collection.

______. Confirmatory Notes: Third Meeting of the Bilateral SADF/MK Working Group, September 30, 1993. Oelschig collection.

______. Communication and Liaison Between the SADF and the Sub-Council on Defence of the Transitional Executive Council. CS/OPS/501/5B. October 1, 1993. SADF HQ, Pretoria.

______. Communication and Liaison Between the SADF and the Sub-Council on Defence of the Transitional Executive Council. Appendix A, October 4, 1993. Chief of South African Defence Force Directive 3/6. SADH HQ, Pretoria.

______. Confirmatory Notes: Fourth Meeting of the Bilateral SADF/MK Working Group, October 6, 1993. Oelschig collection.

______. Notes on the Meeting of the Bilateral Between the SADF and MK, November 2, 1993. Oelschig collection.

______. Meeting of the Bilateral Between the SADF and MK at Simonstown, November 23, 1993. Steijn collection.

______. Conference Notes on Multilateral Talks Held at Fontana, November 26, 1993. Oelschig collection.

______. Confirmatory Notes of Multilateral Talks, November26, 1993. Steijn collection.

______. Conference Notes: Discussions of the Multi-Party Planning Group on the Establishment of the National Peace-Keeping Force, December 9, 1993, South African Military Intelligence College No. 9, December 1993. Directorate of Intelligence, Pretoria, December 1993.

______. Confirmatory Notes: Second Multilateral Meeting of Commanders of Armed Forces. Fax from Colonel C.S. Steijn to Brigadier M. Oelschig, No. 141500B, December 1993. Oelschig collection.

______. Confirmatory Notes of the Meeting of the Special Working Group Held on December 7, 1993, at the South African Military Intelligence College. Steijn collection.

______. Bevestigende Notas: Werkgroep vir Riglyne. No. 21. Fax from Colonel C.S. Steijn to Brigadier M. Oelschig. No. 221400B. Oelschig collection.

______. Confirmatory Notes of the Third Special Bilateral Held at the South African Military Intelligence College on December 17, 1993. Steijn collection.

______. Achievements of the SADF in the Negotiating Process. Chief South African Defence Force, Intneral Communications Bulletin 2, January 2, 1994.

______. Report of the Officer Commanding Second Battalion of the National Peace-Keeping Force. Lieutenant-Colonal Q.B. Painter, 2BN/309, August 19, 1994.

South African Defence Force/National Defence Force. Strategic Management Program 1994. Chief of the South African Defence Force Directive 0/1. January 1994.

______. Memorandum: Chief of the South African Air Force to Chief of the South African Defence Force, January 27, 1994. LMH/HVL/LMS/311/2/TEC.

South African National Defence Force (SANDF). Internal Communications Bulletin, June 1994 to August 1997. Directorate of Corporate Communications, SANDF HQ, Pretoria.

______. *Paratus*. Directorate of Corporate Communications. SANDF HQ, Pretoria.

______. *Salut*, June 1994–August 1997. Directorate of Corporate Communications, SANDF HQ, Pretoria.

______. (Nodal Point). *Submission IRO the Former SADF* Presentation to Truth and Reconciliation Commission by Major General B. Mortimer. n.d.

______. Minutes of the Integration Committee, June 1994–June 1997. SANDF HQ, Pretoria.

______. Minutes of the Integration Work Group. SANDF HQ, Pretoria.

______. Report C/Army/D/TRG/C/504/1. n.d. SANDF HQ, Pretoria.

______. The National Defence Force in Transition: Annual Report, 1994/95. SANDF HQ, Pretoria 1996.

______. Annual Report, 1995–1996. SANDF HQ, Pretoria 1997.

______. Reply to the Joint Parliamentary Standing Committee on Defence, November 9, 1994. February 10, 1995. SANDF HQ, Pretoria.

______. Integration Progress Report to the Parliamentary Integration Oversight Committee, June 12, 1995. SANDF HQ, Pretoria.

______. Integration Progress Report to the Joint Parliamentary Standing Committee on Defence, August 22, 1995. SANDF HQ, Pretoria.

______. South African National Defence Force Reply to the Draft Report on Bridging Course Training to the Joint Parliamentary Standing Committee on Defence, November 23, 1995. SANDF.HQ, Pretoria.

______. Integration Progress Report to the Parliamentary Integration Oversight Committee, February 26, 1996. SANDF HQ, Pretoria.

______. Integration Progress Report to the Joint Parliamentary Standing Committee on Defence, March 19, 1996. SANDF HQ, Pretoria.

______. Integration Progress Report to the Parliamentary Integration Oversight Committee, April 11, 1996. SANDF HQ, Pretoria.

______. Management Directive: Chief Directorate, Equal Opportunities, Personnel Division. CSP/DPD/501/7, July 4, 1996. Directorate of Personnel, SANDF HQ, Pretoria.

______. Report by the Inspector-General, South African National Defence Force on Investigation with Regard to Morale in the South African National Defence Force. 16/SANDF/R/503/2/15, July 15, 1996. SANDF HQ, Pretoria.

______. Briefing to the 11th COD Regarding The Certified Personnel Register Situation by Vice Admiral Loedolff, September 16, 1996. HSP/DIR/C/101/9/2, n.d. September 4, 1996. SANDF HQ, Pretoria.

______. Integration Progress Report to the Parliamentary Integration Oversight Committee, September 16, 1996. SANDF HQ, Pretoria.

______. Evaluation Research on the Psychological Integration Program: Total Sample, Final Report. Military Psychological Institute, Pretoria, December 1996.

______. Psychological Integration Program: Final Report on the Research Findings of Military Culture Perceptions. Military Psychological Institute, Pretoria, 1996.

______. Psychological Integration Program: Analysis Of Questionairre. Military Psychological Institute, Pretoria 1996.

______. Houdings en Meningopnames: Konsolidasie-Verslag van Fokusgroepopnames. Directorate of Intelligence for Effect Analysis, Pretoria, 1997.

______. Submission to the Parliamentary Integration Oversight Committee, January 20, 1997. Directorate of Intelligence. Int/Pers/Util/R/ 103/1.

______. Integration Progress Report to the Parliamentary Integration Oversight Committee, April 14, 1997. SANDF HQ, Pretoria.

______. Integration of TBVC, NSF, and SA Defence Forces, Project INTEGR.18PJ. Revision 25. April 27, 1997. Appendix L to the Minutes of the Eightieth Meeting of the Integration Committee. N.d.

______. Project Jacamar: Investigations into Attitudes and Views of the South African Army. SANDF HQ, Pretoria, May 1997.

______. Enhancement of Representivity on South African Army Leader Group Courses, May 27, 1997. C/Army/D/Pers/101/1/2. Appendix M to the Eightieth Meeting of the Integration Committee, 28th May 1997.

Transitional Executive Council (TEC). Situation Reports.

Transitional Executive Council/Sub-Council on Defence (SCD). Memo to the Third Session of the Joint Military Coordinating Council with Regard to Participation of CDF, BDF, and AVF in the JMCC. February 8, 1994.

______. Memorandum: Issues Arising from the SCD Meeting of March 3, 1994. Appendix D/E to the Minutes of the Sixth Session of the JMCC.

______. Letter to Major General van der Bank, Chief of the Ciskei Defence Force, March 16, 1994. Appendix to the Sixth Session of the Joint Military Coordinating Council.

______. Progress Report on the Strategic Planning Process, the JMCC, and the Integration Process. Submitted as Appendix M to the Seventh Session of the Joint Military Coordinating Council.

United Nations. Study on Defensive Security Concepts and Policies. New York: United Nations Study Series No. 26, 1993.

Newspapers and Journals

Africa Confidential (London)
City Press (Johannesburg)
Die Beeld (Johannesburg)
Eastern Province Herald (Port Elizabeth)
Mail and Guardian (Johannesburg)
Militaria (South African National Defence Force)
New Nation (Johannesburg)
Paratus (South African Defence Force/National Defence Force)
Pretoria News (Pretoria)
Rand Daily Mail (Johannesburg)
Salut (South African Defence Force/National Defence Force)
Sunday Independent (Johannesburg)
Sunday Star (Johannesburg)
Sunday Times (Johannesburg)
The Argus (Cape Town)
The Citizen (Johannesburg)
The Independent (London)
The Observer (London)
The Soweton (Johannesburg)
The Star (Johannesburg)
Windhoek Observer (Windhoek)

Index